KANT ON REPRESENTATION
AND OBJECTIVITY

This book is a study of the second-edition version of the 'Transcendental Deduction' (the so-called 'B-Deduction'), which is one of the most important and obscure sections of Kant's *Critique of Pure Reason*. By way of a close analysis of the B-Deduction, A. B. Dickerson makes the distinctive claim that the Deduction is crucially concerned with the problem of making intelligible the unity possessed by complex representations – a problem that is the representationalist parallel of the semantic problem of the unity of the proposition. Along the way he discusses most of the key themes in Kant's theory of knowledge, including the nature of thought and representation, the notion of objectivity, and the way in which the mind structures our experience of the world.

A. B. DICKERSON is Lecturer in Communication and Media Studies at the University of Canberra.

KANT ON
REPRESENTATION AND
OBJECTIVITY

A. B. DICKERSON

University of Canberra

CAMBRIDGE
UNIVERSITY PRESS

PUBLISHED BY THE PRESS SYNDICATE OF THE UNIVERSITY OF CAMBRIDGE
The Pitt Building, Trumpington Street, Cambridge, United Kingdom

CAMBRIDGE UNIVERSITY PRESS
The Edinburgh Building, Cambridge, CB2 2RU, UK
40 West 20th Street, New York, NY 10011–4211, USA
477 Williamstown Road, Port Melbourne, VIC 3207, Australia
Ruiz de Alarcón 13, 28014 Madrid, Spain
Dock House, The Waterfront, Cape Town 8001, South Africa

http://www.cambridge.org

First published 2004

Printed in the United Kingdom at the University Press, Cambridge

Typeface Adobe Garamond 11/12.5 pt.   *System* LATEX 2ε   [TB]

A catalogue record for this book is available from the British Library

Library of Congress Cataloguing in Publication data
Dickerson, A. B.
Kant on representation and objectivity / A. B. Dickerson.
p.   cm.
Includes bibliographical references and index.
ISBN 0 521 83121 0
1. Kant, Immanuel, 1724–1804 – Contributions in doctrine of representation in
philosophy.   2. Representation (Philosophy)   3. Objectivity.   I. Title.
B2799.R45D53   2003
121′.092 – dc21   2003048480

ISBN 0 521 83121 0

For M.

So stellt der Satz den Sachverhalt gleichsam auf eigene Faust dar.

In this way the proposition presents the situation – as it were off its own bat.

Wittgenstein, Notebooks 1914–1916, 5 November 1914

Nur kann man noch hinzufügen, wie kann ein Inbegriff, Complexus der Vorstellungen vorgestellt werden? Nicht durch das Bewußtsein, daß er uns gegeben sei; denn ein Inbegriff erfordert Zusammensetzen (synthesis) des Mannigfaltigen. Er muß also (als Inbegriff) gemacht werden.

But one may also ask, how can a content that is a complex of representations be represented? Not just through the awareness that it is *given* to us; for such a content requires a *combining* (synthesis) of the manifold. It must thus (*qua* content) be *made*.

Kant, letter to J. S. Beck, 20 January 1792

Contents

Acknowledgments

This book originated as a doctoral dissertation submitted to the School of Philosophy at the University of New South Wales, Sydney, Australia. Many thanks must go to my thesis supervisors – to Genevieve Lloyd, for her patient criticism of early drafts, and to Michaelis Michael, for getting me interested in this project, for valuable philosophical discussion, and for sustaining me with *Wein und Gesang*. I would also like to thank my examining committee – Karl Ameriks, David Cooper and Béatrice Longuenesse – for their constructive criticism. I owe an additional debt of thanks to David Cooper, for his encouragement, and for giving me the opportunity to teach at Durham University whilst I was completing this work.

Note on the text

References to Kant's works are made in parentheses in the body of the text. The *Critique of Pure Reason* (hereafter, simply the *Critique*) is referred to using the standard A and B notation. The Transcendental Deduction in the second edition of the *Critique* is usually referred to simply as the 'B-Deduction'. Other works by Kant are referred to by *Akademie* volume and page number. Where available, I have used (with occasional modifications) the translations of the *Cambridge Edition of the Works of Immanuel Kant*. Interpolations in square brackets are mine, and emphasis is as in the original unless otherwise noted.

Introduction

This book is a study of the argument that lies at the heart of Kant's epistemology: the argument of the 'Transcendental Deduction of the Pure Concepts of the Understanding'. It focuses on the version of that argument given in the second edition of the *Critique of Pure Reason* (i.e., the so-called 'B-Deduction'). The main interpretations of this argument that are to be found in the secondary literature read it as hinging on notions such as personal identity, the 'ownership' of mental states, or the ontological unity of the mind. I, on the other hand, will argue that in the B-Deduction Kant is crucially concerned with the problem of how the 'objective reality' or content of a representation – and, in particular, of a *complex* representation – becomes accessible to the subject that has the representation. In other words, he is concerned with the representationalist parallel of the semantic question of *what it is to understand a complex sign.*

In summary, my interpretation of Kant's argument in the B-Deduction is as follows. In order for the subject to have a unified grasp of a complex representation – or, as Kant puts it, for the 'unity of apperception' to be possible – an act of 'spontaneous synthesis' is required. This is an act of the mind that plays a role in generating the representational content of the subject's experience. Kant then argues that such spontaneity can retain its objectivity – that is, can generate a representation genuinely deserving to be called 'cognition' – only if the synthesis is determined solely by the essential features of the subject *qua* cognising discursive mind, and not by any contingent features of the subject's psychology. The cognising discursive mind is essentially a judging mind, and therefore the spontaneous synthesis must be governed by rules having their source in the essential structure of judgment – that is, by the categories. Hence, the categories make our cognition possible.

What is perhaps my key interpretative claim is that at the core of the B-Deduction is a problem – the problem of making intelligible the unity of complex representations – that is the representationalist parallel of the semantic problem of the unity of the proposition. This problem exercised the early Analytic philosophers, such as Frege and Wittgenstein, and I have drawn on their writings on the deep connections that exist between the notion of understanding a sign, the priority of judgment over concept, the sense in which understanding is active and not passive, and the sense in which the grammar of our language (or, the syntax of signs) is not determined by the nature of things, although, nonetheless, "*Essence* is expressed by grammar".[1] My reading of these philosophers has been strongly influenced by the work of Cora Diamond. In particular, the following passage – from Diamond's essay 'What Nonsense Might Be' – has been important to my understanding of the B-Deduction:

> It would be correct to say that the rules of the language are in a sense permissions, though conditional ones: to make sense of a sentence is to apply such rules, but it is still a *making* sense, and not a mere recognition of what the pieces are and how they are combined, plus a following of the directions-for-use that have been determined for the individual pieces and their mode of combination. We do not just arrive at a result – the meaning – by following such directions, and to make sense of a sentence is not to correlate something with it but to make it make the sense. The hearer's activity in understanding is close to the speaker's in constructing the sentence – the hearer has in a sense to make the sentence *his*, but using *the* rules. The user of language – speaker or hearer – is a thinker of senses according to the rules.[2]

This passage, with its emphasis on the way in which understanding is an active *making* of sense, echoes Kant's provocative remark that 'in order to cognise something in space, e.g., a line, I must *draw* it' (B137). Indeed, if one were to translate what Diamond says here into Kant's representationalist idiom, one would thereby have the main lines of my reading of the B-Deduction. What plays the role of '*the* rules of language' for Kant are of course *the* rules of the discursive mind – the categories. My reading of the B-Deduction could thus be summarised by saying that, for Kant, the cognising subject is a spontaneous grasper of representations according to the categories.

Before beginning my discussion, it should be emphasised that this book is not intended to be a variation on a Kantian theme, but an essay in the history of philosophy. That is, it is an essay in what Robert C. Sleigh calls 'exegetical history', of which he writes as follows.

[1] L. Wittgenstein, *Philosophical Investigations*, trans. G. E. M. Anscombe, 2nd edn (Oxford: Blackwell, 1958), ¶371.
[2] C. Diamond, 'What Nonsense Might Be', in *The Realistic Spirit* (Cambridge, MA: MIT Press, 1991), p. 111.

Useful exegetical history . . . has both a fact-finding component and an explanatory component . . . [T]he goal is to formulate the author's central views on the topic in hand in sentences such that *we* know what propositions those sentences express and those propositions are the very ones our author accepted. Think how often exegetical history fails at this task. Most accounts of Kant's transcendental deduction serve as examples – lucid where Kant is lucid, degenerating to mere paraphrase just where one most wants help.[3]

I have attempted to write in a way that meets Sleigh's two criteria for *useful* exegetical history, and which thus avoids the fate of 'most accounts of Kant's transcendental deduction'. That is, I have attempted to write sentences that, firstly, are comprehensible, and, secondly, express propositions to which Kant is committed. As Sleigh suggests, the difficulty and obscurity of the *Critique* are such that if one merely paraphrases Kant – without having first earned the right to do so, via an explanation of the jargon being used – then one fails to meet the first criterion. And if one engages in any extensive 'reconstruction' of the text, then one fails to meet the second criterion.

In order to avoid these problems, this book has two interlinked components: an attempt to make certain claims intelligible and an attempt to argue that those claims are Kant's claims. Particularly in chapters 1 and 2, the first of these components is emphasised, and I write at quite a distance from Kant's text. This is in order to make certain propositions and inferences as clear as I can – and because if one dives immediately into the text, without having a synoptic view of its overall structure, it is easy to get lost in the complex details of the B-Deduction. In chapter 1 I offer an intuitive model or analogy for understanding what Kant says about representation (and its links with notions such as imagination and judgment), in terms of the notion of seeing something 'in' a picture. In chapter 2 I outline my reading of Kant's argument. In chapters 3 and 4 I increasingly turn to the second component, and work systematically through the B-Deduction in order to demonstrate that my interpretation makes good sense of the details of Kant's text. The book can thus be thought of as like a series of photographs of the B-Deduction taken at ever-increasing magnifications.

[3] R. C. Sleigh, *Leibniz and Arnauld* (New Haven: Yale University Press, 1990), p. 4.

CHAPTER I

Representation

As noted in the introduction, the B-Deduction is so complex that it is important to have a synoptic view of the reasoning at the heart of Kant's argument before descending into the intricacies of the text. The purpose of this first chapter is to begin providing such a synoptic view, via a discussion of Kant's notion of representation. What I am attempting to do here is to make certain conceptual connections appear as intuitive and compelling as I can. As I hope to show in the later chapters of this book, this will help to make intelligible what may otherwise appear to be a series of bewildering *non sequiturs*.

The notion of a representation (*Vorstellung*) is fundamental to Kant's epistemological theory, just as the notion of an idea is fundamental to the theories of his Cartesian and empiricist predecessors. The *Critique*, after all, is a text centrally concerned with what types of representations we have, how we get them, and what we do with them when we have got them. However, despite the crucial role it plays in his arguments, Kant pays little attention directly to the abstract notion of representation in general – tending to concentrate instead on more specific notions like objectivity, cognition and judgment. There is nothing in the *Critique* to compare, for example, with the rich material to be found in the writings of Leibniz on notions like expression and isomorphism. In other words, the notion of representation tends to be treated as a primitive notion in Kant's epistemology. There are therefore no key analyses or definitions in the *Critique* upon which an interpretation of Kant's notion of representation can be grounded. Hence, such an interpretation must instead be justified by its capacity to provide a coherent understanding of Kant's text as a whole. Consequently, this chapter on Kant's notion of representation is the least textually focused of the book. The main evidence for the interpretative hypotheses advanced here will come in the following chapters, as I show how this understanding of representation can help to make sense of the central argument of the B-Deduction.

The main hypothesis advanced in this chapter is, in summary, as follows. Kant is a representationalist, by which I mean that he holds that the immediate objects of consciousness are internal representative states. However, although he shares this representationalist starting point with an indirect realist like Descartes and an idealist like Berkeley, Kant nonetheless has a very different conception of what it is to represent an object. For Kant our internal states constitute the *medium* of representation and to represent an object is to be aware of something *in* that medium. What precisely this means, and the crucial differences such an understanding of representation makes, is explained below.

REPRESENTATIONALISM

Kant announces his representationalist starting point in the opening sentence of the Introduction in B, where he writes as follows.

There is no doubt whatever that all our cognition begins with experience; for how else should the cognitive faculty be awakened into exercise if not through objects that stimulate our senses and in part themselves produce representations, in part bring the activity of our understanding into motion to compare these, to connect or separate them, and thus to work up the raw material of sensible impressions into a cognition of objects that is called experience? (B1)

This passage shows that Kant thinks of the mind (or, the 'cognitive faculty') as occupied in the first place with its own internal representations or impressions. As even a superficial acquaintance with the text reveals, the Cartesian language used in this opening passage runs through the entire *Critique*. Much like Cartesian ideas, Kantian representations are 'in us', are 'determinations' (*Bestimmungen*) or 'modifications' (*Modificationen*) of our mind, and, as the quoted passage indicates, are the objects of a great variety of mental acts. We are, for example, conscious or aware of representations, and variously compare, combine, recognise, synthesise and employ them.

In thus holding that the immediate objects of consciousness or awareness are internal representations, Kant stands in the great Cartesian tradition of representationalism. The origins of this tradition lie in Descartes's rejection of the Aristotelian-Scholastic ontology and its accompanying account of human cognition. In standard Scholastic doctrine, human cognition occurred through, firstly, the reception of the 'sensible forms' or 'intentional species' of objects into the mind, and secondly, the performing of acts of abstraction upon those sensible forms.[1] This doctrine, in which the human mind becomes formally identical with the object of cognition, was accused of being unintelligible mystification by the 'New Philosophy' of the seventeenth century. Leibniz, for example, in the preface to his *New Essays*, writes scornfully of the Scholastics' ' "intentional species" which travel from objects to us and find their way into our souls'. 'If that is acceptable,' he writes, ' "everything will now happen whose possibility I used to deny" (Ovid)'.[2] Kant repeats this stock rejection in § 9 of the *Prolegomena*, where he writes that it is 'incomprehensible how the intuition of a thing that is present should allow me to cognise it the way it is in itself, since its properties cannot migrate over into my power of representation' (4:282). Such 'migration' of properties is precisely what was supposed to occur in the Scholastic account. In the new representationalist view of cognition, it was thought instead that all we have immediately available to our consciousness is the internal effects of objects upon our senses – that is, our ideas, impressions or representations.[3]

Descartes's treatment of ideas combines many themes, but the ontological core of his view is that ideas are *modes* of the mind.[4] This Cartesian terminology is echoed in Kant's own usage. He writes, for example, that 'modification of our sensibility is the only way in which objects are given to us' (A139/B178), and (as pointed out above) repeatedly talks of representations as being 'modifications of the mind' (see, e.g., A97) or equivalently as 'determinations of the mind' (see, e.g., A34/B50). These internal modifications or determinations are then the immediate objects of awareness. The following analogy may help in understanding this jargon. Imagine a hollow globe of soft opaque plastic. The exterior surface of the globe is acted on by external forces and in response takes on various shapes. In the Cartesian and Kantian terminology, each particular shape the globe comes to take on is a *mode* or *modification* of its capacity to receive shapes (its 'receptivity', as it were). This receptivity is a capacity or faculty in the Aristotelian sense of being a range of potentialities that can be actualised (in this case, by

---

[1] For an overview of Scholastic accounts of cognition, see E. Stump, 'The Mechanisms of Cognition: Ockham on Mediating Species', in *The Cambridge Companion to Ockham*, ed. P. V. Spade (Cambridge University Press, 1999), pp. 168–203.

[2] G. W. F. Leibniz, *New Essays on Human Understanding*, trans. Peter Remnant and Jonathan Bennett (Cambridge University Press, 1996), p. 61.

[3] For useful accounts of the motivation for representationalism, see J. P. Carriero, 'The First Meditation', in *Descartes's Meditations*, ed. V. Chappell (Lanham, MD: Rowman & Littlefield, 1997), pp. 1–31, and M. Ayers, *Locke*, vol. 1 (London: Routledge, 1991), part 1.

[4] On the complexities and ambiguities of Descartes's notion of an idea, see R. McRae, ' "Idea" as a Philosophical Term in the Seventeenth Century', *Journal of the History of Ideas* 26 (1965), 175–90, and N. Jolley, *The Light of the Soul* (Oxford University Press, 1990), ch. 2.

the external forces). Or, in the equivalent jargon of 'determinations', we could say that the plastic globe is *determinable* in various ways (i.e., can take on a range of shapes), and in a particular case is *determined* by an external force to take on a certain *determination* (i.e., a certain shape). Let us now imagine a viewer placed within this opaque plastic globe. All she can observe are the internal shapes formed by the globe in response to the external forces. That is, all that is available to her consciousness are the globe's modifications or determinations. The position of this viewer inside the globe is thus analogous to the position of the mind in a representationalist epistemology.

It might be suggested that this analogy of the viewer inside the globe helps to make one thing blindingly obvious, namely, that representationalism is a peculiarly blatant example of the so-called 'homunculus fallacy'.[5] That is, internal representations need a subject – a 'homunculus' – to grasp, or use, or be aware of them. But then this homunculus must itself have its own internal representations and will thus contain a further homunculus, and so on *ad infinitum*. The charge is, in other words, that a theory holding that internal representations mediate the awareness of external things must thereby be committed to holding that further representations are required to mediate the awareness of the former representations, and is thus involved in a vicious infinite regress.

This charge of fallacy, however, does not hold against the views discussed here, for it is based upon a misunderstanding of both the problem to which representationalism is addressed, and the sort of solution it is intended to provide. Certainly, if representationalism were intended as a reductive analysis of awareness or representation, then it would indeed be guilty of the homunculus fallacy. That charge of fallacy is, after all, simply a dramatic way of pointing towards a circularity of explanation. However, it seems clear that Kant and the other major figures in the representationalist tradition think of the capacity to represent as a primitive property of the mental. Hence, what motivates them is not a felt need to provide a reductive analysis or explanation of the notion of representation itself. As pointed out above, the central motivation for the postulation of internal representations in fact lies in the rejection of the Scholastic account of cognition. For the Scholastics, the mind as it were reaches right out to the objects themselves, by becoming formally identical with them. With this kind of immediate contact between mind and object rejected as unintelligible, it seemed to the representationalist thinkers that the only possible basis for the cognition

---

[5] See D. Dennett, *Brainstorms* (Brighton: Harvester Press, 1978), pp. 122ff.

of objects could be the effects of those objects upon the mind (i.e., the mind's own modifications). But there is no reason why the mind should not have the immediate access to its own modifications that is ruled out in the case of external objects. Hence, the representationalists can take the step of postulating internal representations as the immediate objects of consciousness, without thereby falling into any regress. In other words, only one 'homunculus' – the mind itself – is required, and there is therefore no fallacy.

Representationalist views are sometimes accused of a further supposed error, namely, that of 'reifying' representations, and it is worth briefly discussing this accusation. To recapitulate, by the term 'representationalism' I mean that family of epistemological theories committed to the core belief that the immediate objects of consciousness are the mind's own ideas, impressions, or representations. In such theories, consciousness or awareness is, in other words, conceived of as being primarily reflexive in nature. This, however, does not entail that the mind's ideas, impressions, or representations are independent entities. To say that an idea is 'the object of my awareness' is simply a grammatically convenient way of saying that the idea is 'that which I am aware of'. It is not the same as saying that an idea is an object *per se*, in the sense of being an entity that could exist independently of the mind. As pointed out above, in the Cartesian model followed by Kant, ideas or representations are not internal entities but rather internal states. That is, they are modes or modifications of the mind, or ways in which the mind exists. In such a model, representations are therefore not reified into independent entities, but instead have an 'adjectival' mode of being. They could be compared with other states of a subject, such as a state of irritation. The subject can become reflexively aware of being in this state, and can thereby make the state an object of consciousness, but this does not entail that the state of irritation is an independent entity. Hence, whether or not the reifying of ideas is an error, it is not a necessary consequence of accepting representationalism. Whilst no doubt representationalists like Hume and (perhaps) Berkeley do think of ideas as independent entities, there seems no reason to think that Kant is committed to such a view.

There is one more error that representationalist epistemologies are sometimes accused of that I will also pause briefly to dismiss. This is the claim that representationalism is wrong for the simple reason that we are usually aware of external things (like cats) and not of internal things (like our ideas of cats). As G. E. M. Anscombe puts it: 'When one reads Locke, one wants to protest: "The mind is not employed about ideas, but about things – unless ideas are what we happen to be thinking about" '.[6] This protest, although tempting, is not a valid criticism of representationalism, for it is, in effect, simply a repetition of the truism that when I think about X it is X itself that I am thinking about, and not some proxy that stands in for it. Representationalism is not an absurd attempt to deny this truism by asserting that, despite appearances, we really spend all our time thinking about our own internal states – it is, rather, an attempt to provide a philosophical account of just how it is possible for us to think about X itself.

Now, it should be mentioned here that, despite the language used throughout the *Critique*, there have been some attempts to deny that Kant is a representationalist, and to interpret him as being instead some kind of direct realist. In direct realism, representations or ideas are not thought of as being themselves the immediate objects of awareness, but instead as constituting the act or state of awareness itself. Hence, at least in the case of veridical perception, the immediate object of awareness is the external thing itself and not a representation of that thing. Richard Aquila, one of the proponents of this sort of reading of Kant, puts this point as follows.

Cognitive states [i.e., representations], in the sense that was new with Kant, are not cognitive relations with objects, nor are they themselves peculiar objects supposed to mediate the occurrence of cognitive relations. They are simply the perceiver's awareness of possible objects.[7]

Derk Pereboom also endorses a direct realist reading of Kant, claiming that 'for [Kant] the immediate object of awareness is always the ordinary object and not some special object', and that therefore, for example, 'Intuitions . . . are the immediate awarenesses of . . . ordinary objects', rather than themselves objects of awareness.[8] A third attempt to see Kant as a direct realist is Arthur Collins's *Possible Experience*, in which he writes that, according to Kant, 'Having representations *is* our way of apprehending perceivable objects . . . we are conscious, in the first place, not of *them*, but of . . . outer things'.[9]

The fundamental problem with this direct realist reading of Kant is that it does not do justice to his use of an 'act-object' grammar in talking of representations. As mentioned above, Kant persistently talks of representations as being themselves the objects of our mental acts – as objects of

[6] G. E. M. Anscombe, 'The Intentionality of Sensation: A Grammatical Feature', in her *Metaphysics and the Philosophy of Mind* (Minneapolis: University of Minnesota Press, 1981), p. 5.
[7] R. E. Aquila, *Representational Mind* (Bloomington: Indiana University Press, 1983), p. xi.
[8] D. Pereboom, 'Kant on Intentionality', *Synthese* 77 (1988), 326, 338.
[9] A. W. Collins, *Possible Experience* (Berkeley: University of California Press, 1999), p. 35.

consciousness or awareness, as well as of a great variety of other mental acts. Kant's language thus constantly implies that for him, as for most of the major philosophers of the seventeenth and eighteenth centuries (such as Descartes, Malebranche, Leibniz, Locke, Berkeley and Hume), human cognition is understood as involving the mind's reflexive grasp of its own internal representations. Hence, to read the *Critique* as expressing a direct realism is, at most, to compose a variation on a Kantian theme rather than to seek to understand the historical Kant. In fairness, it should be said that the direct realist reading of Kant is largely motivated by an attempt to do justice to the *anti*-Cartesian themes that are clearly evident in the *Critique*. One of the things I hope to show in this book is that it is possible to do justice to those themes, whilst nonetheless taking Kant's representationalism seriously.

If the historical Kant is thus a representationalist, it must now be asked how he answers the obvious and fundamental question that any such epistemology faces, namely, how it is possible to cognise external objects, given that all that is immediately available to the mind is its own internal representations. That is, having denied the immediacy of contact between mind and world that is provided by the Scholastic account, representationalism needs an account of how any contact at all can be re-established. Put in its most general terms, the problem is this. Our cognition is, most usually, not of our own internal states, but of a world that is, in an important sense, independent of us. A representationalist epistemology needs to account for this intuitively obvious fact. It thus needs to explain how the mind's awareness of its own internal states can yet amount to, or provide the basis for, an awareness of an independent reality. At least two familiar models for understanding this can be found in the representationalist tradition. The first I shall call the 'indirect realist' model, and the second the 'idealist' model. By 'indirect realism' I mean a position that thinks of representing objects as involving (*i*) an act of awareness of an idea (or representation, impression, etc.) and (*ii*) an inference to the external cause of that idea. By 'idealism' I mean a position that thinks of representing objects as involving (*i*) an act of awareness of an idea and (*ii*) constructive acts in which that idea is linked with other ideas.

In the indirect realist model of cognition, the ideas or representations are thought to stand for external things via a relation of natural resemblance or symbolism, and in the case of veridical perception the ideas are caused in us by the influence of external things. Our knowledge of external things is thus indirect, in that it is mediated by the ideas, which are as it were clues to, or evidence for, the external things that act on our senses. An epistemology of this sort is often associated with the views of Descartes and Locke (although whether or not this is an accurate interpretation of those thinkers is a moot question). Marjorie Grene, for example, writes that Descartes holds that 'it is through judgment . . . that I stretch my ideas from their own undoubted existence as modes of mental life and take them to be copies of things outside'.[10] As this quote makes clear, on an indirect realist model our judgments about the external world become hypothetical identifications of the causal origins of our own ideas. It is through such an act of judgment/inference that the mind breaks through the so-called 'veil of ideas' and re-establishes contact with independent reality.

In the idealist model of cognition, by contrast, the ideas do not signify or stand for something beyond themselves. Instead, the things of the external world are identified with or constructed out of ideas (whether actual or possible), and veridical perceptions are those complex arrays of ideas that obey certain rules of coherence and consistency. On this model (famously propounded by Berkeley) being aware of reality is not a question of *leaping beyond* one's ideas through an inference to their causes, as in the previous model. Rather, it is a question of *enriching* the content of one's ideas by connecting them with one another. This is clear in Berkeley's *A New Theory of Vision*. He argues there that through an unconscious process of 'suggestion' our two-dimensional visual ideas are linked with tactual ideas, via habits of association built up through experience, to produce our experience of a three-dimensional world. The ideas are, as Berkeley puts it, 'most closely twisted, blended, and incorporated together'.[11] It is through this unconscious, constructive process that our reflexive awareness of our own inner states comes to have the richness of the perceived world.

This picture of the contrast between the indirect realist and idealist models of representing objects is of course simplified. It is offered only with the aim of pointing out some well-known landmarks in the philosophical landscape, in order to help locate Kant's views in relation to them. Perhaps the most straightforward way to sum up the contrast presented here is to say that it is the contrast between thinking of our knowledge of the world as either *inferred from* or *reduced to* knowledge of our own representations or ideas. If we now turn to the secondary literature on Kant, it is possible to find commentators who read him as an indirect realist and those who read him as an idealist (as I am using those terms). A clear example of the former can be

[10] M. Grene, *Descartes*, 2nd edn (Indianapolis: Hackett, 1998), p. 10.
[11] G. Berkeley, *An Essay Towards a New Theory of Vision*, § 51, in *A New Theory of Vision and Other Writings* (London: J. M. Dent, 1910), p. 35. Cf. G. C. Hatfield and W. Epstein, 'The Sensory Core and the Medieval Foundations of Early Modern Perceptual Theory', *Isis* 70 (1979), 379–82.

found in Paul Guyer's *Kant and the Claims of Knowledge*. That Guyer views Kant as committed to some kind of indirect realism comes out particularly clearly in his discussion of the Second Analogy. According to Guyer, the problem of the Analogy is how we pass from knowledge of our subjective mental states (i.e., our representations) to knowledge of objective states of affairs. And Guyer explicitly treats this problem as a question of how we can be justified in making inferences based on the evidence constituted by our representations. As Guyer remarks, for Kant we make 'judgments about empirical objects . . . on the basis of our representations of them'.[12] An explicit example of an interpretation of Kant as holding to the idealist model is given by Jonathan Bennett in *Kant's Analytic*, who writes that 'Kant thinks that statements about phenomena are not merely supported by, but are equivalent to, statements about actual and possible sensory states'.[13] That is, according to Bennett, Kant thinks that our knowledge of the (phenomenal) world reduces to knowledge of our own representations, or 'sensory states'.

The secondary literature thus contains interpretations of Kant as an indirect realist and as an idealist (I am not saying that Guyer and Bennett are the only such readings – I use them simply as illustrative examples). However, it is well known that both interpretations face some major problems. Firstly, the interpretation of Kant as an indirect realist seems plainly to contradict an important claim that he makes in the Refutation of Idealism, where he writes as follows.

Idealism assumed that the only immediate experience is inner experience, and that from that outer things could only be *inferred*, but, as in any case in which one infers from given effects to *determinate* causes, only unreliably . . . Yet here it is proved that outer experience is really immediate. (B276)

Here Kant explicitly denies that we infer our knowledge of external objects from knowledge of our own inner states (ideas or representations), and thus explicitly denies that he is committed to indirect realism. Secondly, the interpretation of Kant as having an idealist model of object representation – and thus as holding that our knowledge of the objective world reduces to knowledge of our internal representations – seems inconsistent with his repeated fervent denials that he is an empirical idealist like Berkeley. Furthermore, whilst Berkeley at least offers some sketches for how such an idealist reduction might proceed, there is nothing equivalent to be found in

---

[12] See P. Guyer, *Kant and the Claims of Knowledge* (Cambridge University Press, 1987), ch. 10. The quote is from p. 246.
[13] J. Bennett, *Kant's Analytic* (Cambridge University Press, 1966), p. 22.

Kant's text.[14] Hence, both the indirect realist and the idealist interpretations seem to conflict with salient features of the *Critique*. This does not mean that there are no ways of dealing with these apparent conflicts, for the secondary literature offers many such attempts. But it does suggest that it is worth looking for a reading of Kant's notion of representation that avoids having to deal with those conflicts in the first place.

In summary, the position reached so far is as follows. A representational-ist epistemology needs to give an account of our awareness of independent reality that is consistent with the claim that the only immediate objects of our awareness are the mind's internal representations. What I called the 'indirect realist' model saw the key to this account as lying in an act of *inference* to the external cause of the idea. What I called the 'idealist' model saw the key as lying in an act of *construction*, in which representations were linked together. I have suggested that there are reasons to believe that Kant rejects both the indirect realist and the idealist model of representation. My interpretative hypothesis is that Kant sees the key to an account of representation as lying in an act of *synthesis*, which is something crucially different from both inference and construction. It is a model that allows him to hold consistently that representations are the immediate objects of our awareness, and that our knowledge of an independent reality is neither inferred from nor reduced to our knowledge of those representations. The crucial point for understanding this is to see that for Kant the 'determina-tions' or 'modifications' of the mind constitute the *representational medium*, which must not be assimilated with the object represented *in* that medium. In the following section I attempt to explain what this means.

SEEING THINGS IN PICTURES

In order to fill out and clarify my interpretative hypothesis, I will consider what it is to see something in a picture, and will show how this can help provide us with a clear and intuitive model for understanding Kant's notion of representation. In the case of pictures, the representational medium is various spatial configurations of marks on a page, rather than certain 'determinations' or 'modifications' of the mind. Nonetheless, I hope to show that it is an analogy worth pursuing. Before I begin, it should also be emphasised that nothing in what follows is intended to be an *explanation* of the notion of representation, pictorial or otherwise – if this means a

---

[14] For a useful summary of the evidence against assimilating Kant to Berkeley, see S. Gardner, *Kant and the Critique of Pure Reason* (London: Routledge, 1999), pp. 271–8.

reduction of it to non-representational notions. As mentioned above, Kant uses the notion of representation as a primitive, which suggests that he thinks of it as a ground-floor property of the mental and in no need of reductive explanation. Hence we can expect Kant to be exploiting in his own discussions the conceptual resources contained in our ordinary notion of representation. The central point of the discussion in this section is to emphasise that those resources can provide Kant with a richer notion of representation (and thus a richer notion of what it is to be conscious of a representation) than that which is at work in the indirect realist and idealist models of cognition discussed above.[15]

In discussing pictorial representation, it will help to have a concrete example of a picture before us. So here is one:

This is a picture of a smiling face. We could say, 'These black dots here are eyes, this curved line is a mouth', and so forth. So much is obvious. We might then ask, 'What is the relation between the collection of lines and dots on the page and the smiling face?' But this question is potentially misleading, and any talk of there being a relation here between two things does not make for clarity. For the smiling face is not a separate object that lies 'behind' or 'outside of' the configuration of lines and dots. That is, the configuration of lines and dots is not like a signpost that points beyond itself to some further object (i.e., the smiling face). Nor is the configuration of lines and dots as it were evidence for, or a natural sign of, the smiling face. For I do not *infer* to the smiling face from the lines and dots, as a doctor might infer the presence of a certain bacterial infection from a rash on the skin. For the smiling face is precisely *in* the picture.

If the smiling face is therefore not something lying beyond the picture, which the configuration of lines and dots goes proxy for, then it might be suggested that the face in the picture is identical to the configuration (or to some part thereof). But this suggestion will not do either. For example, the face in the picture is smiling, but the configuration of lines and dots is not smiling – for that is nonsensical. The configuration is composed of ink

---

[15] My discussion is highly indebted to R. Pitkänen, 'The Resemblance View of Pictorial Representation', *British Journal of Aesthetics* 16 (1976), 313–23, and to two papers by H. Ishiguro: 'Imagination – II', *Aristotelian Society (Supplement)* 41 (1967), 37–56, and 'On Representations', *European Journal of Philosophy* 2 (1994), 109–24.

marks on paper, but the face is not composed of ink marks on paper – it is composed of eyes, a nose and a mouth. Therefore the face in the picture and the configuration of lines and dots on the page are not identical. A two-dimensional depiction of a three-dimensional object makes this fact even more obvious (and on this, see the discussion of the cube below). A more general way of putting this point is that the 'is' of representation is not the 'is' of identity; similarly, the 'in' of 'the face is in the picture' is not the 'in' of physical inclusion.[16] This is most manifestly true if the picture is of an existing thing. For example, it is clear that the Prime Minister is not *in* the Parliament House in the same way that he is *in* a photo of the Prime Minister that appears in a newspaper.

There are thus two points that need to be held on to. Firstly, the phrase 'the smiling face' as I have used it here concerns only something *in* the picture and not something outside of the picture (it is, e.g., obvious that the picture I gave above is not a picture of a particular, existing smiling face – such as the Prime Minister's). Secondly, in using the phrase 'the smiling face' I am not talking about the ink marks on the page, but about what is presented by those ink marks. We could sum up these two points by saying that the picture above does not stand proxy for something outside of itself, but rather *presents* something to us *off its own bat* – or '*auf eigene Faust*', as Wittgenstein has it.[17] Kant's German term for 'representation' captures this sense nicely, for a *Vor-Stellung* is literally a *before-putting*. (This is different from the German term '*Repräsentation*', which tends to carry the sense of one thing going proxy for another.) The configuration of lines and dots above – the representational medium – precisely serves to put a smiling face before us. As a matter of terminology, it is worth pointing out that where I have used the phrase 'the smiling face' I could also have used more general phrases like 'what is in the picture', 'the depicted object' or, more portentously, 'the intentional object of the picture'. As I use them here, these phrases are independent of any questions about the existence of anything over and above the existence of the picture. That is, to say that there is a such-and-such in a picture does not entail that there exists a such-and-such; it entails only that there exists a picture of a such-and-such. But the crucial point is that this latter statement says a good deal more

---

[16] On the 'is' of representation, see H. Ishiguro, 'Representation: An Investigation Based on a Passage in the *Tractatus*', in *Forms of Representation*, ed. B. Freed *et al.* (Amsterdam: North Holland Publishing, 1975), pp. 189–202. On the 'in' of 'in the picture', see V. C. Aldrich, 'Mirrors, Pictures, Words, Perceptions', in *New Representationalisms*, ed. E. Wright (Aldershot: Avebury, 1993), pp. 117–35.

[17] L. Wittgenstein, *Notebooks 1914–1916*, 2nd edn (University of Chicago Press, 1979), entry for 15 November 1914.

than just that there exists a certain configuration of ink marks on a page. For a picture is not a mere cluster of ink marks that may or may not stand in relation to some further thing – it is not 'flat' or 'dead' in this way, but rather a 'before-putting' in the sense I have tried to make clear.

The point of repeating these truisms here is to show that our concept of pictorial representation has a certain richness about it, in that it embodies a distinction between the representational medium (i.e., the configuration of lines and dots) and the depicted object (i.e., what is in the picture). My interpretative hypothesis is that we should read Kant as insisting upon the importance of this distinction in the case of mental representations as well. It is, I suggest, because he is making use of a richer conception of representation that he can avoid having to choose between an indirect realist and an idealist model of cognition. The notion of mental representation at work in those models of cognition is of something that is effectively 'flat' or 'dead', in that it does not present something 'off its own bat'. Using a different sort of language, this is to say that such models neglect the intentionality of sensation.[18]

I will try to explain this by taking the example of visual representations. In this case, collapsing the notion of the depicted object into the notion of the representational medium produces the familiar concept of a 'mental image', the *esse* of which is *percipi*. Take, for instance, another simple picture:

In the standard early modern representationalist accounts of visual perception, the mind is thought of as being immediately aware of representations that are two-dimensional 'mental images' like this.[19] On the indirect realist model of cognition, the two-dimensional image provides part of the evidential basis upon which the mind makes judgments (i.e., inferences) about the three-dimensional cube in the external world. On the idealist model of cognition (i.e., Berkeley's model), the two-dimensional image is associated with (or 'suggests') various tactual ideas, so as to make up a complex idea that constitutes the three-dimensional cube.

Both the indirect realist and idealist models of cognition thus share a conception of what is available for immediate apprehension by the mind, and this conception is the product of collapsing the distinction between

---

[18] See Anscombe, 'Intentionality of Sensation', *passim*.
[19] See, e.g., Hatfield and Epstein, 'Sensory Core'.

representational medium and depicted object. That is, the models have no conception of a representation as something that 'presents off its own bat' (in the sense discussed above). Hence, a mental representation becomes something that is apprehended and then must either be thought of in relation to some further object through an act of inference (in the indirect realist model), or thought of as partially constituting the object itself (in the idealist model). But if instead the distinction between medium and depicted object is maintained, then a different account of representation can be given. In the analogous case of the above picture, rather than simply having a two-dimensional image available for apprehension, we have the following: a representational medium (i.e., a certain configuration of ink marks) that is indeed (effectively) two-dimensional, and also a three-dimensional object (i.e., a cube) *in* or *presented by* the representational medium. In other words, seeing the picture is not a question of simply apprehending the representational medium, but of seeing something *in* the medium. It is something analogous to this act of 'seeing in' that is the key to Kant's account of representation – that is, its equivalent with respect to the reflexive grasp of mental representations, namely, the act Kant calls 'synthesis'. I want to suggest that it is this act of synthesis that replaces the acts of inference and construction that play the crucial role in the indirect realist and idealist models.

Before going on to discuss this notion of 'seeing in', it is worth saying something about what may lie behind the 'flattening' of the notion of representation that is characteristic of the indirect realist and idealist models of cognition. When considering representation, it is very tempting to treat it from a third-person rather than from a first-person perspective, and then the crucial notion of 'presenting off its own bat' tends to be lost from view. To think of representation from a third-person perspective is to have a model like this before one's eyes:

Mind → Representation →

Given such a model, it is natural to ask how the mind gets from the representation to the object – how it breaks through the 'veil of ideas' to the world beyond. An obvious choice is via an act of inference, as in the indirect realist view. The idealist view, on the other hand, argues that the problem is unreal because there is nothing beyond the representations: the supposed 'veil' is in fact reality itself. As I have argued, what is common to both of these views is the conception of a representation as something 'flat', rather than as a 'before-putting' or '*Vor-Stellung*'. The model above makes such a view almost irresistible, but this model is from the perspective of someone who is, as it were, observing another person representing a cat. If instead one takes up a first-person perspective (i.e., of the subject that has the representation), then what one has is simply this:

In this case the questions one will be led naturally to ask are rather different from the former case. They will concern not how the mind can get from one thing (the representation) to another thing (the cat), but how the representation functions to *present* the object *to oneself*. This is one reason why it is worth taking seriously Kant's remark in the first-edition Paralogisms that 'it is obvious that if one wants to represent a thinking being, one must put oneself in its place, and thus substitute one's own subject for the object one wants to consider' (A354). Since the *Critique* is itself a representation of a thinking being (or, more precisely, is a representation of the cognising human mind in general), Kant's remark is an instruction for reading the book. By following this instruction and taking up a first-person perspective we will, to put things in more Kantian language, be led to consider what is involved in something being able to appear to us *in* our representations, and thus 'become an object for us'.

I now return to take up the main thread of my discussion. I argued above that the awareness of a representation (as a 'before-putting') will involve not simply an apprehension of the representational medium, but also an act of seeing something in that medium. One way of clarifying this notion of 'seeing in' is by using the Aristotelian jargon of 'matter' and 'form'. I am not claiming that this fits with Kant's own use of that distinction (which appears in a bewildering variety of contexts in the *Critique*); only that it may help to make clearer what I am saying. In a hylomorphic analysis of pictorial representation, the representational medium (i.e., the ink marks in their spatial arrangement) could be called the *matter*. It could then be said that to see the depicted object (e.g., the smiling face or the cube) in that spatial arrangement of ink marks is not to apprehend an object separate from the medium, but rather to see those lines and dots as *informed* in a certain way. This may help one to think of the connection between the representational medium and the depicted object in the correct way, and not as two separate things in a relation.[20]

---

[20] W. Charlton makes a similar use of the matter–form distinction in *Aesthetics* (London: Hutchinson, 1970), ch. 3.

A comparison with the notion of seeing a meaningful gesture (such as a greeting or an insult) may also help in this respect. An account of this in the Cartesian style would run something like this. We begin with the seeing of a physical movement of a body in space. Identifying this as the meaningful, purposive action of a person then becomes a matter of identifying a certain mental occurrence (an intention or an act of will) as the efficient cause of that movement. In this way, seeing the movement as meaningful becomes an *inference*, an attempt to identify by hypothesis a hidden, mental cause that we postulate to lie behind the mere physical movement (which is all that is immediately accessible to us). Such a view is thus analogous to what I have called the 'indirect realist' model. We could also imagine a reductive empiricist analysis, which would run something like this. Again we begin with the seeing of a mere physical movement, but associate or connect it with various other actual and possible movements and such like, and thus enrich it into the complex notion of a voluntary act. Such an account would thus be analogous to what I have called the 'idealist' model. It will be noticed that both share the assumption that all that is available for immediate observation is a 'mere physical movement'. A hylomorphic analysis, on the other hand, is an attempt to recapture the realism that has disappeared in these Cartesian and empiricist accounts.[21] On a hylomorphic account, the intention does not lie hidden behind the physical movement, nor is talk of intention simply an abbreviated way of talking about complex patterns of physical movements. Rather, the intention is thought of as *embodied in* the physical movement (the matter of the gesture), or as *informing* it. A gesture is, as we might say, 'filled with meaning'. We thus see the intention *in* the physical movement. In other words, the hylomorphic view holds that the Cartesian and empiricist models involve an impoverished conception of what is accessible to immediate observation. I want to suggest that, in an analogous fashion, Kant has a much richer conception of what is available to the mind in its reflexive grasp of its own representations than do the indirect realist and idealist versions of representationalism.

This appeal to the distinction between matter and form, and the comparison with seeing a meaningful action, has I hope helped to clarify further the closely connected notions of 'presenting off its own bat' and 'seeing in'. They were another way of making the point that seeing a configuration of lines as, for example, presenting a face (i.e., seeing the face in the picture),

---

[21] Cf. J. Haldane, 'A Return to Form in the Philosophy of Mind', in *Form and Matter*, ed. D. S. Oderberg (Oxford: Blackwell, 1999), p. 59.

is not an act of making an inference about something that lies behind or beyond the picture, but nor is it a matter of *merely* seeing a configuration of lines. In order to see the depicted object in the picture we must of course apprehend the matter – that is, the lines and dots in their spatial arrangement. But this is not sufficient, for we must also grasp the form – that is, see those lines as presenting something to us.

To say that apprehending the configuration of ink marks is not sufficient for seeing the object in the picture follows from the earlier point that the depicted object is not identical to that configuration, but it is worth emphasising. Looking at the two examples of pictures that I gave previously, we can imagine a person who was aware of all the lines and dots standing in their spatial arrangement, but yet who failed to see the face or the cube in those lines and dots (i.e., who was unable to see that the configuration composed a picture of a face or of a cube). We could imagine that person able to draw an identical copy of each picture – that is, able to produce a spatial configuration of ink marks that was indistinguishable from the original – thus demonstrating that she had accurately apprehended that configuration in all its details. Yet that person would be bewildered by (could make no sense of) any remarks about the face or the cube in the picture. No doubt the two pictures used above are so simple and familiar that this failure to see what was in them would probably strike us as very odd. However, in the case of more complex pictures such an occurrence is not so uncommon. The difference between merely seeing the picture as a collection of ink marks and seeing what is in the picture is made especially clear in the case of trick pictures, in which a face, for example, may be hidden in a tangle of lines. In such cases we may need to have things explained to us – 'You see, this line here is the nose and these the eyes', before we 'get it' and see the face.[22]

In these cases that I have imagined, a person has failed to see the depicted object, yet she has not failed to apprehend any aspect of the representational medium. That is, there are no lines, dots, patches of colour, or whatever, that she has failed to see, nor has she failed to see the spatial configuration in which they stand. Using the hylomorphic jargon, it could be said that she has thus apprehended the matter of the picture, but has failed to grasp its form. This situation could also be described by using some Kantian jargon. It seems quite natural to say of this person that what she is suffering from is not a failure of *receptivity*, for there is nothing wrong with her eyesight, nor is there anything obscuring her vision. Rather, what she is suffering from is

---

[22] Cf. Wittgenstein's discussion of 'aspect seeing' in *Philosophical Investigations*, part 2, § xi.

a failure of *imagination* – where I am using this word in the original (and Kantian) sense of a capacity for 'image-making' (i.e., '*Einbildungskraft*'). We could also say of such a person that she is *blind* to something that lies before her, but that her blindness is not a defect of receptivity but of imagination.

There is, in other words, a conceptual gap between simply apprehending the representational medium (the lines and dots in their spatial arrangement) and actually seeing what is in it (the depicted object). But, as I hope my discussion in this section has made clear, what bridges that conceptual gap is not an act of inference from the configuration of lines and dots to some further object that lies outside of them (in the manner of indirect realism). Nor is it an act of constructing or compounding a complex of lines and dots (in the manner of idealism). Rather, it is an imaginative act of seeing something *in* the configuration of lines and dots.

This concludes my discussion of the notion of 'seeing things in pictures'. In it, I have briefly attempted to do two things. Firstly, I have attempted to draw out some of the conceptual resources in our ordinary notion of representation (or, at least, of pictorial representation). Secondly, I have attempted to suggest how those resources may allow for the construction of an account of mental representation that differs in important ways from both the indirect realist and idealist models. In the next section I start to fill out my interpretative hypothesis that Kant is making use of just such an account of representation.

REPRESENTATION AND SYNTHESIS

In the first section of this chapter it was emphasised that Kant, like most of the major philosophers of the seventeenth and eighteenth centuries, was a representationalist. That is, he held that the immediate objects of consciousness or awareness were the mind's internal representations or ideas. For Kant, in cognition these internal representations are modifications or determinations of the mind's sensibility (i.e., of its capacity for receptivity). I now turn to explore some of the consequences of marrying this basically Cartesian model to the conception of representation outlined in the previous section. Once again I should emphasise that in this chapter I am simply making a hypothesis about Kant's notion of representation rather than arguing for its truth. Although I consider here the occasional passage from the *Critique*, the real evidence for my interpretation will come in the following chapters, through a demonstration of its capacity to make good sense of the main argument of the B-Deduction.

A useful way of approaching these matters is to return to my earlier analogy, in which the representationalist cognising subject was compared to a viewer placed inside a hollow opaque globe of soft plastic. The globe (sensibility) takes on various shapes (modifications) in response to external forces (independent reality), and these shapes are observed from within by the viewer (are grasped reflexively by the mind). Let us now modify this analogy slightly, and think of the external forces as resulting in a cartoon film being projected on the inside of the globe. That is, available for the viewer's observation is a sequence of various arrangements of colour patches. However, the viewer does not merely see a sequence of colour patches, but rather sees a cartoon story, with various characters engaged in various actions (e.g., Wile E. Coyote engaged in dastardly plots to catch the Road-Runner, etc.). That is, the spatially arranged colour patches (the modifications of sensibility) make up the representational medium, and the viewer does not simply apprehend the patches, but sees things *in* them. Hence, on a model of representation like this the cognising mind is immediately conscious of its own modifications, but this reflexive grasp is not a grasp of them simply as internal modifications, but as representations. Crucially, this involves neither an inference nor a constructive act, but rather an exercise of the imagination akin to the act of 'seeing in' discussed above.

As already mentioned, part of my general interpretative hypothesis is that this exercise of the imagination is what Kant calls 'synthesis' or 'combination', and I shall use this terminology henceforth. Kant's explicit definition of synthesis is as follows.

By *synthesis* in the most general sense, however, I understand the action of putting different representations together with each other and comprehending [*begreifen*] their manifoldness in one cognition. (A77/B103)

This definition is, taken by itself, compatible with many different accounts. This includes the common view that synthesis is a process in which mental entities are put into relations with one another, and wholes thus formed out of parts. Such a conception of synthesis assimilates it to the constructive acts involved in the idealist model of cognition. However, the term '*begreifen*' in the passage suggests that Kant thinks of synthesis as primarily an act of comprehending or understanding something. This in turn indicates that the 'putting together' or 'combining' that is mentioned should be understood in a metaphorical sense. My hypothesis is thus that the act of synthesis involved in cognition is the act of grasping the object presented in the representational medium (the modifications of the mind). As such, it is analogous to the act of seeing the depicted object (such as the smiling face) in a picture – the act of comprehending the configuration of lines and dots by seeing what it depicts. Hence, through synthesis the mind grasps its representations as representing things, and not simply as its own modifications.

This talk of being aware of a representation 'as representing' rather than merely 'as a modification of the mind' is closely related to the important Cartesian distinction between the formal and the objective reality of an idea.[23] Descartes famously distinguished between ideas 'considered simply as modes of thought' (i.e., considered with respect to their formal reality) and 'considered as images which represent different things' (i.e., considered with respect to their objective reality).[24] In Kant's hands, I suggest, this becomes the distinction between sensation (*Empfindung*) and intuition (*Anschauung*). I will briefly consider these two notions in turn.

Near the beginning of the *Critique*, Kant writes that an intuition is 'that through which [cognition] relates immediately to [objects]' (A19/B33). By this I suggest Kant means simply that it is in virtue of my grasping an intuition that an object is presented to me as if it were here before me at this very moment. In other words, the reflexive grasp of intuitions is involved in perceiving something, rather than merely thinking about it in its absence. As Charles Parsons puts it, 'immediacy for Kant is direct, phenomenological presence to the mind, as in perception'.[25] This 'immediacy' is thus the same phenomenological quality of an experience which Hume appeals to when talking of the greater 'vivacity' possessed by an impression over an idea. The presence of this quality is decided on the basis of (to borrow Nagel's useful phrase) what it is like to have that experience – that, after all, is the point of calling it 'phenomenological'. It is thus that Kant writes in the *Prolegomena* that 'an intuition is a representation of the sort which *would* depend immediately on the presence of an object' (4:281; my emphasis). It should be noted that Kant uses the subjunctive 'would' (*würde*) in this statement, rather than the indicative. This is because it is in virtue of grasping one's intuitions that one has experiences in which it seems *as if* something were present to one's senses (i.e., putative perceptual experiences). The use of 'as if' here is to emphasise that an experience can possess this property of immediacy independently of whether or not there really is

[23] The importance of this distinction for Kant's philosophy is emphasised by W. Sellars, *Science and Metaphysics* (Atascadero: Ridgeview, 1992), p. 31.
[24] R. Descartes, *Third Meditation* in *The Philosophical Writings of Descartes*, trans. J. Cottingham *et al.* (Cambridge University Press, 1985–91), vol. II, pp. 27–8.
[25] C. Parsons, 'The Transcendental Aesthetic', in *The Cambridge Companion to Kant*, ed. P. Guyer (Cambridge University Press, 1992), p. 66.

something before me – that is, independently of whether that experience is veridical or non-veridical. It is thus that Kant writes that 'it does not follow that every intuitive representation of outer things includes at the same time their existence, for that may well be the mere effect of the imagination (in dreams as well as in delusions)' (B278). This passage does more than suggest that Kant's concern is less with how we represent the world rightly than with how we represent it at all (wrongly or rightly). I will return to this point below.

I now turn to consider the notion of sensation. Kant defines it by saying that the 'effect of a object on the capacity for representation, insofar as we are affected by it, is *sensation*' (A20/B34), and that 'a *perception* that refers to the subject as a modification of its state is a *sensation*' (A320/B376). These two passages show that Kant thinks of sensations as representations considered simply as effects on, or modifications of, the subject. In this way Kant is closer to Malebranche than to Descartes. Whilst Descartes sometimes seems to treat sensations as confused representations of bodily events, Malebranche argues that sensations (or '*sentiments*') are not representational but simply modifications of the subject.[26]

I thus suggest the following definitions for Kant's terms. A sensation is a modification of the sensibility, insofar as it is merely a subjective state. An intuition is a modification of the sensibility, insofar as it plays a role in presenting an object in cognition. Now, it is important to be careful with intensional constructions like the 'insofar as' that features in these definitions (and with equivalents like 'considered as' and '*qua*'). So, to say that 'intuitions, but not sensations, represent objects' is not to say that there exist two classes of mental states, one of which (intuitions) is intentional and the other (sensations) non-intentional.[27] The sentence does not say this, because the terms 'sensation' and 'intuition' as defined above are not terms for classes of things. Rather, what this sentence means is that one does not cognise objects by grasping one's sensations, but by grasping one's intuitions. That is to say, one does not cognise objects by grasping one's mental modifications simply *as* mental modifications, but by grasping them *as* representing something.

What I mean by this can be made clearer by talking of the ambiguity in the notion of the 'object of sight' in the case of pictorial representation. If I am looking at a picture and am asked 'What do you see?', it is clear that I can answer this question in at least two different ways. I can say either that I see

[26] See Jolley, *Light of the Soul*, ch. 4. On the connection between Kant and Malebranche, see also R. George, 'Kant's Sensationism', *Synthese* 47 (1981), 229–55.

[27] George ('Kant's Sensationism') seems to make this mistake.

a certain configuration of ink marks, or that I see a smiling face (or whatever the picture happens to be of).[28] In the first case the object of sight is the representational medium (or, the matter, to use the hylomorphic jargon). In the second case the object of sight is the representational medium seen as presenting an object (or, the matter seen as informed in a certain way). Now, in the case of mental representation, the mind becomes reflexively aware of its own modifications (internal states), which are thus the immediate objects of consciousness. However, in cognition, the mind is not aware of its modifications simply as states of itself – that is, simply as *sensations*. Rather, in virtue of an act of synthesis the mind is aware of those modifications as presenting something, or as putting something before it – that is, as *intuitions*. In this way, an intuition can indeed be 'that through which our cognition relates immediately to objects' (see A19/B33). In other words, the grasp of an intuition (i.e., the bringing of the modifications of our sensibility to consciousness via an act of synthesis) just *is* the immediate awareness of the object *in* that intuition. This is because an intuition is not merely a mental state. If so, it would be a 'flat' or a 'dead' thing, at which our awareness would 'terminate' as it were, and we would thus require something like an act of inference to 'get beyond' it (as in the indirect realist model of cognition). Rather, the grasp of an intuition is the awareness of a representation *as representing* – and this is not simply awareness of a mental state, but awareness of what is *in* that representation.

An understanding of this fundamental point shows why the act of synthesis can be thought of as resulting in a *judgment*. This may sound peculiar to modern ears, which are perhaps accustomed to associate the term 'judgment' with the notion of something like an asserted proposition – an abstract entity that can be the content of a 'that' clause. But I doubt that Kant has any clear understanding of a judgment in this sense.[29] Judgment for him is primarily an awareness *of* things *as* being thus and so, rather than an awareness *that* things are thus and so. If we are to grasp what Kant is doing with this notion of judgment it is, once again, important to remember the Cartesian heritage that he is adapting and transforming. According to Descartes, the *cogito* reveals an internal realm of ideas and their contents, a realm which is immune from sceptical doubt. It is the act of judging, Descartes holds, that leaves us vulnerable to error, precisely because to judge is to leap beyond the immediacy and certainty of ideas and their contents, and make a claim about the external world. To repeat

---

[28] For a useful discussion of this, see Ishiguro, 'Imagination – II', pp. 43–5.

[29] See, e.g., Kant's discussion of the contrast between 'the black man' and 'the man is black' in a letter to Beck, 3 July 1792 (11:347).

Grene's remark (quoted above), for Descartes 'it is through judgment . . . that I stretch my ideas from their own undoubted existence as modes of mental life and take them to be copies of things outside'.[30] Thus the fundamental role that judgment is playing in Descartes's representationalism can be roughly characterised as follows. It is the mental act of as it were getting out to the world beyond one's internal states and saying something about it (and thus opening oneself to the possibility of error). Now, given Descartes's indirect realist model of cognition, for the act of judgment to play this role it must effectively become an act of inference – an attempt to identify by hypothesis the efficient cause of an idea, like a doctor attempting to diagnose an infection from a rash on the skin.

For Kant, on the other hand, the notion of synthesis (as I have interpreted it) can play a key part in 'getting out to the world'. Synthesis is the act of, as it were, seeing the depicted object in the representational medium. Now, the representational medium that is grasped in the act of synthesis is mental, in that it is constituted by modifications of the mind. But what is 'seen' or cognised *in* the medium is not therefore mental. On the contrary, it may be (and often enough is) an object in three-dimensional space – a coyote chasing a road-runner, for example. This is in some ways an obvious point, but it has nonetheless been a source of confusion. For example, David Bell, in expounding Brentano's and Husserl's conception of representation, argues as follows: an object exists in our representations; representations are mental; therefore the object in the representations (the so-called 'intentional object') is itself mental. This confuses the notion of being in a representation with the mereological notion of being a proper part of.[31] It is like arguing as follows: there is a cat in this picture (i.e., this is a picture of a cat); this picture is made of ink and paper; therefore the cat in this picture is made of ink and paper. But the picture is not a picture of an ink-and-paper cat, but of a warm-blooded, furry, bad-tempered creature whose breath smells of fish. Bell, in other words, is implicitly committed to the reductive view of a representation as something 'flat' or 'dead', rather than as a 'before-putting'. It is certainly the case that facts about things in pictures are (identical to) facts about what pictures there are. (At least, as I am using phrases like 'things in pictures'.) But this does not mean that facts about what pictures there are reduce to facts about ink marks, for, as I have repeatedly argued, pictures are not merely configurations of ink marks.

---

[30] Grene, *Descartes*, p. 10.
[31] D. Bell, *Husserl* (London: Routledge, 1990), pp. 9ff. Michael Dummett discusses Bell's confusion in 'Frege and Husserl on Reference', in *The Seas of Language* (Oxford University Press, 1993), pp. 224–9.

Extending this model to mental representations means that the act of synthesis can thus produce the awareness of a world beyond, or independent of, one's own mental states. In grasping its representations *as* representing, the mind's awareness thereby goes beyond its own subjective states. For such a synthesis does not result in the grasp of something that is 'merely intentional' or a sort of 'mental shadow'. Rather, the object that is cognised in the representations can be cognised as spatial, as having an *esse* distinct from its *percipi*, and so forth. In other words, in this richer view of representation, the modifications of the mind can come to function not as a veil of ideas needing to be penetrated but as a point of view on an objective world.[32] It is through the synthesis of the modifications of sensibility that this world is revealed as being thus and so. Such an act of synthesis thus results in a *judgment* – a claim about how things are in an independent world. Individual cognitions may be veridical or non-veridical, but in either case they represent or are about that world.

This is very different from the two-stage procedure implicit in Descartes's indirect realist model. In that model the first stage was an immediate consciousness of the content of our ideas. Ideas being modes of our existence as a thinking thing, this consciousness is protected against any possibility of error by the *cogito*. It is only if we choose to affirm those ideas of the world (via an act of judgment) that we step outside this internal realm of thought and thus open ourselves to the possibility of error. There is thus, in Descartes's account, a sharp split between (*i*) grasping the content of an idea (an act free from sceptical doubt) and (*ii*) affirming that content of the world in an act of judgment (an act vulnerable to sceptical doubt). This may, perhaps, be thought of as an act of apprehending a 'mental image', followed by a hypothesis that this image 'resembles' or 'copies' an external object, and that therefore our apprehension of the image is a reliable basis for judgments about that object.[33] Now, in this chapter I have sketched a conception of representation that is certainly deeply Cartesian in many respects, in that internal modifications are the immediate objects of the mind's awareness. However, it nonetheless rejects this Cartesian model of self-awareness and the split between (*i*) and (*ii*). For in the model sketched

---

[32] Cf. John McDowell's remark that 'impressions are, so to speak, transparent' in his *Mind and World* (Cambridge, MA: Harvard University Press, 1994), p. 145. The point of my discussion of pictures is precisely to offer an intuitive model of how representations can be 'transparent'. Gerold Prauss's '*Deutung*' model of Kantian representations is another attempt to clarify this difficult notion: see his *Erscheinung bei Kant* (Berlin: Walter de Gruyter, 1971).

[33] Think, e.g., of Locke's famous claim that 'the ideas of primary qualities of bodies are resemblances of them', in *An Essay Concerning Human Understanding*, ed. P. H. Nidditch (Oxford University Press, 1979), book 2, ch. 8, § 15.

here the mind is aware of its internal modifications of sensibility via an act of synthesis, and this results in a cognition of the world. The synthesis of the internal modifications thus produces a judgment – something that is as it were inherently assertive. The synthesis does not result in something akin to the grasp of a descriptive phrase, which the mind may then choose to 'compare' against the world. It is thus that Kant holds that the notion of a judgment is logically prior to the notion of a concept – a view which will be discussed in chapter 3. Descartes, on the other hand, does think of grasping the content of an idea as akin to grasping the meaning of a descriptive phrase, and to think like this is precisely to collapse the depicted object into the representational medium. It is by doing this that Descartes produces the familiar notion of an indubitable, internal world of ideas that we immediately apprehend, and which are the evidential foundation of our judgments about the external world.

Kant's conception of representation thus generates questions about objectivity (our 'relation to objects', as Kant puts it) that are very different from those that face someone who, like Descartes, is committed to an indirect realist model of cognition. In the indirect realist model, the central problem of objectivity is how inferences from one's ideas to their efficient causes in the external world are to be justified, and how we know if our ideas are reliable indicators of that external world. (It was, of course, an awareness of the problems besetting any attempt to answer these questions that, in part, generated Berkeley's idealism.) How we represent the world thus becomes for the indirect realist a question of justification and knowledge. Now, if we instead use the richer conception of representation sketched above, then things look rather different. From this point of view, the indirect realist model is guilty of putting questions of justification and knowledge in the wrong place, for those questions come *after* the fact of representation and not *before* it. Through synthesis, the internal modifications of our sensibility function to present a world to us. They may present it as it is or as it is not, and we can thus ask whether particular perceptions are veridical or not. But this question presupposes an answer to a prior one, namely, the question of how our internal modifications can function to present anything to us in the first place. This question is not a question of justifying an inference, but rather of how the act of synthesis (analogous to the act of 'seeing in') results in awareness of an objective world. That is, it concerns what must govern and constrain the synthesis of our internal states if that act is to produce cognitions – or, as Kant sometimes puts it, it concerns the conditions of possible experience. This point can be put in modern linguistic garb as follows. We can ask of a sentence whether we are justified in believing the proposition expressed by it. But before this question can be asked, we must understand what the sentence means. In other words, prior to any epistemological questions there is a semantic question to be answered. Namely, how does the sentence come to relate to the world – not in the sense of saying something *true* about it, but in the sense of saying anything at all, *true or false*. One of the central claims of this book is that the representationalist equivalent of this is the key problem of the Transcendental Deduction.

CONCLUSION

The text of the *Critique* makes it clear that Kant is a representationalist, in that he thinks that the immediate objects of awareness are the mind's internal states or modifications. However, this core thesis can be developed in a number of different ways, and how one develops it depends crucially upon one's conception of representation in general. In this chapter I have advanced a hypothesis that Kant has a conception of representation that differs in crucially important ways from that to be found in the familiar indirect realist and idealist models of representationalism. I have sketched this conception above, and have also attempted to provide an intuitive model for understanding it, by linking it closely with our ordinary notion of pictorial representation. I suggested that, for Kant, cognition occurs in virtue of the mind's reflexive awareness of its intuitions. However, cognition involves neither an act of inference (like the indirect realist model) nor an act of construction (like the idealist model). Rather, the reflexive awareness of intuitions involves an act of synthesis, which is an act of grasping the object represented by the intuition. Synthesis is thus analogous to the act of seeing something *in* a picture, for it is the awareness of a representation as a representation and not simply as an internal state. I suggested that this richer, non-reductive conception of representation, modelled on the notion of pictorial representation, would allow Kant consistently to hold (*i*) that the immediate objects of awareness are representations, and (*ii*) that we are immediately aware of things that do not reduce to mere mental states.

I am now in a position to explain something I said near the beginning of this chapter. It was mentioned there that there are some commentators who attempt to read Kant as a direct realist, despite all the textual evidence for his representationalism. That is, they argue that Kant held that representations constitute the acts of awareness themselves, rather than being the immediate objects of awareness. I suggested that one thing motivating this reading was a desire to make sense of the anti-Cartesian, realist themes in the

Critique. Part of that realism is that Kant seems to argue for neither an indirect realist nor an idealist model of cognition. That is, he does not seem to hold that our knowledge of the objective world is either inferred from or reduced to knowledge of our own mental states. Yet if the only objects of awareness are mental states then these two models may seem jointly to exhaust Kant's options. The fact that he chooses neither may then seem to suggest that, despite the representationalist idiom in which he writes, Kant is in fact committed to a direct realism. As should be clear, the problem with this argument is that it implicitly assumes that representations are identical to subjective mental states – which is like assuming that pictures are merely configurations of ink marks. If Kant does not hold this impoverished, reductive conception of representation, then he is not faced with the dilemma of choosing between indirect realism and reductive idealism. It would thus be possible to make sense of the realist themes in the *Critique* without implausibly denying that Kant is a representationalist.

Before beginning the next chapter, it should be emphasised that, as I noted at the start of this chapter, the purpose of the above discussion was simply to outline a certain way of thinking about the notion of representation, and also to begin suggesting how that account of representation may link with important themes in the B-Deduction. Hence, all I have attempted to do is to provide a sketch that, I hope, begins to make certain conceptual connections – for example, between the notions of representation, the object *in* a representation, imagination, synthesis, judgment, and objectivity – appear intuitive and intelligible. I am well aware that I have not yet dealt with those connections in the detail that they require, but I will be returning to discuss them again and again throughout this book. The account above, in other words, is offered only with the aim of starting to shed some light on Kant's representationalism and his argument in the B-Deduction.

It is worth pointing out that there are therefore at least three things that I have *not* attempted to do in this chapter. Firstly, I have not attempted to argue that the model of representation sketched above is in fact the correct way to analyse perception. Indeed, perhaps representationalism and the very notion of a mental medium of representation is ultimately incoherent – but that possibility will not concern me in this book. Secondly, I have not attempted to argue that the reductive model of representation is an incorrect way to analyse perception, nor do I deny that there are perhaps good philosophical reasons for holding a reductive rather than a non-reductive account. Thirdly, I have not yet attempted to provide detailed textual justification for my claim that the model of representation outlined here is in fact Kant's model. As was noted in the introduction to this chapter, Kant treats the notion of representation as a primitive, and thus any interpretation of his views on it has to be justified by its capacity to provide a perspicuous account of his epistemology as a whole. Obviously such a complete account is beyond the scope of this book, but in the chapters that follow I offer an interpretation and close reading of Kant's central argument in the B-Deduction – an argument which constitutes the heart of his transcendental idealism. These following chapters are intended to show how the conception of representation sketched here allows us to make good sense of that difficult argument.

CHAPTER 2

Spontaneity and objectivity

The previous chapter introduced my reading of Kant's notion of representation. The rest of this book gives my reading of the central argument of Kant's Transcendental Deduction in B. In the two chapters following this one (i.e., chapters 3 and 4) my interpretation of this argument will be filled out and defended via a close reading of the main sections of the B-Deduction. The relation of my interpretation to the secondary literature will also be considered in those chapters. In the present chapter, however, I simply attempt to sketch out and explain the main lines of my interpretation, in order to provide the reader with a synoptic view of my reading of this complex argument, before I make the descent into close textual analysis.

In brief, my reading of Kant's argument in the B-Deduction can be summarised as follows. My fundamental claim is that the B-Deduction is primarily an analysis of the concept of cognition. I should note that it would be more precise to say that the B-Deduction is an analysis of the concept of human cognition, considered as a species of *discursive* cognition in general, which Kant distinguishes from another logically possible form of cognition, the *intuitive*. However, this is a subtlety which I will defer discussing until a later chapter; in this chapter, I will simply use the terms 'cognition' and 'cognising mind' as a convenient shorthand for 'discursive cognition' and 'discursive cognising mind'. Now – to return to my summary – Kant's analysis aims to show that cognition should be analysed as involving the two faculties of receptivity and spontaneity. The argument is that grasping a unified complex representation entails *spontaneity*, but if spontaneity is to be made compatible with objectivity, and thus with *receptivity*, then it must be governed by a priori rules derived from the essential structure of the act of judging – that is, it must be governed by the categories. In this way, Kant argues, the categories are shown to be necessary conditions of experience, and thus their objective validity is proved.

That Kant has a two-faculty model of cognition has been noted many times before in the secondary literature. However, the nature of his model has often been misinterpreted, and its importance for an understanding of the B-Deduction has not been emphasised enough. Furthermore, Kant's commitment to this model is sometimes treated as if it were a mere 'postulate' on his part – in other words, as a dogmatic assumption about the structure of the human mind, for which he provides no argument.[1] I will be arguing that (fortunately) this is not the case: Kant has an interesting argument for that model, and that argument is the central argument of the B-Deduction.

SPONTANEITY AND THE TWO-FACULTY MODEL

Before turning to the text of the B-Deduction, it is important to say something about what I have referred to above as Kant's 'two-faculty' model of cognition. This is the doctrine that cognition involves both receptivity (i.e., the faculty of sensibility) and spontaneity (i.e., the faculty of understanding). A clear statement of this doctrine occurs at the beginning of the Transcendental Analytic, where Kant writes as follows.

Our cognition arises from two fundamental sources in the mind, the first of which is the reception of representations (the receptivity of impressions), the second the faculty for cognising an object through [*durch*] these representations (spontaneity of concepts); through the former an object is *given* to us, through the latter it is *thought* in relation to that representation (as a mere determination of the mind). (A50/B74)

Kant is claiming here that to cognise an object through one's representations (i.e., to grasp one's representations as representing; or, in more Kantian jargon, to bring one's intuitions to consciousness) necessarily involves not only the reception of impressions, but also what he calls the 'spontaneity of concepts'. This doctrine is of great importance to Kant – indeed, it is the heart of his transcendental idealism. It is thus not surprising to find him locating his central difference from his great predecessors, Leibniz and Locke, precisely in this two-faculty model of cognition. For he writes in a famous passage that

Leibniz *intellectualised* the appearances, just as Locke *sensualised* the concepts of understanding . . . Instead of seeking two entirely different sources of representation

[1] See, e.g., L. Falkenstein, *Kant's Intuitionism* (University of Toronto Press, 1995), p. 28. The term *postulate* is his.

in the understanding and the sensibility, which could judge about things with objective validity *only in conjunction*, each of these great men holds on only to one of them. (A271/B327)

This chapter, and indeed the rest of this book, is largely about spontaneity, receptivity, and how the conjunction of them is necessary to 'judge about things with objective validity'. The purpose of this section is to introduce those notions and make some initial points in explanation of them. These points will be returned to in the rest of the book, and filled out in more detail.

Before discussing Kant's two-faculty model of cognition, it is worth saying something briefly about the notion of a faculty in general. Faculties have had bad press since the Cartesian attack on Scholasticism, and by now 'faculty psychology' is largely a term of abuse. Despite this, there is nothing intrinsically problematic about the notion of a faculty. For a faculty is simply a capacity or an ability; in other words (simplifying somewhat), if it is possible for me to do X, then I have the faculty of doing X. This is made even clearer in Kant's German, in which, along with synonyms like 'power' (*Kraft*), and 'capacity' (*Fähigkeit*), the word he habitually uses for 'faculty' is '*Vermögen*', which is simply the nominalised form of the verb 'to be capable of'.

Bearing this point in mind, it is worth considering the following passage from a recent paper by Edwin McCann:

> In my interpretation [*sc.*, of the B-Deduction] . . . the hoary transcendental psychology in terms of which Kant tended to put his points is, as far as is possible, dispensed with; the argument is no longer seen to rely on such claims as that . . . faculties of mind such as understanding and sensibility operate upon one another [etc.].[2]

The reconstructive zeal this passage exhibits is inappropriate, for there is nothing particularly dubious or incoherent about the notion of a 'transcendental psychology' – or, transcendental *logic*, to give it its correct Kantian title. The difference between transcendental logic and psychology is the difference between an a priori, conceptual (and thus properly philosophical) enterprise, and an a posteriori, empirical inquiry. As this book should make clear, the B-Deduction is not concerned with contingent psychological features of human beings (no matter how universally shared those features may be), but only with the essential features of the cognising mind. That is, Kant is not engaged in any observational inquiry, but in the logical

---

[2] E. McCann, 'Skepticism and Kant's B Deduction', *History of Philosophy Quarterly* 2 (1985), 71.

analysis of the concept of (human) cognition. Another way of putting this is to say that he is concerned with what it is to have the ability to cognise. And a conceptual account of this will involve analysing that ability into the relations of various subabilities – that is, it will involve the question of what *faculties* are involved in cognition.

Now, it might be asked at this point how Kant can consistently treat receptivity or sensibility as a faculty, as it hardly seems as if we are active or exercising an ability simply in being receptive. Thus Robert Pippin, for example, writes that it 'seems to be stretching the senses of *Vermögen* and *Fähigkeiten* quite thin to say that receiving impressions is something we have the ability to *do*'.[3] But this accusation does not hold, for Kant is in fact using the notion of a faculty in a perfectly standard and traditional way, namely, in the minimal Aristotelian or Scholastic sense of the potentiality to take on a certain range of determinations. In that tradition, for a faculty to act was simply for one of those potentialities to be actualised (and thus for the possessor of the faculty to be determined in a certain way).[4] Thus it can sensibly be said, for example, that opium has a 'dormitive' faculty, which *acts* upon us in putting us to sleep. Of course, to attempt to explain the fact that opium puts one to sleep by appealing to the 'dormitive' faculty would be circular and thus vacuous. This circularity was what the 'New Philosophers' claimed to find (and perhaps not without reason) in Scholastic explanations of natural phenomena. But this is simply a bad use to which the notion of a faculty was put, and does not impugn the notion itself. As I shall be arguing, Kant's appeal to 'faculties' is not part of an attempted naturalistic explanation of human psychology, but is instead his way of stating the results of a conceptual analysis of the notion of cognition. Whatever problems may be found with that analysis, the use of the notion of faculties is not one of them.

In his analysis, Kant argues that cognition involves both receptivity (which is as one would expect) and spontaneity (which is the interesting claim). Put in Kant's jargon of 'determinations', it could be said that in receiving impressions the subject is determined in certain ways; in being spontaneous, the subject determines its experience in certain ways. What precisely Kant means by this 'spontaneity' should become much clearer over the course of this chapter and the next, but it is worth saying something briefly about it here. To begin with, it can be noted that the doctrine of spontaneity echoes in some important ways Aquinas's doctrine of the

[3] R. B. Pippin, *Kant's Theory of Form* (New Haven: Yale University Press, 1982), p. 32.
[4] Cf. Kenneth Winkler's response to the similar objection that Berkeley is guilty of inconsistency in thinking of 'passive acts', in *Berkeley* (Oxford University Press, 1989), p. 9.

'agent intellect' (*intellectus agens*). This is not surprising, given that Kant received his philosophical education in a milieu that was a 'stronghold' of the Aristotelian-Scholastic heritage.[5] According to Aquinas's doctrine, in cognition the intellect is not simply determined by the reception of the sensible forms of objects, but also acts upon them. As Eleonore Stump writes, 'For Aquinas, the agent intellect is a top-down causer; that is, it initiates causal chains without itself being caused to do so by anything else'.[6] Robert Pippin, in one of the few discussions in the secondary literature to focus on the Kantian notion of spontaneity, makes Kant's doctrine sound very close to that of Aquinas, writing that 'for Kant a spontaneous activity is always a "self-causing" activity'.[7] However, I think this assimilation is misleading, for, despite certain similarities, Kant is not thinking, as Aquinas was, in terms of efficient causation.

What Kant *is* thinking of can be made clearer by appealing to the model of representation outlined in the previous chapter. In that model, cognition involved the mind reflexively grasping its own modifications, but not grasping them simply as internal states of itself. Rather, through an act of synthesis (analogous to the act of 'seeing in') the mind grasps its modifications as representing something. This act can also be thought of as the representationalist equivalent of the act of understanding a sign, or grasping its meaning. Hence, in cognition the mind can be thought of as being given certain 'signs' via its receptivity, and then understanding them, or as it were 'reading' them. Now, as shall be argued in detail below, Kant's claim that cognition involves spontaneity is in more specific terms the claim that cognition involves a *spontaneous synthesis*. That is, what is spontaneous is the mind's grasp of its own modifications (or, impressions) as representing. The meaning of this claim, and Kant's argument for it, are the subject of the following chapter. For now, this fundamental point can be roughly stated as follows: the act of synthesis must be spontaneous because the mind's impressions do not determine their own interpretation, or what the mind grasps *in* them. As the discussion in the rest of this chapter should make clear, this does not necessarily mean that the spontaneous act involves 'an element of choice' (as Ermano Bencivenga, for example, suggests[8]). To call the synthesis 'spontaneous' is simply to say that the way

[5] Falkenstein, *Kant's Intuitionism*, p. 31. The first chapter of this book contains some useful discussions of Kant's relation to the Aristotelian-Scholastic tradition.

[6] Stump, 'Mechanisms of Cognition', pp. 172–3.

[7] R. B. Pippin, 'Kant on the Spontaneity of Mind', *Canadian Journal of Philosophy* 17 (1987), 450.

[8] E. Bencivenga, 'The Metaphysical Structure of Kant's Moral Philosophy', in *My Kantian Ways* (Berkeley: University of California Press, 1995), p. 33. The same confusion infects S. L. Hurley's

the synthesis proceeds is determined by the nature of the subject rather than by the nature of the subject's given mental modifications. Thus, Kant holds that our cognition must involve an act in which the mind grasps or comprehends its own mental modifications, and that this act is spontaneous rather than receptive – that is, it is not simply an act of passively recognising or revealing something that is as it were already there in those modifications.

It is thus important to emphasise that Kant's two-faculty model is not simply the claim that concepts as well as intuitions are required for cognition. The point is rather that *spontaneity* is required. Kant argues, as I will show below, that this spontaneity entails the spontaneous use of certain concepts, namely, the categories. By calling their use 'spontaneous' it is meant that their use is not grounded upon the (passive) recognition of repeatable features of what is given in experience. That is, in using the categories the subject determines its experience, rather than being determined by experience. In other words, Kant's claim is that cognition involves not simply intuitions and concepts, but rather intuitions and *a priori* concepts. This is made clear in the following important remark from § 22 of the B-Deduction.

To *think* an object and to *cognise* an object are thus not the same. For two components belong to cognition: first, the concept, through which an object is thought at all (the category), and second, the intuition, through which it is given. (B146)

Here Kant makes it absolutely clear that the 'two components' belonging to cognition are not simply intuition and concept, but intuition and *category* – that is, a very special kind of concept indeed, namely, one which is used a priori.

This point is worth emphasising because it is often missed or blurred in discussions in the secondary literature, which in turn can lead to confusion over the structure of Kant's argument. That Kant holds a two-faculty model of cognition is a salient feature of the *Critique*, and has been much discussed. However, many discussions of it are marred by a lack of close attention to the text, which leads such commentators to suggest that the two-faculty model is the claim that cognition involves intuition and concept, rather than intuition and category. Bennett, for example, thinks that Kant's two-faculty model is the bland point that cognition involves, on the one hand, 'factual raw material' (i.e., intuitions), which, on the other hand, we have 'to organise intellectually . . . by classifying, discriminating,

discussion in 'Kant on Spontaneity and the Myth of the Giving', *Proceedings of the Aristotelian Society* 94 (1994), especially 160–1.

judging, comparing'.[9] Similarly, for P. F. Strawson the two-faculty model is simply the point that cognition involves both sides of 'a certain fundamental duality', namely, 'the duality of general concepts, on the one hand, and particular instances of general concepts, encountered in experience, on the other'.[10] If this is all Kant's two-faculty model comes to, then it is altogether mysterious how he could have thought that it constituted the important difference between his epistemology and those of his predecessors.

This is because if Kant were saying merely that cognition involves intuition and concept, then he would not be saying anything fundamentally different from the standard views of the time. To begin with, the claim that cognition or perception involves both given sensory input (i.e., 'intuition' in Kant's terminology) and conceptualisation was a standard part of both Scholastic and Cartesian theories of cognition. After all, it is an obvious point that in order, for example, to perceive a triangle as a triangle, the subject must possess the concept of triangularity. Furthermore, at least with regard to empirical concepts, Kant in fact fundamentally shares the abstractionist model that was the received view of his time (i.e., the seventeenth and eighteenth centuries). This model is trenchantly defined by Peter Geach as being

the doctrine that a concept is acquired by a process of singling out in attention some one feature given in direct experience – *abstracting* it – and ignoring the other features simultaneously given – *abstracting from* them.[11]

Or, as the Port-Royal *Logic*, the standard logic textbook of Kant's day, says after discussing the various types of abstraction, 'through these sorts of abstractions, ideas of individuals become common, and common ideas become more common'.[12]

That Kant shares this abstractionist view, at least insofar as empirical concepts are concerned, is made clear in his *Logic* (i.e., the so-called '*Jäsche Logik*'). Here he asks the question '*Which acts of the understanding constitute a concept?* or what is the same, *Which are involved in the generation of a concept out of given representations?*' (9:93). Kant's answer to this question is in terms of what he calls the three 'logical *actus* of the understanding,

[9] Bennett, *Kant's Analytic*, p. 53.
[10] P. F. Strawson, *The Bounds of Sense* (London: Routledge, 1966), p. 20. For two more examples of such readings, see Gardner, *Kant and the Critique of Pure Reason*, pp. 66–8, and N. Kemp Smith, *A Commentary to Kant's 'Critique of Pure Reason'*, 2nd edn (New York: Humanities Press, 1962), p. 168.
[11] P. T. Geach, *Mental Acts*, 2nd edn (Bristol: Thoemmes Press, 1992), p. 18.
[12] A. Arnauld and P. Nicole, *Logic or the Art of Thinking*, trans. J. V. Buroker (Cambridge University Press, 1996), ch. 5, p. 38.

through which concepts are generated as to their form', namely, the acts of comparison, reflection, and abstraction (9:94). The following example that Kant gives of the generation of a concept could easily have come straight from the pages of the Port-Royal *Logic*:

> I see, e.g., a spruce, a willow, and a linden. By first comparing these objects with one another I note that they are different from one another in regard to the trunk, the branches, the leaves, etc.; but next I reflect on that which they have in common among themselves, trunk, branches, and leaves themselves, and I abstract from the quantity, the figure, etc., of these; thus I acquire a concept of a tree. (9:94–5)

One can hardly get a clearer commitment to the standard abstractionist views of concepts than that given here. Of course, Kant's *Logic* must be used with caution, as it was not written by Kant but assembled from his lecture notes by Jäsche.[13] However, I see no evidence in the *Critique* that Kant wavered from this view of empirical concepts. See, for example, the passage at A271/B327, in which Kant talks in one breath of 'empirical or abstracted concepts', where the 'or' seems clearly intended to express an equivalence (i.e., a choice between synonyms) rather than a disjunction.

Kant's abstractionism means that he thinks of empirical concepts in what is essentially a very traditional manner, as being capacities for recognising repeatable features in experience. Of course, Kant does have interesting and less traditional views about how we go about recognising these features, with his talk of such things as 'rules' and 'schemata'. Nonetheless, according to Kant the use of empirical concepts is still fundamentally grounded on recognition. In itself, then, the use of such concepts is non-spontaneous – a case of the subject being determined by experience, rather than determining experience (although, as will be shown in what follows, for Kant even the use of empirical concepts will turn out in the end to depend upon a prior spontaneity). Hence, if Kant's two-faculty model were simply the claim that cognition involves intuition and concept (as, e.g., Bennett and Strawson think), then he would not thereby be committing himself to anything either new or interesting. However, as I have argued here, Kant's two-faculty model is in fact much more radical and idealist. For it involves the claim that in cognition the subject must not simply be determined by experience, but also determining of experience – that is, spontaneous. The problem with readings like those of Bennett and Strawson is that this demand for spontaneity disappears from view, and is replaced with the demand simply for conceptualisation. The crucial notion of spontaneity is

---

[13] See T. Boswell, 'On the Textual Authenticity of Kant's *Logic*', *History and Philosophy of Logic* 9 (1988), 193–203.

thus blurred with notions of mental activity in general, and is assimilated to the use of any concept. But it is of crucial importance to emphasise that the two-faculty model involves the demand for spontaneity rather than simply for conceptualisation, because, as I will show, it is from the necessity of spontaneity that Kant will argue to the objective validity of the categories.

This concludes my preliminary explanatory comments on Kant's two-faculty model of cognition. As noted above, the themes that have been touched on here will be returned to and expanded on in the rest of the book. The main purpose of this section was to emphasise the role of spontaneity in that model, and to insist that it should not be confused, as it often is, with the notion of conceptualisation in general. This is crucial for understanding the argument of the Transcendental Deduction, to the text of which I now turn.

AIM AND STRATEGY OF THE DEDUCTION

The Transcendental Deduction (in both editions of the *Critique*) begins with two introductory sections, entitled 'On the principles of a transcendental deduction in general' and 'Transition to the transcendental deduction of the categories' (i.e., A84–95/B116–29). In these sections Kant tells us what the aim of the Deduction is, what general task it is supposed to perform, and sketches the general strategy that he intends to use in order to fulfil this aim. In what follows I am working from the reasonable assumption that Kant has an accurate understanding of his own argument. Therefore an examination of what he says in these introductory sections of the Deduction should provide a general picture of the argument, and thus some general constraints that an interpretation of it ought to meet. I will argue that such an examination will support my claim that the Deduction is most centrally an argument for the two-faculty model of cognition, with its two components of receptivity and spontaneity.

At the beginning of the introductory sections of the Deduction, Kant tells us that the term *deduction* is being used in a (now archaic) legal or juridical sense, rather than a logical one.[14] He explains this as follows.

Jurists, when they speak of entitlements or claims, distinguish in a legal matter between the questions about what is lawful (*quid juris*) and that which concerns the fact (*quid facti*), and since they demand proof of both, they call the first, that which is to establish the entitlement or the legal claim, the *deduction*. (A84/B116)

---

[14] For a discussion of the history of the legal term *deduction*, see D. Henrich, 'Kant's Notion of a Deduction and the Methodological Background of the First *Critique*', in *Kant's Transcendental Deductions*, ed. E. Förster (Stanford University Press, 1989), pp. 30–6.

As an example, let us imagine a dispute over a piece of land. In such a case the *quid facti* would concern the current facts of ownership, such as who is now occupying the land, or who now collects the rent for it. The *quid juris*, on the other hand, would concern the question of who is legally entitled to the land or the rent, and a 'deduction' would be an argument that such-and-such possesses that right. In the Transcendental Deduction the 'entitlements or claims' that Kant is concerned with are certain concepts, namely the categories – concepts such as substance, cause, and so forth. The *quid facti* in this case concerns the point that, as Kant puts it in the introduction to the *Critique*, 'we are in possession of certain a priori cognitions' (B3). That is, we employ certain concepts (the categories) in synthetic a priori judgments. For example, we claim to know a priori that every event must have a cause, and that all outer things are modifications of an underlying substance (matter in space). In the Deduction it is the legitimacy or lawfulness of these claims of reason (the *quid juris*) that is in question; that our reason actually makes these claims (the *quid facti*) is not in question.

Kant now goes on to say that 'I call the explanation of the way in which concepts can relate to objects a priori their *transcendental deduction*' (A85/B117). That is, our possession of these 'a priori cognitions' calls for an explanation. Three possible explanations or justifications of our a priori employment of the categories are ruled out by Kant. Firstly, the claims in question are synthetic, and therefore this use of the categories cannot be justified by appeal to a process of conceptual analysis. For example, Kant, like Hume, thinks that no analysis of the concept of event can show that it contains the concept of cause. As Kant writes in the *Prolegomena*, Hume 'indisputably proved that it is wholly impossible for reason to think such a connection [*sc.*, a causal connection] a priori *and from concepts* [i.e., from concepts alone]' (4:257; my emphasis). Secondly, the claims in question are made a priori, and therefore this use of the categories cannot be justified by claiming that these concepts are derived from experience via a process of abstraction. Locke in his *Essay* had attempted abstractionist explanations of concepts like cause, substance, God, infinity, and the like.[15] However, as Kant notes, 'a *deduction* of the pure a priori concepts can never be achieved in this way' (A86/B117). For if the categories were abstracted from experience, and were therefore ordinary empirical concepts, their use would be founded upon the recognition of features of what is given in experience. But this would mean that, for example, we could not claim to know that

[15] See Locke, *Essay*, book 2.

all events must have a cause, but at most only that all the events we have encountered in experience have been found to have causes. If the categories had their origin in abstraction, then this would thus reduce our supposed a priori judgments to mere a posteriori generalisations. Thirdly, Kant claims that we cannot justify the a priori use of the categories by appeal to our form of receptivity, as he thinks we can justify the a priori use of the concepts of space and time. In other words, according to Kant we must represent objects as in space and time in virtue of our form of receptivity. But although we must also represent objects as causally interacting modifications of substance, this does not hold in virtue of our form of receptivity. As Kant says, 'The categories . . . do not represent to us the conditions under which objects are given in intuition at all' (A89/B122). 'Thus,' as Kant says, 'a difficulty is revealed here that we did not encounter in the field of sensibility, namely how *subjective conditions of thought* should have *objective validity*' (A89/B122).

This last passage shows that what is concerning Kant in the Deduction, or what raises the 'difficulty' requiring explanation, is the spontaneity of the categories. Both empirical concepts and the a priori concepts of space and time lack this spontaneity, for the use of both is grounded in features of what is given to us in experience. Of course the concepts of space and time are still a priori, in that they are grounded in the form of what is given, and the given has that form in virtue of the constitution of our sensibility. But nonetheless the use of these concepts, like the use of empirical concepts, is grounded upon the way in which we are determined in experience – that is, it is grounded upon the recognition of and abstraction from features of our experience.[16] The categories, however, are not like this, for they are ways in which *we determine experience*. That is, the categories are spontaneous in that the subject imposes these concepts in its experience (i.e., determines its experience according to them), rather than as it were 'reading them off' its experience. Their use, in other words, is not a response to what is given in experience.

The spontaneity of the categories, however, raises a problem concerning their objectivity – a problem that is easy to see. If the categories are used in a spontaneous way, then it becomes very difficult to see how their use can constitute genuine knowledge or cognition at all. After all, knowledge is surely a question of finding out how the world is independently of us, and

---

[16] Note that I am not talking here of what Kant calls the 'original representations' of space and time, which are a priori intuitions (see A25/ B40), but of our use of the *concepts* of space and time, which are grounded upon the way in which we intuit a priori. (For a defence of this point, see Falkenstein, *Kant's Intuitionism*, ch. 5.)

this seems incompatible with our simply imposing certain concepts in our experience. For then it must be asked what distinguishes that imposition from us merely making things up, fantasising, or otherwise falsifying what is given to us in cognition. As Kant puts it, if we do indeed use those concepts in a spontaneous way, rather than as a response to features given to us in our experience, then those concepts start to look as if they are 'a mere fantasy of the brain' (A91/B124), the product of subjective habits of the imagination which we project onto the world. In other words, for cognition to be objective (i.e., for it to be genuinely cognition) it appears as if the subject must be determined by experience rather than determining of experience. That is, the spontaneous use of concepts in cognition appears to be incompatible with their objectivity.

This thought is precisely what is underlying Hume's conclusion about the concept of necessary connection. In his well-known discussion in the *Treatise*, Hume searches for an objective ground for our idea of causality, by looking at the impressions (i.e., what is given in experience) upon which that idea could be based. Famously, he finds that the impressions only licence what could be called the 'objective core' of the notion of cause – namely, constant conjunction and spatio-temporal contiguity. Subtracting this objective core from the notion of cause leaves us with a remainder, namely, the idea of necessary connection. Because our use of this idea is based neither upon conceptual analysis nor upon any corresponding impression of external reality (i.e., has no grounds in experience) Hume argues that it must therefore be something merely subjective, and founded upon our habits of association.[17] As Kant writes of him, Hume 'could not explain at all how it is possible for the understanding to think of concepts that are not combined in the understanding [i.e., not analytically connected] as still necessarily combined in the object', and he was thus 'driven by necessity' (B127) to argue that the connection was a 'merely subjective necessity' (B5). Hence, as Kant writes in the *Prolegomena*, for Hume the concept of necessary connection 'is really nothing but a bastard of the imagination', and in using it we pass off the 'subjective necessity (i.e., habit) for an objective necessity (from insight)' (4:258). These passages make it clear that Kant sees Hume's destructively sceptical account of the notion of cause, and his consequent rejection of the possibility of synthetic a priori judgments like 'every event must have a cause', as stemming from an inability to see how something could be explained. Namely, Hume

---

[17] D. Hume, *A Treatise of Human Nature*, ed. L. A. Selby-Bigge and P. H. Nidditch, 2nd edn (Oxford University Press, 1978), book 1, part 3.

'could not explain at all' how the *spontaneity* of our concept of necessary connection (i.e., its use in the absence of any grounds in experience) is compatible with the *objectivity* claimed for it (e.g., in making synthetic a priori judgments). And this problem about causality arises with respect to all the categories.

Hence, an examination of the 'entitlements and claims' of reason, or the *quid facti*, shows that there is an apparent conflict between two of reason's claims, namely, its claim that the categories are spontaneous and its claim that they are objective. This is what Kant calls the problem of the 'objective validity' of the categories. In his discussion in the introductory sections of the Deduction, Kant treats both Locke and Hume as responding to this apparent conflict between spontaneity and objectivity. Locke's abstraction-ist account responds to the problem by denying the spontaneity of the categories, and maintaining their objectivity at the cost of reducing them to merely empirical concepts (i.e., concepts grounded in a recognition of what is given in experience). And, as we have seen, Hume's response to this conflict, in the case of the idea of necessary connection, consists of denying the objectivity of that idea, and retaining its spontaneity at the cost of reducing it to a mere subjective projection of the human imagi-nation. Locke and Hume thus share the presupposition that spontaneity and objectivity are incompatible, and that one of these claims of reason must thus be relinquished. In other words, each offers us a reductionist account in response to an apparent conflict between our intellectual com-mitments. Now, if anything characterises Kant's philosophy as a whole, then it is his anti-reductionism – that is, his resolute attempt to do justice to *all* our intellectual commitments, both theoretical and practical. The project that Kant undertakes in the Deduction can thus be expected to be a non-reductionist resolution to the question of the 'objective validity' of the categories.

In other words, the aim of the Transcendental Deduction is to show how the categories can be both objective *and* spontaneous. Therefore, ac-cording to Kant, the apparent dilemma to which Locke and Hume were responding is a false one. We do not have to choose between the objectivity and the spontaneity of the categories, for it is in fact possible to have both. That is, the task for the Transcendental Deduction is to show how the apparent conflict between spontaneity and objectivity can be reconciled; or, equivalently, to show how this apparently inconsistent combination can be made intelligible. As Kant puts it in the passage previously quoted, the Deduction's task is to show 'how *subjective conditions of thought* should have *objective validity*' (A89/B122).

Now, Kant's statements of the aim of the Deduction tell us that the task it is intended to perform has an important explanatory dimension. This is an obvious point – after all, a 'transcendental deduction' is defined by Kant as 'the *explanation* [*Erklärung*] of the way in which concepts can relate to objects a priori' (A85/B117; my emphasis) – but nonetheless worth emphasising. Kant himself emphasises the point repeatedly. In the preface to the first edition, for example, he writes that the Deduction 'is supposed to demonstrate *and make comprehensible* the objective validity' of the categories (Axvi; my emphasis). And in § 26 of the B-Deduction Kant claims that 'in the transcendental deduction . . . their [*sc.*, the categories'] possibility as a priori cognitions of objects of an intuition in general was *exhibited* [*dargestellt*]' (B159; my emphasis). So, in the Deduction a possibility (i.e., the combination of spontaneity and objectivity) is being explained, made comprehensible, or exhibited to us.

Hence, the Deduction is not intended simply as a *proof* of the objective validity of the categories – if by 'proof' is meant 'something that takes us from certain things we know to certain things we did not know'. This is not a correct formulation of the intended task of the Deduction, because, as Kant sees it, we *already* know that the categories have objective validity, for this is a matter of the *quid facti* which provided us with our starting point. That is to say, to repeat the passage quoted above, 'we are in possession of certain a priori cognitions, and even the common understanding is never without them' (B3). We are committed to holding that the categories are both objective and spontaneous, because we make synthetic a priori judgments – in science and mathematics, for example. A philosophical 'proof' that we are entitled to do this would be pointless, because it would be as nothing compared to the real existence and success of such bodies of knowledge as Newtonian science. The Deduction's task is not to provide such a proof; rather, it is to provide a satisfactory response to the problem generated by the fact that, on the one hand, we find ourselves with these commitments to both spontaneity and objectivity, and, on the other hand, these two commitments seem incompatible with one another. Hence, to be successful the argument of the Deduction must not leave us with the brute fact that the categories just do apply a priori to the world, but must make that fact *intelligible* to us. This is what it is to answer the *quid juris* with respect to the claims and entitlements of reason. That is, just as a legal deduction must satisfy a court of law, a deduction of the claims of reason – a transcendental deduction – must satisfy reason itself.

The explanatory role of the Transcendental Deduction has been noticed by other commentators. P. F. Strawson, in his seminal work *The Bounds of*

Sense, pointed out long ago that the Deduction 'is not only an argument [but] also an explanation, a description, a story'.[18] However, the phrase 'not only' and the dismissive term 'story' used here betray a narrow view of what philosophical argument is and what it can achieve. This presupposition lies behind Strawson's view that the Deduction can be divided into two parts. The first part is an austere 'analytical argument' deserving of serious discussion, which can be excised from the second part, which is 'an essay in the imaginary subject of transcendental idealism'[19] – a mere 'story' unfit for adult consumption. In other words, Strawson treats the explanatory role that Kant clearly ascribes to the Deduction as an inessential and thus separable part of the discussion. Stephen Engstrom, in an important paper, argues instead that to understand the Deduction it must be seen as essentially fulfilling an explanatory role.[20] Oddly enough, however, Engstrom seems to share the presupposition underlying Strawson's view, for he (Engstrom) thinks that because the Deduction provides an explanation it is therefore not an argument for the categories. This presupposition that an argument for the objective validity of the categories cannot simultaneously play the required explanatory role is groundless, and should be rejected. Rather, Kant's statement of the aim of the Deduction provides a criterion that ought to be met by any proposed interpretation of its argument. That is, any interpretation must show how the argument for the categories demonstrates, or makes intelligible, the compatibility of spontaneity with objectivity.

It is worth noting here that in its attempt to explain the compatibility of spontaneity and objectivity, the Deduction is part of Kant's response to scepticism – at least as he uses the word *scepticism*. This term, and its correlative term *dogmatism*, feature in what could be called Kant's natural history of reason, and refer to two extremes between which human reason invariably oscillates, until given peace by the critical philosophy. Scepticism and dogmatism are not particular theories, but rather attitudes that reason takes up to its own 'claims and entitlements', namely, its own a priori principles. Dogmatism is the taking of those claims of reason for granted, without any prior critical examination of their possibility (or, without answering the *quid juris*). As Kant writes, 'the dogmatist . . . continues gravely along his path without any mistrust of his original objective principles, i.e., without critique' (A763/B791). Scepticism, on the other hand, occurs when reason ceases to takes its 'original objective principles' for granted, and comes to

[18] Strawson, *Bounds of Sense*, p. 86.   [19] Ibid., p. 32.
[20] S. Engstrom, 'The Transcendental Deduction and Skepticism', *Journal of the History of Philosophy* 32 (1994), especially 376–80.

doubt and then deny their legitimacy. Kant claims that scepticism, however, 'is not . . . itself *satisfying* for questions of reason' (A769/B797). For reason finds itself unable simply to give up its claims, and it thus tends once again to lapse back into dogmatic assertions of them.

We can see this tendency of reason played out in the work of Hume, who, according to Kant, was 'the most ingenious of all sceptics' (A764/B792). Unable to comprehend how the spontaneity of the notion of necessary connection could be made compatible with its objectivity, Hume argues that we must deny the latter. However, his 'sceptical solution' is not really a solution, and even Hume admitted as much – pointing out that our 'natural propensities' do not allow us to take the conclusions of his arguments seriously. We must thus remain dogmatists, except whilst in the midst of philosophical perplexity.[21] It is no wonder that Kant thinks that such scepticism is

a mode of thinking in which reason moves against itself with such violence that it never could have arisen except in complete despair as regards satisfaction of reason's most important aims. (4:271)

What Kant thinks will be able to satisfy reason's aims is, of course, the critical philosophy. If the Deduction can make it intelligible how the spontaneity of the categories can be combined consistently with their objectivity, then it will mean that reason's claims will no longer be made dogmatically and thus the root cause of scepticism, or the source of reason's 'despair', will have been removed. It is the fact that we find the combination unintelligible that drives us into various reductionist 'explanations' (e.g., Hume's empiricism) that end up denying that to which we wanted to do justice.

This view of the Deduction can perhaps be made clearer by comparing the aim of the Deduction with the aim of a theodicy – a comparison that is made by Engstrom in the paper mentioned above.[22] A theodicy aims to justify the ways of God to human beings. That is, a theodicy is addressed to a person who finds a tension between her belief in a benevolent God and her awareness of the evil in the world. As such it is not addressed to an unbeliever, and is thus not an attempt to prove the existence of God. In a similar fashion, the Deduction is addressed to human reason, which (so Kant thinks) finds itself with commitments to both the spontaneity and objectivity of the categories, and yet cannot see how these can be made compatible. We find ourselves at a loss as to *how* this compatibility can be possible, even though we believe – know – that it *is* possible. In other

---

[21] See Hume, *Treatise*, book 1, Part 4, § 7.   [22] Engstrom, 'Transcendental Deduction', 377.

words, what we lack is a clear view, or understanding, of our own intellectual resources – the 'claims and entitlements of reason'. Hence, to resolve
this problem, we do not need philosophy 'to strut about with a dogmatic
gait and to decorate itself with the titles and ribbons of mathematics' –
by pretentiously attempting to 'prove' that, for example, the great edifice
of Newtonian science is 'adequately grounded'; what we require is some
'modest but thorough self-knowledge by means of a sufficient illumination
[*Aufklärung*] of our concepts' (A735/B763). I thus suggest that the aim of
the Deduction is to dispel the appearance of conflict between the objectivity
and spontaneity of the categories, by providing a philosophical account –
that is, a conceptual analysis – which will make clear how it is possible
for them to be compatible (and this, in turn, will be an important part of
showing just how it is possible for us to make synthetic a priori judgments).

In the introductory sections of the Deduction, Kant tells us not only his
aim but also the general strategy that he intends to follow in order to fulfil
that aim. This strategy is as follows. Kant writes that the Deduction needs
to demonstrate that the categories 'must be recognised as a priori conditions of the possibility of experiences' (A94/B126), because a 'representation
is . . . determinant of the object a priori if it is possible through it alone
to *cognise something as an object*' (A92/B125). That is, Kant claims that the
way to reconcile the objectivity and the spontaneity of the categories is to
show that the spontaneity of the categories is *essential* to their objectivity,
and in fact to the objectivity of our cognition in general. This is, as Kant
puts it, to show that the categories are 'a priori conditions of the possibility
of experience'.

Taken by itself, this statement of the Deduction's strategy could mean
many things, depending upon the sense given to terms like 'conditions' and
'experience'. However, despite the potential ambiguity, it does suggest that
the two-faculty model of cognition will be a central topic of the Deduction.
For Kant is claiming that the way to explain the objective validity of the categories is to understand the way in which spontaneity, as well as receptivity,
is essential to our cognition in general. This, he is suggesting, will dissipate
the appearance of tension that is felt to exist between spontaneity and objectivity, and will thus remove the root cause of that intellectual conflict of
which both Locke's empiricism and Hume's scepticism are symptoms. This
in turn implies that Kant holds that the apparent incompatibility of spontaneity with objectivity is generated by a natural misunderstanding of the
nature of objectivity in general, or, as he also puts it, of the nature of what
it is 'to cognise something as an object'. As I will discuss in much greater
detail below, the key thing that generates the apparent incompatibility is

the intuitively tempting assumption that for a concept to be objective its use must be grounded in, or justified by, what is given in experience. For without this grounding, it seems as if our use of the concept must float free from any constraint in experience, and thus become completely arbitrary and subjective. I thus suggest that what Kant is promising to provide in the Deduction is a clearer understanding of 'cognising something as an object', via an analysis of the concept of our cognition that will show spontaneity and the categories to play a key role. By thus providing a clearer view of our own intellectual resources, the Deduction will show how the tension between them is only apparent, and thus give reason a 'perpetual peace' (A752/ B780) – freeing it from the endless oscillation between dogmatism and scepticism.

Before turning to consider my interpretation of the main argument of the B-Deduction, it is worth briefly summing up the results of this discussion of Kant's own characterisation of his aim and strategy. I have argued that Kant is thinking as follows.

1. We employ certain concepts (i.e., the categories) in synthetic a priori judgments.
2. Hence, our use of the categories is not based on a recognition of features of that which is given – as our use of empirical concepts (i.e., those based on abstraction) is. In other words, in using the categories the subject determines its experience, rather than being determined by experience.
3. That is, our use of the categories is *spontaneous*.
4. However, this fact seems incompatible with the *objectivity* that we claim for the categories (in using them in synthetic a priori judgments).
5. This is because it seems that objectivity demands that our use of concepts be receptive to, or constrained by, reality, rather than spontaneous. For how can the subject's spontaneity be distinguished from the projection of mere imaginary fantasies onto the world (as Hume had argued was in fact the case with our idea of necessary connection)?
6. The task of the Transcendental Deduction is thus to show how the spontaneity and objectivity of the categories are compatible.
7. This task will be fulfilled by showing that spontaneity is in fact *essential* to objectivity in general (i.e., what it is to 'cognise something as an object'). That is, the spontaneity of the categories in fact makes cognition possible.

This indicates that the argument of the B-Deduction will involve a reconsideration of the reasoning behind point 5 above, and thus of the connections between objectivity, receptivity, and spontaneity. Hence, as I have suggested, the B-Deduction can be expected to contain a consideration of the two-faculty model of cognition, in which cognition is seen as involving both spontaneity and receptivity.

The main constraints that this reading of the aim and strategy of the Deduction places on an interpretation are as follows. Firstly, it needs to be shown how the Deduction attempts to exhibit the necessity of the categories in a way that makes their spontaneity and their objectivity (and thus their use a priori) intelligible, rather than leaving it as a brute fact. Secondly, it needs to be shown how Kant's announced strategy (i.e., a consideration of objectivity in general) is intended to contribute towards achieving this aim. If the a priori use of the categories is left as a brute fact, then the problem to which the Deduction is intended as a response will remain unresolved. For Kant's argument would then simply be another piece of dogmatism, rather than an attempt to remove the root cause that generates reason's fruitless oscillation between dogmatism and scepticism. For example, a proof that either presupposed the objective validity of the categories or concluded simply that we must use them in cognition leaves them looking arbitrary or like mere psychological features. And this would leave the ground open for a sceptic like Hume to respond that, although we certainly must use the categories, for all we know they might simply be fantasies of ours which the imagination projects onto the world because of a built-in mechanism – in which case, they would have no objective validity.

SKETCH OF AN INTERPRETATION

In the previous section I argued that, according to Kant, the basic aim of the Transcendental Deduction was to reconcile the apparent conflict between the spontaneity and the objectivity of the categories, by way of an analysis of the notion of cognition. In this section I sketch a reading of the B-Deduction that fits with this description of its aim and strategy. In order to provide an uncluttered summary of the argument I will develop it here without a line-by-line commentary on the main text of the B-Deduction, and in fact make use mainly of Kant's own summary of that argument in the *Prolegomena*. The two chapters that follow this one will contain a detailed reading of §§ 16–20 and § 26 of the B-Deduction that is intended to provide the required detailed textual support for the interpretation given here.

In highly summarised form, Kant's argument in the B-Deduction can be presented in the form of two premises and a conclusion, as follows.

α. All our cognition must involve a spontaneous synthesis.

β. If our cognition involves a spontaneous synthesis then this synthesis must be governed by the categories.

$\therefore$. The categories make our cognition possible.

By itself, of course, this summary is not very helpful. The meaning of the premises (α) and (β) and of the conclusion needs to be examined, as does the claimed implication itself. However, the summary does indicate how the argument that I am attributing to Kant fits with his own description of the aim and strategy of that section of the *Critique* – that is, it is an attempt to demonstrate how the categories can be both objective and spontaneous by showing that they are in fact necessary conditions of experience, or of 'cognising something as an object'. How exactly the argument does this, and, in particular, how it fulfils the crucial explanatory role of the Transcendental Deduction, will be discussed below.

The first premise, (α), which is the heart of Kant's argument for the two-faculty model of cognition, is the subject of the following chapter. However, it will help my discussion in this section to summarise very briefly what will be discussed in detail there. Kant argues that cognition must involve a spontaneous synthesis, from a consideration of what he calls the 'necessary unity of apperception'. This, as I shall argue, is the representationalist equivalent of the problem later discussed in the history of philosophy as the problem of the unity of judgment or the unity of the proposition. It concerns the question of what understanding a sign (or, grasping a representation as representing) must be like, given that it is possible to understand complex unified signs or representations. Kant argues that for this to be possible, the grasp of a complex representation must be holistic rather than atomistic. That is, the understanding must proceed from an understanding of the whole to an understanding of each part, rather than from parts to whole. This entails that the mind's impressions do not determine their own interpretation, and that grasping a complex unified representation as representing – the act of synthesis – is therefore spontaneous. In other words, if the mind's synthesis or understanding of its mental modifications were a passive reception or recognition of something already there, then complex unified representations (or, the unity of apperception) would be impossible.

Another way of putting this is to say that the act of synthesis is the mind's application of a method or rule of projection to its mental modifications, and the spontaneity of that synthesis is demanded by the fact that these modifications do not by themselves reveal how they are to be projected (i.e., which rule or method is to be applied). This is to adopt the language of the *Tractatus Logico-Philosophicus*, in which Wittgenstein writes that 'We use the perceptible sign of a proposition (spoken or written, etc.) as a projection of a possible situation. The method of projection is to think the sense of the proposition.'[23] For the mind to apply a method (or rule) of projection is for it to grasp a representation as representing (to 'think the sense'), which in turn is for the mind to cognise something *in* its mental modifications (to 'use them as a projection of a possible situation'). The spontaneity of cognition means that the mind itself determines the method of projection, rather than that method being determined by the given mental modifications (the 'perceptible sign').

This summary of Kant's argument for the first premise of his argument should already indicate that the central problem raised by the doctrine of spontaneity is that previously raised in connection with the categories, namely, the problem of objectivity. Let us return to my prior analogy for the representationalist subject: the person trapped inside a hollow globe of opaque plastic. I pointed out in the previous chapter that Kant's subject is like a person watching a cartoon film that is caused to be projected on the inside of that globe by external forces. The subject then apprehends the projected sequence of coloured patches as representing various characters (coyotes, road-runners, and the like) – that is, she sees things *in* the cartoon. But now let us add the doctrine of spontaneity to this model. In this case, if the subject's act of 'seeing in' is spontaneous, then it may seem that she is free to see what she likes in the film. It is as if what she is being shown is not a cartoon but a sequence of Rorschach ink blots, which she can respond to as she pleases, in accordance with whatever passing whim she has, or whatever they happen to remind her of. We can therefore imagine various subjects being shown the same sequence of coloured patches (i.e., receiving the same mental impressions), yet each one would see different things in the sequence (i.e., would represent different objects).

The spontaneity of cognition thus appears to threaten the objectivity of experience, and would seem to entail that each subject's so-called 'cognition of an objective world' must degenerate into solipsistic fantasising or free association. For a fundamental aspect of the concept of objectivity is the idea that in experience we are receptive to something that is in some sense independent of us, or, in other words, that the character of our experience is

23 Wittgenstein, *Tractatus Logico-Philosophicus*, trans. D. F. Pears and B. F. McGuinness (London: Routledge, 1961), prop. 3.11; translation modified.

determined to some extent by an independent reality. Kant thus writes in the A-Deduction that

our thought of the relation of all cognition to its object carries something of necessity with it, since namely the latter is regarded as that which is opposed to our cognitions being determined at pleasure or arbitrarily rather than being determined a priori. (A104)

As this passage notes, for my cognition to have any claim to objectivity it cannot be something that I determine 'at pleasure or arbitrarily'. Such 'cognition' would have no right to demand the agreement of others. Like an ink blot's suggesting a malevolently grinning face to me, it would have only what Kant calls 'mere subjective validity', and not 'objective validity'. Yet it would seem that if the subject's synthesis is spontaneous, then cognition must be something that is determined 'at pleasure or arbitrarily'. Hence, spontaneity and objectivity seem incompatible.

Kant's solution to this problem is hinted at in the passage just quoted from the A-Deduction – in the claim, namely, that our concept of objective cognition 'carries something of necessity with it'. The 'necessity' mentioned here alludes to Kant's claim, premise (β), that cognition involves the a priori use of the categories. Kant's argument for this, the second premise of the B-Deduction, is the subject of the rest of this section's discussion. The argument can be summarised briefly, as follows. Given that cognition involves spontaneity, as claimed in (α), the question becomes how the objectivity of cognition is to be defended, and the spontaneous act of synthesis (or the 'method of projection') not degenerate into something merely personal and arbitrary. Kant's answer to this problem is precisely to argue that if cognition is to be possible at all, then we must recognise that the spontaneous act of synthesis is governed a priori by certain rules – namely, the categories.

That Kant is concerned with this problem can be seen from his discussion of the notion of objectivity, or 'objective validity', in the *Prolegomena*. Here Kant writes that 'the objective validity of a judgment of experience means nothing other than its necessary universal validity' (4:298).[24] What Kant means by saying that a cognition (a 'judgment of experience', as he puts it here) should have *universal* validity he explains by saying that it is a 'connection of perceptions' that we intend should not 'hold only for us, i.e., for our subject', but 'should also be valid at all times for us and for

---

[24] Note that in the discussion that follows I omit any consideration of the distinction between judgments of experience and judgments of perception that Kant makes in the *Prolegomena* (see 4:298–301), as this distinction is not mentioned in the B-Deduction.

everyone else' (4:298). The term *connection* in the phrase 'connection of perceptions' is one of Kant's terms for the act which he elsewhere calls 'combination' and 'synthesis'. So what he is saying is that insofar as it is to be objective, the synthesis of perceptions that occurs in cognition must be 'valid for everyone'. In other words, as was suggested above, for it to result in an objectively valid judgment the synthesis should not be dependent upon any personal peculiarities of the subject. And therefore any other subject, on being presented with these perceptions, would have synthesised or connected them in precisely the same fashion – that is, would have grasped them as presenting the same thing. In other words, for the act of synthesis (or the method of projection) to be objective (i.e., for it to result in an objective judgment, or cognition) is for it not to be grounded upon anything personal or subjective – such as, for example, the particular psychological make-up or habits of association of the subject.

Now, Kant says above not simply that an objective judgment should possess universal validity, but rather that it should possess *necessary* universal validity. By this he does not mean the absurd claim that judgments must be necessarily rather than contingently true in order to be objective (and on this, see Kant's remark at 4:305n). What he means is as follows. Universal validity demands that any subject, upon being presented with certain given mental modifications, would synthesise them in one and the same way. Necessary universal validity therefore demands that any subject, upon being presented with certain given mental modifications, not only would (as a matter of fact) synthesise them in one and the same way, but *must* do so. To understand why this is required, it needs to be recalled that Kant's problem concerns what conditions a subject's spontaneous act of synthesis must meet if it is to result in something deserving to be called a cognition (i.e., something with a claim on the agreement of all cognisers). With this in mind, let us compare the following two conditions for objectivity, the weaker and the stronger.

A. To be objective, the spontaneous act of synthesis must not be grounded upon any personal peculiarities of the particular subject in question. (Universality)
B. To be objective, the spontaneous act of synthesis must not be grounded upon any contingent features of the particular subject in question, even if (as a matter of fact) these features are shared by all subjects. (Necessary universality)

The weaker condition (A) suffices to rule out the obviously subjective. If what a subject 'sees in' its mental modifications is dependent upon personal peculiarities of that subject, then the result can hardly count as a putative cognition of an objective world – to claim so would be like my insisting that everyone must see just what I see in a certain ink blot. As Kant would put it, the result would be merely 'subjectively valid', rather than 'objectively valid'.

The reason why Kant requires the stronger condition (B) is less obvious, but if Hume's discussion of causality is recalled, the point of it should become clearer. Hume argues that the mind comes to project the idea of necessary connection onto the world as the result of the workings of what he variously refers to as 'habit', 'instinct' and 'custom'. That is, the human mind happens to possess certain psychological dispositions. These dispositions are such that if we repeatedly experience the constant conjunction of events of type X with events of type Y, then we will come to associate the idea of X with the idea of Y. This association is the subjective source of the idea of necessary connection. As Hume writes,

after a repetition of similar instances, the mind is carried by habit, upon the appearance of one event, to expect its usual attendant, and to believe that it will exist. This connexion, therefore, which we *feel* in the mind, this customary transition of the imagination from one object to its usual attendant, is the sentiment or impression from which we form the idea of power or necessary connexion.[25]

Our use of the idea of necessary connection, according to Hume, is thus grounded upon certain very general facts about human psychology. It therefore meets the weaker condition (A) for objectivity, the demand for universality. For, on Hume's view, when I think of two events as being necessarily connected, then this is not the result of any personal peculiarities of mine, but of certain innate psychological tendencies that are common to all human beings. However, as Hume gleefully emphasises, the idea of necessary connection is still clearly subjective for all that, and cannot claim to represent an objective feature of the world. This is because, although human minds may universally possess certain innate habits or instincts, this would be a merely contingent fact about them. Thus the fact that our experience incorporated the experience of necessary connections would be dependent upon the fact that it was the experience of a mind that contingently happened to possess certain features (i.e., certain habits of association). But because the possession of those features by the mind is a contingent fact, it would be logically possible for there to be minds that did not possess those features. Such (possible) minds, in response to precisely the same given

---

[25] Hume, *Enquiries Concerning Human Understanding and Concerning the Principles of Morals*, ed. L. A. Selby-Bigge, 3rd edn (Oxford University Press, 1975), § 7, Part 2, p. 75.

sensory input, would not have the experience of necessary connections, and yet there would be no sense in which they would thereby be missing any aspects of that input. Our use of the idea of necessary connection, on Hume's account, therefore reflects only accidental facts about our subjective psychological constitution and thus cannot be seen as objectively grounded. Hence, merely meeting the weaker condition (A) is not sufficient for objectivity.

The stronger condition (B) for objectivity that Kant holds – that is, the demand for *necessary* universal validity – rules out an account (like Hume's) that would ground the spontaneous synthesis upon universal but contingent facts about the human mind. For condition (B) says that a subject's act of spontaneous synthesis can only be objective insofar as any other possible cognising mind, on being presented with certain mental modifications, would necessarily have synthesised them in just the way the subject in question did. As Kant puts it in the *Prolegomena*, 'I want therefore that I, at every time, and also everyone else, would necessarily have to connect the same perceptions under the same circumstances' (4:299). In other words, to be objective the spontaneous synthesis must be grounded not in any contingent features of the cognising subject (no matter how universally shared those features happen to be), but in the features that the subject necessarily shares with any other possible cognising subject. That is, in order to result in cognition the spontaneous synthesis must be grounded only upon *essential* facts about the cognising mind. In this way the method of projection applied in the act of synthesis is not determined by the given sensory data, but by the subject itself, and is thus spontaneous (as demanded by the first premise of Kant's argument in the B-Deduction). However, the method of projection is determined by the nature of the subject *qua* cognising mind, and is thus free from anything merely personal, arbitrary, or, in a word, subjective. Only thus, by meeting the stronger condition for necessary universal validity can the synthesis be objective, in that it results in a judgment that can legitimately lay claim to the assent of any other possible cognising mind, and which thus can be called 'cognition'.

If, as I have argued, the simultaneous spontaneity and objectivity of synthesis demand that the synthesis be grounded only in essential facts about the cognising mind, then it must be asked what those essential facts are. This is to demand a logical analysis of the abstract concept of cognition, or, equivalently, of the notion of a cognising mind in general. The method of projection applied in the act of synthesis must be shown to follow simply from a very abstract description of the cognising mind – that is, from the nature of the mind *qua* cognising. Now Kant holds (and some of the reasoning for this was outlined in the previous chapter) that cognition is essentially a form of judging; hence, a cognising mind is, in essence, a judging mind. Kant thus writes of himself in the *Prolegomena* that

I cast about for an act of the understanding that contains all of the others, and that only differentiates itself through various modifications or moments in order to bring the multiplicity of representation under the unity of thinking in general; and there I found that this act of the understanding consists in judging. (4:323)

From this it follows that the essential nature of the cognising mind can be discovered by attending to the essential nature of the act of judgment itself. The essential nature of judgment is given by the different possible logical forms of judgment, which, according to Kant, are contained in the so-called 'table of judgments' given in the Metaphysical Deduction (see A70/B95). Kant thus continues the passage from the *Prolegomena* just quoted, by writing as follows.

Here lay before me now, already finished though not yet wholly free of defects, the work of the logicians, through which I was put in the position to present a complete table of the functions of the pure understanding. (4:323)

Kant's claim is, in other words, that the spontaneous synthesis involved in cognition must be grounded upon the basic possible structures (i.e., logical forms) of the act of judgment. That is, the forms of judgment, or the 'logical functions' as Kant also calls them, are the basic methods of projection that are applied in the act of synthesis – they are, if you like, the fundamental, essential resources required of the imagination for 'seeing' *objects* in the mind's internal modifications. These basic methods of projection, or resources of the imagination, are of course the categories. Kant thus writes in § 26 of the B-Deduction that 'in the *metaphysical deduction* the origin of the a priori categories in general was established through their complete coincidence with the universal logical functions of thinking' (B159). It is through this appeal to the 'logical functions of thinking' that Kant attempts to provide a ground for the spontaneous synthesis that is objective because it is not based upon any contingent psychological facts, but solely upon the essential nature of the cognising mind. The forms of judgment, as applied in the spontaneous synthesis involved in cognition, thus come to play a constitutive role in experience by partially determining what the subject cognises *in* its given mental modifications.

This argument is briefly summarised by Kant in the *Prolegomena*. He writes there that in order to cognise it is not sufficient for me (i.e., the subject) simply to have 'a connection of perceptions within *my* mental state', for that has 'only subjective validity'; rather, I must 'connect them in a consciousness *in general*' (4:300; my emphasis in both cases). That is, objectively valid judgments are those in which representations 'are united in a consciousness in general, i.e., are united necessarily therein' (4:305). As noted above, terms like the *Critique*'s ubiquitous 'in general' (*überhaupt*) or 'as such' signify a discussion of abstractions. Hence, Kant is saying in these remarks from the *Prolegomena* that, for cognition to be possible, I must connect or synthesise my internal states in a way that is determined by the nature of my consciousness only insofar as my consciousness is a consciousness in general. In other words, the way in which I connect my internal states must be determined solely by the *essential* nature of a (cognising) consciousness, and not by any merely contingent features of my consciousness. It is in this way that the representations 'are united *necessarily*' in a cognition. For the way in which they are synthesised (i.e., grasped as hanging together to present an object) is the way they *must* be synthesised if that synthesis is to result in an objective claim. That is, if the perceptions were synthesised any differently the result would no longer be a cognition, but instead something with mere 'subjective validity'. Now, as I have suggested, Kant holds that a spontaneous yet objective synthesis must be governed by the categories. He summarises his argument for this in the following dense sentence from the *Prolegomena*.

The given intuition must be subsumed under a concept, which determines the form of judging in general with respect to the intuition, connects the empirical consciousness of the latter in a consciousness in general, and thereby furnishes empirical judgments with universal validity; a concept of this kind is a pure a priori concept of the understanding, which does nothing but simply determine for an intuition the mode in general in which it can serve for judging. (4:300)

This sentence can be interpreted as follows. Kant says that for cognition to occur the subject must 'subsume' an intuition under a logical function of judgment. That is, the subject grasps an intuition as presenting an object by synthesising the intuition in a way determined by the essential structure of the act of judgment. This 'subsumption' under a category determines for the intuition 'the mode in general in which it can serve for judging'. In other words, it is in virtue of this objective synthesis (i.e., application of a method of projection grounded in the forms of judgment) that the subject cognises an object *in* its internal modifications, and thus makes a judgment. This in turn is, in the sense explained above, to 'connect' or synthesise the representations composing the intuition 'in a consciousness in general'.

The following mathematical analogy may assist in understanding the general structure of Kant's argument, as sketched above. The given mental modifications of the mind (i.e., sensations) can be thought of as *arguments* to which a cognising subject applies a *function* (i.e., synthesises them) in order to produce a *result* (i.e., experience or cognition of the phenomenal world). With this in mind, imagine a game in which a list of numbers, the arguments, is read out to all logically possible players, who have to apply a function to each number they hear in order to produce another list of numbers, which is the result. However, the arguments do not determine which function the player is to apply to them (i.e., the synthesis is spontaneous); hence, which function is applied is determined by features of the player. Let this function be determined in each case by contingent features of the player (e.g., by personal whims, innate psychological dispositions, etc.). In such a case, given all logically possible players of the game, we could expect all possible functions to be applied to the arguments, and thus all possible results to be produced. For any set of arguments can be mapped onto any set of results depending upon which function (i.e., mapping) is chosen. In such a case, therefore, any sense of all the players being receptive to one and the same independent reality (i.e., the list of numbers that was read out to them all) has disappeared. As Kant would put it, what has been lost is any sense of 'the unity of the object – an object to which they all refer, with which they all agree, and, for that reason, also must all harmonise among themselves' (4:298). If *any* results can legitimately be obtained, then there is no genuine sense in which the players as a whole are dependent upon or constrained by the arguments that were initially read out – the arguments thus effectively drop out as irrelevant. In order to maintain a sense of the players as all being receptive to one and the same reality (i.e., to be genuinely cognising) then which function is applied, although determined by features of the players, must be one and the same for every logically possible player. Therefore, in a conclusion analogous to the one reached above, which function is applied must be determined only by the features essential to being a player of that game (i.e., essential to being a cognising mind).

This reading of Kant's argument helps to make sense of that section of the appendix to the *Prolegomena* in which he discusses Berkeley. I am not concerned with the question of whether or not this is a fair reading of Berkeley; only with the question of what Kant's discussion reveals about his own philosophy. In the discussion in the *Prolegomena* Kant claims that Berkeley's philosophy degrades our experience to 'sheer illusion'. However, the interesting feature of this discussion is that although Kant thus echoes the standard complaint about Berkeley, he does not do so for the standard reason. For Kant does not say that Berkeley degrades bodies to mere illusion in virtue of his immaterialism (the claim that their *esse* is *percipi*). Instead, Kant locates Berkeley's error in a different place, namely, in Berkeley's failure to recognise that objective experience essentially involves the use of certain concepts a priori. Kant thus writes that

> since truth rests upon universal and necessary laws as its criteria, for *Berkeley* experience could have no criteria of truth, because its appearances (according to him) had nothing underlying them a priori; from which it then followed that experience is nothing but sheer illusion. (4:375)

My interpretation of Kant's argument in the B-Deduction makes this claim about Berkeley comprehensible. If the mind did not make use of any a priori rules grounded in its essential structure (i.e., the categories) in spontaneously synthesising its internal states, then its experience could have no claim to objectivity. For its experience would become the application of a purely arbitrary and subjective method of projection, and the appearances (i.e., what the subject grasped in its representations via the act of synthesis) would therefore be the results of mere fantasising or subjective association. They would, in other words, be 'sheer illusion', and there could thus no longer be any question of the truth or falsity of the mind's supposed 'cognition'. It is thus that Kant tells us in the *Prolegomena* to 'heed well the distinction of experience from a mere aggregate of perceptions' (4:310). For he thinks that if the appearances have 'nothing underlying them a priori', as in Berkeley's account, then the mind's so-called 'experience' collapses into a 'mere aggregate' of subjective states. Without the categories, the spontaneous synthesis would be arbitrary, and there would thus no longer be any grounds for seeing one's experience as the experience of an objective world (i.e., something independent of oneself and one's personal whims, which one can therefore get right or wrong).

This interpretation of Kant's argument for the categories allows me to resolve the problem of how intuitions can both be non-conceptual and yet function as a constraint on our experience. This problem has often been noted in the secondary literature. Richard Aquila, for example, writes of it as follows.

> It has often been assumed that on Kant's views intuitions are as such devoid of conceptual or descriptive content. This has led to the supposition that intuitions, as such, represent some sort of mysterious 'bare particulars'. It also leads in turn to puzzlement as to how a Kantian intuition could have any epistemological relevance.[26]

---

[26] Aquila, *Representational Mind*, p. 48; footnotes omitted.

The opening chapters of John McDowell's book *Mind and World* are also concerned with this problem, and it will be useful to compare his solution with the solution that I find in Kant's Transcendental Deduction. McDowell points out that there must be some rational external constraint on cognition, if it is to be thought of as constituting experience of a reality that is even minimally independent of ourselves – that is, if we are to consider ourselves as being genuinely *receptive* in any way. If this is not the case then, he suggests, our applications of concepts in experience 'threaten to degenerate into moves in a self-contained game'.[27] That is, McDowell is suggesting that there must be some sense in which what is given to us in experience justifies or constrains the application of various concepts to it. For otherwise it seems that we would be left free to apply whatever concepts we liked in experience, in which case we could no longer consider ourselves as being receptive to an independent reality. We would, in other words, be left with the absurdity of a solipsistic idealism ('a self-contained game'), in which our experiences would be spun completely out of our own heads. Hence, it seems that if intuitions are thought of as non-conceptual, then they can no longer play the role in our epistemology that they were introduced to play – namely, as what is given to us by our receptivity – and indeed must ultimately drop out of the theory as an irrelevance.

In response to this problem, it is sometimes argued that we must accept that Kantian intuitions are conceptual if we are consistently to conceive of our experience as receptive. As McDowell puts this conclusion, 'Experiences are impressions made by the world on our senses, products of receptivity; but those impressions already have conceptual content'.[28] Wilfrid Sellars, moved by similar considerations to McDowell, also suggests that intuitions should be considered as constituting 'a special class of representations of the understanding' which 'belong, as such, to spontaneity'.[29] By thus making intuitions conceptual, McDowell and Sellars avoid the collapse into complete idealism. For if intuitions are already conceptual then they can obviously serve to justify our use of concepts in experience. Now, neither McDowell nor Sellars is engaged in Kantian exegesis in any straightforward sense, and both are thus free to make such conscious deviations from Kant's own position. However, it is important for my purposes (which are exegetical) to show why their view that intuitions are conceptual is not an adequate interpretation of Kant. The problem is essentially the reverse of that

---

[27] McDowell, *Mind and World*, p. 5. Cf. R. P. Wolff, *Kant's Theory of Mental Activity* (Cambridge, MA: Harvard University Press, 1963), p. 152n.

[28] McDowell, *Mind and World*, p. 46.

[29] Sellars, *Science and Metaphysics*, p. 9. Aquila follows Sellars, arguing that intuitions are 'informed' by concepts (see *Representational Mind*, ch. 2).

which is motivating McDowell and Sellars, and is that if intuitions are conceptual then genuine spontaneity becomes impossible. As I have argued,
for Kant the subject is spontaneous when it determines its own experience rather than being determined by that experience. If intuitions were
conceptual then, given Kant's fairly traditional understanding of empirical
concepts (as pointed out above), our use of concepts in experience would
reduce to a passive recognition of features of what is given to us. Hence,
our cognition would be, in Kant's terms, merely receptive – all the mind
would have to do would be to 'read off' the data given to it. There would
therefore be no space left for his transcendental idealism, which depends
on the claim that we apply the categories spontaneously.

Kant thus seems to be faced with a dilemma in explaining how it is
possible for the cognising subject to be both spontaneous and receptive.
In summary, the dilemma is as follows. Kant must hold that intuitions are
either non-conceptual or conceptual. (1) If intuitions were non-conceptual
then our use of concepts in experience would be totally unconstrained,
and Kant would thus be committed to an absurd idealism in which we
were spontaneous in cognition but not receptive. (2) If intuitions were
conceptual then we would be receptive in cognition but not spontaneous,
which is inconsistent with Kant's 'two-faculty' model of cognition, and
his transcendental idealism. Now, my interpretation of the argument of
the B-Deduction shows how Kant can avoid this supposed dilemma, by
denying the truth of (1). In other words, it is possible for intuitions both to
be non-conceptual and to function as constraints on our experience. This
is because, as I have argued, the cognising subject's spontaneity will not be
arbitrary or subjective if (and only if) it is grounded in the essential nature
of the mind. Intuitions are non-conceptual, so they do not determine how
the subject will synthesise them. But if the synthesis (the 'seeing in', as I have
also called it) is governed solely by rules derived from the essential structure
of the cognising mind (i.e., by the categories) then any possible cognising
mind would, on being presented with just these intuitions, necessarily have
synthesised them in the same way. The mind would thus be spontaneous
(in applying the categories) without thereby being free to apply concepts
without constraint; hence, the slide into an absurd idealism is avoided. In
this fashion it is possible for Kant to hold that in cognition we are both
receptive and spontaneous.

To recapitulate, I have been concerned here with the reasoning for the
second premise of Kant's main argument in the B-Deduction, which is
the proposition (β) *if our cognition involves a spontaneous synthesis then
this synthesis must be governed by the categories*. This premise is, in other

words, the claim that a necessary condition of the claim made in the first premise of the B-Deduction's argument – namely, (α) *all our cognition must involve a spontaneous synthesis* – is that that synthesis must be governed by or grounded in the categories. In summary form, the argument that I have suggested Kant has for the second premise is as follows.

1. Necessarily, a spontaneous act of synthesis can result in a judgment with a claim to objectivity (i.e., a cognition) only if that synthesis is governed solely by what is essential to the cognising mind.
2. The cognising mind is essentially a judging mind.
3. The essential structures of the act of judgment are the logical functions listed in the 'table of judgments'. [From the Metaphysical Deduction.]
∴. Necessarily, a spontaneous act of synthesis can result in a cognition only if that synthesis is governed solely by the logical functions.
4. The logical functions, insofar as they govern the synthesis involved in cognition, are the categories.
∴. Necessarily, a spontaneous act of synthesis can result in a cognition only if that synthesis is governed by the categories.
∴. (β) If our cognition involves a spontaneous synthesis then this synthesis must be governed by the categories. QED.

Of course much more needs to be said, both in explanation of this argument and, most importantly, in justification of my claim that this is in fact Kant's argument in the B-Deduction. The purpose of the discussion so far was to give an overall sense of the structure and logic of the argument that my interpretation proposes. In the remaining sections of this chapter I will develop this argument in more detail by discussing a number of points that it raises.

However, before ending this section it is important to point out how the argument sketched here fulfils the crucial explanatory role of the De-duction. In the previous section it was argued that the central aim of the Deduction was to explain how the categories can be both objective and spontaneous, in the face of the strongly intuitive view that those two prop-erties are incompatible. As I said there, simply showing that we must use the categories in experience fails to fulfil this aim, for such a proof fails to make their objectivity intelligible. This is because such a result does not show how the categories are to be distinguished from merely sub-jective psychological habits or compulsions, and thus leaves a door open for a sceptic like Hume. Kant's argument, as I have interpreted it here, at-tempts to shut that door by showing that the categories 'must be recognised as a priori conditions of the possibility of experiences' (A94/B126). The argument flows from the claim (made in Kant's premise (α), which I am taking for granted in this chapter) that all cognition must involve a spontaneous act of synthesis – in other words, the claim that cognition involves two faculties, namely, receptivity and spontaneity. Now, as I have argued, for the subject to be genuinely receptive (i.e., for its experience to be determined by something independent of it) and also spontaneous (i.e., determining of its experience), then the determining act of the subject (i.e., synthesis) must be such that any possible mind that was determined in a certain way, would necessarily determine its experience in one and the same way. Therefore the nature of that determining act cannot depend upon any contingent facts about the subject, but only upon what is essential to a mind that is both determined and determining (i.e., a discursive mind). Hence, given the truth of the two-faculty model of cognition, then for the subject to be genuinely receptive to an independent reality it must synthesise according to rules that have their ground solely in the essence of the discursive cognising mind. Given Kant's further argument that these rules are the categories, then it follows that the categories actually make objective experience ('cognising something as an object') possible. In this way, then, the spontaneity of the categories, which had seemed incompatible with their objectivity, turns out to be the essential source of objectivity in general. In other words, the objectivity of the act of cognising (i.e., its being something more than an imaginary projection or the result of mere habits of association) is rescued *only* by recognising the existence of a priori laws that govern the act of synthesis or of 'seeing in'. Hence, from Kant's argument it follows that empiricism (by which I here mean the denial that there can be any concepts both spontaneous and objective) can be maintained only at the cost of relinquishing any objectivity at all. In other words, as Kant said, we come to understand the objectivity of the categories only by seeing them as essential to *all* cognition. It is thus that he writes that 'concepts that supply the objective ground of the possibility of experience are necessary *for just that reason*' (A94/ B126; my emphasis).

At the end of the B-Deduction (in § 27), Kant discusses an alternative method of attempting to reconcile the objectivity and spontaneity of the categories. Although they are not mentioned by name, this alternative method is strongly suggestive of both Leibniz's doctrine of 'pre-established harmony' and Descartes's argument in the *Meditations*, in which the objectivity of our innate ideas of extension and thought is guaranteed by the fact that we 'have perceived that God exists . . . and that he is no deceiver'.[30]

---

[30] Descartes, *Fifth Meditation* in *Philosophical Writings*, vol. II, p. 48.

For Kant imagines someone suggesting that instead of being conditions of possible experience, the categories are 'subjective dispositions for thinking, implanted in us along with our existence by our author in such a way that their use would agree exactly with the laws of nature along which experience runs' (B167). Now, in § 27 Kant does not attack this suggestion on the standard grounds that it cannot be proven – that, for example, Descartes's arguments for a non-deceiving God are unsound, or that we lack criteria for telling which 'innate ideas' might be trustworthy. Rather, Kant tells us that 'in such a case the categories would lack the *necessity* that is essential to their concept' (B168). In other words, Kant is claiming that *even if* the Cartesian arguments (or similar) were sound, they would still not suffice for demonstrating the objective validity of the categories. We can make sense of this if the crucial explanatory role of the Transcendental Deduction is recalled. Let us suppose that we know that God has made us such that we synthesise in a way that must match the nature of independent reality. Now, even if we know this claim to be true, the categories are still left looking like mere 'brute facts' – modes of synthesis that God has arbitrarily decided to attach to our natures. The Cartesian argument, even if sound, would thus fail to make it intelligible just why the categories *must* apply to the world; it only tells us that they do so because God has commanded it. In other words, the appeal to a 'pre-established harmony' or to God's benevolence no more explains the necessity of the categories, than does an appeal to a universal psychological disposition (Hume's 'custom'). The only way to make that necessity intelligible is to show how our spontaneous (and thus a priori) use of the categories follows intrinsically from our essence – that is, to show that we apply them simply *qua* discursive cognising minds, and not *qua* God's creatures.

PURE PRACTICAL REASON AND AUTONOMY

Kant's argument for his premise (β), as I have interpreted it above, is intended to demonstrate that the spontaneity of the categories is not only not in conflict with their objectivity, but is in fact essential to that objectivity. Further light can be shed on this argument by showing how it parallels an important argument in Kant's practical philosophy, in which he argues that what could be called the 'spontaneity' of the moral law – that is, its being grounded on something internal rather than external to the subject – is essential to its objectivity. Hence, the autonomous nature of moral action, which had seemed to threaten the objectivity of the moral law, is shown to be a necessary condition of that objectivity. An examination of this parallel should indicate how it is possible to see both Kant's theoretical and moral philosophy as profound treatments of Rousseau's famous claim that 'obedience to a law which we prescribe to ourselves is liberty'.[31]

It is well known that the notion that the moral law is a law that we prescribe to ourselves is fundamental to Kant's practical philosophy. He writes, for example, in the *Groundwork of the Metaphysics of Morals* that

> If we look back upon all previous efforts that have ever been made to discover the principle of morality, we need not wonder now why all of them had to fail. It was seen that the human being is bound by laws to his duty, but it never occurred to them that he is subject *only to laws given by himself but still universal.* (4:432)

This passage echoes the remarks that Kant makes about Hume and others in the introduction to the Deduction in the first *Critique* (remarks that were discussed above). Kant says there that Hume failed to give an adequate account of the categories because he (Hume) could not understand how something grounded on our own nature (and thus spontaneous) could simultaneously be objective. In much the same way, Kant is saying in this passage from the *Groundwork* that previous discussions of morality have failed because they do not see that the moral law could be both a law that we give to ourselves and 'still universal'.

Kant argues that the moral law *must* be a law that reason prescribes to itself, because this is the only way in which the moral law can be genuinely objective or universally binding. That is, just as in the case of the categories, Kant holds that the spontaneity of the moral law is essential to its objectivity. The reasoning behind this claim is familiar, and I will only summarise it here.[32] Kant argues that an analysis of our ordinary notion of morality shows that we recognise the moral law as unconditionally and universally obligatory. In Kant's famous terminology, this is to say that it imposes categorical rather than hypothetical imperatives upon us. That is, the moral law specifies simply what I must do, and not what I must do *if* I want to achieve such-and-such. But if I am to recognise the moral law as unconditionally obligatory in this way, then it cannot bind me to act in virtue of any particular, contingent desires or motivations I happen to have. For in that case the law would not be binding upon an agent that lacked those desires or motivations. Hence, for example, the moral law cannot be thought of as God's commands, or as a specification of the best method

---

[31] J.-J. Rousseau, *The Social Contract*, trans. G. D. H. Cole (London: J. M. Dent, 1993), book 1, ch. 8.
[32] I have benefited from the discussions in R. C. S. Walker, *Kant* (London: Routledge, 1978), ch. 11, and L. W. Beck, *A Commentary on Kant's Critique of Practical Reason* (University of Chicago Press, 1960), chs. 10–11.

to achieve happiness. For if this were possible then we could imagine a rational agent that did not wish to obey God, or did not wish to achieve happiness, and that agent would thus not be bound by the moral law – which, Kant argues, is an absurd conclusion. Therefore, he argues, we must conceive of the moral law as binding on rational beings simply in virtue of their essence – that is, their rationality – and not in virtue of any particular desires, motivations, or psychological dispositions they might have. Kant thus writes in the *Groundwork* that

unless we want to deny to the concept of morality any truth and any relation to some possible object, we cannot dispute that its law is so extensive in its import that it must hold not only for human beings but for all *rational beings as such* [i.e., *qua* rational beings], not merely under contingent conditions and with exceptions but with *absolute necessity*. (4:408)

In other words, if the moral law is to be objective, then it must bind us *qua* rational beings (rather than, for example, *qua* seekers of happiness, or *qua* servants of God). Kant argues that a number of things about the nature of the moral law follow from this conclusion (e.g., that it binds us always to treat other rational beings as ends and never simply as means), but these further developments of Kant's moral theory do not concern me here.

Kant also puts this conclusion by saying that if the moral law is to be possible then there must be such a thing as pure practical reason. That is, it must be possible for there to be something that a subject recognises as binding on her will (i.e., it is practical) solely in virtue of its appeal to her rationality (i.e., it is purely rational). Thus Kant asks rhetorically,

how should laws of the determination of *our* will be taken as laws of the determination of the will of rational beings as such [i.e., *qua* rational], and for ours only as [i.e., *qua*] rational beings, if they were merely empirical and did not have their origin completely a priori in pure but practical reason? (4:408)

In this passage Kant is repeating the same sort of solution that, I have argued, he gives in the field of theoretical reason: the moral law can be spontaneous and objective only if it is grounded in something completely non-empirical or a priori. That is, it can be spontaneous and objective only if it is grounded in 'pure but practical reason'. As I have argued above, if the moral law had its source in something inessential to the subject's own reason (e.g., in God's commands or in a desire for happiness) then it would not be binding on all possible rational beings that possess a will. Hence the moral law can only be universally valid if it has its source in the essential structure of reason alone. It is only in this way that, as Kant writes in the *Critique of Practical Reason*, this principle of morality, just on account of the universality of the law-giving that makes it the formal supreme determining ground of the will regardless of all subjective differences, is declared by reason to be at the same time a law for all rational beings insofar as they have a will. (5:32)

In other words, the moral law is a law for all rational willing beings precisely because it has its source in self-legislation by pure practical reason. Hence, according to Kant, the internal and a priori source of the moral law is a necessary condition of its objectivity, just as the internal and a priori source of the categories (in the essential structure of judgment) is a necessary condition of their objectivity.

This argument of Kant's practical philosophy entails that insofar as a subject acts morally, that subject is autonomous. Autonomy is when the subject determines itself to act, and for Kant this means being determined to act solely by what is essential (or 'internal') to oneself – that is, one's reason. Hence, autonomy is possible if it is possible for pure reason to be practical. For if autonomy were impossible, then reason alone could not cause us to act. In such a case the moral law could bind us only in virtue of our psychological motivations or desires (e.g., in virtue of our desire for happiness). But because no such particular psychology is essential to a rational being, the moral law would in such a case not be universally valid. In other words, without the possibility of autonomy there could be no objective moral law; or, equivalently, the possibility of autonomy is a necessary condition of objective morality. Kant thus writes in the Deduction in the second *Critique* that 'freedom is necessary because those laws [*sc.*, moral laws] are necessary' (5:46), and that 'the moral principle . . . itself serves as the principle of the deduction of an inscrutable faculty . . . , namely, the faculty of freedom' (5:47). The moral law binds me simply by virtue of my rationality, and this act of self-legislation is the source of both my potential autonomy as a rational being, and of the objectivity of the moral law. In this way, what looked to be incompatible with the objectivity of the moral law is in fact shown to be essential to it; and the attempt to ground the moral law on something external (which seemed the way to defend its objectivity) in fact destroys that objectivity.

From this summary it should be clear how this argument in Kant's practical philosophy parallels the argument for the objectivity of the categories in his theoretical philosophy. The objective validity of the categories is secured by showing how their spontaneity (as it were, their status as the products of the subject's 'self-legislation') is essential to objective cognition in general. Similarly, the objectivity of the moral law is made compatible with its spontaneity (i.e., its being a law that reason prescribes to itself, rather than some external command) by showing that the spontaneity is essential to that law's being universally binding. Although the moral law is a law I prescribe to myself, it is one which binds me not by virtue of any contingent desires I may have, but by virtue of my essence as a rational willing being. Similarly, the categories, although spontaneous, are not simply arbitrary or personal habits of my imagination, but are grounded on my essence as a cognising (and therefore judging) mind. In both the theoretical and practical cases the general solution is the same: the constitutive act of mind is objective (and not merely personal, subjective or arbitrary) because it is grounded in the essential structure of rationality rather than in any contingent psychological features of the subject. With this parallel in mind, consider the following passage from the *Prolegomena*.

> To think, however, is to unite representations in a consciousness. This unification either arises merely in relation to the subject and is contingent and subjective, or it occurs without condition and is necessary and objective. (4:304)

We are told here that for the synthesis or 'unification' involved in cognition to be objective is for it to occur *without condition*. To echo the language of Kant's practical philosophy, it could be said that an objective synthesis must, as it were, occur categorically rather than hypothetically. That is, a synthesis that I would perform only *if* I happened to possess such-and-such habits of association (or whatever) could not result in a cognition with any claim to objectivity.

In his insightful discussion of Kantian ethics in the final chapter of *Science and Metaphysics*, Sellars makes the following remark.

> The central theme of Kant's ethical theory is, in our terminology, the *reasonableness* of intentions. In what sense or senses, if any, can *intentions* be said to be reasonable, i.e., have a *claim* on the assent of a rational being? Kant clearly construes this task as parallel to the task of defining in what sense or senses, if any, *beliefs* can be reasonable, i.e., have a *claim* on the assent of a rational being.[33]

I have argued here that Kant does indeed construe his task in the theoretical philosophy as parallel to his task in the practical philosophy. According to Kant, for a belief or an intention to possess objective validity (i.e., for it to be 'reasonable', as Sellars puts it) is for it to be the product of a mental act (a synthesis or an act of 'self-legislation') that the subject performs solely in virtue of being rational. In the field of theoretical reason, Kant argues that this entails that the synthesis involved in cognition must be grounded

---

[33] Sellars, *Science and Metaphysics*, p. 208.

a priori on rules having their source in the form of judgment – that is, the categories. In this section I have briefly exhibited how this argument that I find in the first *Critique* parallels a central argument of Kant's practical philosophy. The purpose of doing this was twofold: firstly, to add further support to my interpretation of the Transcendental Deduction, and secondly, further to clarify the logical structure of the argument that I claim to find there.

CONCLUSION: REPRESENTATION AND IDEALISM

In this chapter I have attempted to sketch out what I hold to be Kant's central argument in the Transcendental Deduction. I have suggested that the argument looks like this:

α. All our cognition must involve a spontaneous synthesis.

β. If our cognition involves a spontaneous synthesis then this synthesis must be governed by the categories.

$\therefore$. The categories make our cognition possible.

This chapter has focused particularly on attempting to explain the structure of the reasoning for (β), Kant's crucial argument to the objective validity of the categories from the spontaneity of cognition. The next chapter is a detailed discussion of Kant's argument for his first premise, (α), and includes a close examination of § 16 of the B-Deduction. The final chapter discusses in detail the remaining important sections of the B-Deduction (§§ 17–20 and § 26) and attempts fully to support and defend the interpretation that has been laid out so far. Before proceeding to these more detailed textual discussions, however, in the rest of this section I want to provide an overview of the conclusions reached so far and, as part of this, give a brief picture of the sort of interpretation of transcendental idealism that my understanding of Kant's position implies.

I have suggested that the best way to understand Kant's representationalism is as follows. In experience we are *receptive*, in that the mind's sensibility is modified or determined in certain ways by an independent reality. Cognition then involves the mind's awareness of its own modifications. I argued in the previous chapter that this reflexive act is best treated neither as an act of compounding the states together into complexes (as in the idealist model of cognition), nor as an act of inferring beyond them (as in the indirect realist model). Rather, this act, which Kant calls 'synthesis', is an act in which the mind grasps or comprehends its internal states as representing something (i.e., as complex signs), and not simply as internal states.

I have suggested that this act of synthesis is best understood on the analogy of seeing something *in* a picture. However, the mind's modifications do not, of themselves, determine how they are to be synthesised – which is to say that in cognition we are not only receptive but also *spontaneous*. It was argued above that receptivity and spontaneity can be consistently combined (i.e., Kant can hold a two-faculty model of cognition) only if the spontaneity is governed a priori by the categories. Hence, it is in virtue of a category-governed synthesis that the modifications of sensibility function to present an objective world to the subject (and in our – human – case, an objective spatio-temporal world). The categories are thus 'concepts of an object in general' (B128) in that they are the most basic, fundamental resources of the imagination for 'seeing' objects 'in' a manifold of sensations given to the mind. The categories are spontaneous in that they are not simply capacities for recognising features of what is given in experience, or for bringing clarity and distinctness to ideas that are obscure and confused. Rather, they are partially constitutive of what we cognise, for they are the rules of projection which are applied to the manifold of sensation in the act of synthesis. However, despite this spontaneity, the categories are also objective because they are grounded in the essence of judging itself.

This summary of my interpretation can be illustrated by considering a passage from the Second Analogy, in which Kant is concerned with what it is for a representation to present something to us (i.e., what it is for us to grasp an internal modification as signifying). Kant begins this passage with an explicit statement of his representationalist starting point, and then asks the obvious question that any representationalist epistemology must answer, as follows.

We have representations in us, of which we can also become conscious. But let this consciousness reach as far and be as exact and precise as one wants, still there always remain only representations, i.e., inner determinations of our mind … Now how do we come to posit an object for these representations, or ascribe to their subjective reality, as modifications, some sort of objective reality? (A197/B242)

This passage demonstrates clearly that Kant is thinking of representations – at least insofar as they are only 'inner determinations of our mind', which have a 'subjective reality' – as internal to our minds, and as being the immediate objects of awareness or consciousness. He then makes the obvious point that if we think of representations only in this fashion, it becomes altogether mysterious how they can have any 'objective reality'. That is, it becomes mysterious how they can be a means of our being aware of something other than a mere 'inner determination' – how they are able, as it were, to reach out to the world.

Now, the indirect realist and idealist (i.e., Berkeleyan) models of cognition provide two answers to that problem, but Kant's own answer is given in the final sentence of the paragraph just quoted. Here he writes that

> If we investigate what new characteristic is given to our representations by the *relation to an object*, and what is the dignity that they thereby receive, we find that it does nothing beyond making the combination of representations necessary in a certain way, and subjecting them to a rule. (A197/ B242)

Kant claims here that for our representations to relate to an object – that is, for them to present an objective realm to us – two conditions must be met. Firstly, the representations must be 'combined', and secondly, that 'combination' must be 'made necessary in a certain way', by being 'subjected to a rule'. My interpretation of Kant makes the meaning of this claim reasonably clear. The first condition is that a spontaneous act of combination, synthesis, or 'seeing in' is required in order for us to comprehend the mental modifications as presenting something. However, in order for this spontaneous synthesis to result in a cognition with a claim to objectivity, then it must be necessary. That is, the synthesis *must* be performed just as any other possible discursive mind would have performed it (in grasping the very same intuitions), so that the result is in no way personal, subjective or arbitrary. This, as I have argued, is possible only if the synthesis is subjected to (or performed in accordance with) an a priori rule or category.

This conclusion is repeated in a slightly different form in a well-known passage from earlier in the Second Analogy, which is also worth examining. Kant is concerned in this passage with the question of how it is possible to make sense of the notion of the object of a representation, given that that object is not a 'thing in itself'. He asks:

> what do I understand by the question, how the manifold may be combined in the appearance itself (which is yet nothing in itself)? Here that which lies in the successive apprehension is considered as representation, but the appearance that is given to me, in spite of the fact that it is nothing more than a sum [*Inbegriff*] of these representations, is considered as their object . . . Appearance, in contradistinction to the representations of apprehension, can thereby only be represented as the object that is distinct from them if it stands under a rule that distinguishes it from every other apprehension, and makes one way of combining the manifold necessary. (A191/ B236)

To understand what is being said in this passage, it will be helpful to recall my earlier discussions of Kant's notion of representation, and my analogy for his model of the subject. That is, we should imagine a person inside an opaque plastic globe and watching a film that is being projected on the inside surface of that globe. In this case the representational medium is simply a temporal series of various spatial arrangements of colour patches, and yet this medium serves to present a 'world' to the subject (the world of the film, as it were). It could thus be said to echo the passage just quoted, that there is a sense in which the various things and events that the subject sees in the film (the 'appearances') are 'nothing in themselves' and 'nothing more than a sum' of the various changes in the representational medium. Yet at the same time the things or events in the film are not identical with any collection of colour patches. As Kant puts it above, the appearances are 'represented by the subject as objects distinct from the representations of apprehension'. In other words, the subject does not simply see a series of colour patches, but instead sees things *in* that series.

Kant is thus concerned, in the quoted passage, to explain how it is possible for our imaginative act of 'seeing in', or synthesis, to be applied to a private collection of mental modifications and yet result in the cognition of an objective world. His answer is, as might now be expected, that there must be a 'rule' that 'makes one way of combining the manifold necessary'. Although we are spontaneous in synthesising or combining our manifold of representations, there cannot be any 'free-play' in this act of spontaneity, insofar as it is to result in objective cognition. For any such 'free-play' would render the result of the synthesis arbitrary or, in other words, subjective. Therefore, given a certain manifold of representations, any cognising subject must combine or synthesise those representations in just one way (i.e., must determine them in just *this* way), for the result to be a cognition with any claim to objectivity. Hence, as I have argued in this chapter, the synthesis must be performed according to an a priori rule or a category.

The purpose of the discussion in this section so far has been to recapitulate the main details of my interpretation of Kant's views on the notions of representation and objectivity. Now, given the closely knit nature of the *Critique*, it is hardly surprising that my interpretation of these notions implies certain consequences for an understanding of Kant's transcendental idealism. I will conclude this section by outlining and briefly defending some of those consequences. I should emphasise here that I am not proposing to discuss these complex issues in the detail which a full consideration of them would demand, for such a discussion would require another book. All that I am attempting to do here is to say just enough to show that my interpretation of the B-Deduction does not commit me to a view of Kant's idealism that is *obviously* indefensible, either textually or philosophically.

A clear statement of the doctrine of transcendental idealism occurs in the first edition version of the Paralogisms, where Kant writes, 'I understand by the _transcendental idealism_ of all appearances the doctrine that they are all together to be regarded as mere representations and not as things in themselves' (A369). The meaning of three important terms in this statement – namely, 'representations', 'appearances' and 'things in themselves' – needs to be considered in the light of the interpretation of Kant that I have outlined in this book so far. I begin with the closely connected notions of representation and appearance. According to Kant's representationalist epistemology, in cognition our faculty of sensibility is determined or modified in certain ways, and, via the act of synthesis, we grasp the modifications of our sensibility as presenting an objective world to us. The modifications (our internal mental states) thus make up the representational medium, and _appearances_ (or 'phenomena') are the objects that the mind cognises _in_ that medium. As Kant puts this point, an appearance 'can exist only in the representation of it' (A375n). Now, it is notorious that Kant also repeatedly says that appearances are 'mere representations'. This occurs not only in A, as in the sentence from the Paralogisms just quoted, but in both editions of the _Critique_ – as, for example, in the Antinomies where Kant writes that 'all objects of any experience possible for us, are nothing but appearances, i.e., mere representations' (A491/B519). However, as I hope the previous chapter has already made clear, this claim should not be taken to mean that Kant holds that appearances are 'mere representations' in the sense of being identical to (collections of) representations _qua_ subjective mental states, as in Berkeley's idealism. Rather, appearances are 'mere representations' in the sense that facts about appearances are reducible to facts about representations _qua_ representing.[34] This is just as facts about 'things in pictures' (where this last phrase is used without existential commitment to those things) are reducible to facts about pictures _qua_ representing, but not to facts about pictures _qua_ spatial arrangements of ink marks. This view, which is in some ways close to the so-called 'intentional object' interpretation of transcendental idealism,[35] does raise some very difficult questions – for example, concerning precisely how to specify the sense in which appearances supervene on our representations, and how the relation between the empirical and the transcendental self is to be understood. However, to

---

[34] Cf. ibid., ch. 2.
[35] For an example of the 'intentional object' interpretation see Aquila, _Representational Mind_, ch. 4. Cf. E. Bencivenga, _Kant's Copernican Revolution_ (Oxford University Press, 1987), ch. 4, and the interpretation of Leibniz's phenomenalism in R. M. Adams, _Leibniz_ (Oxford University Press, 1994), ch. 9.

reiterate what I said above, I do not have the space to go into such questions here; all I am attempting to do is to demonstrate that my reading of the B-Deduction does not imply an *obviously* absurd interpretation of transcendental idealism.

I now turn to consider the notion of things in themselves. The things in themselves are, as Kant repeatedly tells us, 'the non-sensible, and to us fully unknown ground of the appearance' (8:203). What is meant by this is that the things in themselves constitute the independent reality which ultimately grounds the modifications of our sensibility – that is, which provides the ultimate explanation of why our experience is thus and so. The existence of things in themselves is demanded if our experience is to be considered as being in any way receptive. This can be shown as follows. As all readers of the *Critique* know, Kant holds that the phenomenal realm has its spatio-temporal character in virtue of our (human) form of sensibility. Hence, that the phenomena or appearances are arranged in three dimensions of space and one dimension of time holds in virtue of a fact about our form of sensibility. However, that the phenomenal realm contains just *these* things arranged in just *this* way in space and time does not hold in virtue of any facts about us. For this would be an absolute idealism, in which all the facts about the entire spatio-temporal world would be spun out of our own minds. Hence, if this sort of idealism is to be avoided, then there must be a reality independent of us – the things in themselves – that determines our sensibility in cognition. One of the clearest expressions of this doctrine in the *Critique* is the following passage.

The sensible faculty of intuition is really only a receptivity for being affected in a certain way with representations . . . The non-sensible cause of these representations is entirely unknown to us, and therefore we cannot intuit it as an object . . . Meanwhile we can call the merely intelligible cause of appearances in general the transcendental object [i.e., thing in itself], merely so that we may have something corresponding to sensibility as a receptivity. To this transcendental object we can ascribe the whole extent and connection of our possible perceptions, and say that it is given in itself prior to all experience. (A494/ B522)

An even more unmistakable statement of this view about things in themselves is given in Kant's reply to Eberhard in '*Über eine Entdeckung*', where he (Kant) writes as follows.

Having asked 'Who (what) gives sensibility its matter, namely, the sensations?' he [*sc.*, Eberhard] believes himself to have spoken against the *Critique* in that he says: 'We may choose whatever we want – we nevertheless arrive at *things in themselves*'. Now this is precisely what the *Critique* constantly asserts; the only difference is that it places this ground of the matter of sensible representations not itself again in things as objects of the senses, but in something super-sensible, which grounds the sensible representations, and of which we can have no knowledge. It says: the objects as things in themselves *give* the matter to empirical intuition (they contain the ground of the determination of the faculty of representation in accordance with its sensibility) but they *are not* the matter of those intuitions. (8:215)[36]

As Kant emphasises in the final sentence of this passage, the proposition

(1) things in themselves *ground* our sensible representations

does *not* entail

(2) our sensible representations *represent* things in themselves.

Proposition (2) says that in experience we cognise things in themselves rather than appearances, which contradicts one of the central claims of the *Critique*. Hoke Robinson, for example, in a recent discussion of transcendental idealism, mistakenly assumes that this entailment does hold. For he claims that Kant cannot consistently hold that our sensibility is affected by (i.e., its modifications grounded in) things in themselves, for the reason that 'Kant explicitly denies that the object [*sc.*, of a sensible representation] can be a thing in itself'.[37] In other words, Robinson takes it as obvious that (1) entails (2). However, this is not the case, and Kant can therefore consistently claim, as he does, both (1) and not-(2). To understand why this is so, think again of the Kantian subject as a person inside an opaque plastic globe and watching a film projected on the internal surface of that globe. In this analogy, the 'things in themselves' make up the external reality that provides the ultimate explanation or ground for just why this particular film is being shown to the subject. But what the subject sees are not those 'things in themselves', but the things in the film – that is, the appearances. Indeed, the subject can draw *no* conclusions about the external reality on the basis of what she sees in the film – except for the trivial fact that that reality is such as to produce this particular film in interaction with her 'sensibility'. It is in this way that the things in themselves, although the grounds of our experience, are nonetheless entirely beyond the limits of that experience.

Despite all the textual evidence in its favour, this view of things in themselves as affecting our sensibility has been attacked on the grounds that

---

[36] Kant's internal page references have been omitted. I have largely followed Henry Allison's translation, from *The Kant–Eberhard Controversy*, ed. and trans. H. E. Allison (Baltimore: Johns Hopkins University Press, 1973). For further textual support for this view, see the discussion in notes 1 and 2 to § 13 of the *Prolegomena* (4:288–94).

[37] H. Robinson, 'Two Perspectives on Kant's Appearances and Things in Themselves', *Journal of the History of Philosophy* 32 (1994), 415.

it is inconsistent with Kant's claims about the categories. A clear summary of this argument is provided by Vaihinger, who writes that if

one understands by the affecting objects the things in themselves . . . one falls into the contradiction discovered by Jacobi, Aenesidemus and others that one must apply beyond experience the categories of substantiality and causality which are only supposed to have meaning and significance within experience.[38]

That is, to suppose that things in themselves ground our sensible representations is, it is claimed, to think of things in themselves as *substances*, and of their interaction with our sensibility as *causal* in nature. And this supposedly contradicts Kant's claim that 'the categories . . . have no other use for the cognition of things except insofar as these are taken as objects of possible experience [i.e., appearances]' (B147–8). In response to this argument it is worth repeating Sellars's warning that 'It can scarcely be overemphasised that the difficulty that Kant finds with things-in-themselves is that, considerations of morals and religion aside, our conception of them is *empty* – not that it is *incoherent*'.[39] Or, as Kant himself puts it in the Preface to B, 'even if we cannot *cognise* these same objects as things in themselves, we at least must be able to *think* them as things in themselves' (Bxxvi). That is, the problem with the argument summarised above is that it neglects Kant's distinction between thought and cognition, and his claim that the categories *can* be thought of as applying beyond the boundaries of possible experience (cognition) – but only in their 'unschematised' forms, that is, as mere logical functions. For example, he tells us that

from the concept of cause as pure category (if I leave out the time in which something follows something else in accordance with a rule), I will not find out anything more than that it is something that allows an inference to the existence of something else. (A243/B301)

In other words, it is possible, and thus neither contradictory nor meaningless, to *think* of non-temporal things (such as things in themselves) as standing in causal relations – but this means simply to think of things as being logically dependent upon one another (in the most abstract sense). Kant's point is that nothing of interest can be *known* about things in themselves on the basis of this sort of thought – all that can be done is to deduce 'obvious tautologies' (A244/B302). Amongst these 'obvious tautologies' is the claim that there is an independent reality, which is the ultimate explanation of why the phenomenal world is the way it is – for this follows

[38] H. Vaihinger, *Commentar zu Kants Kritik der reinen Vernunft* (Stuttgart: W. Spemann, 1881–92), vol. II, p. 53. I take this quote from H. E. Allison, *Kant's Transcendental Idealism* (New Haven: Yale University Press, 1983), pp. 247–8.
[39] Sellars, *Science and Metaphysics*, p. 59.

analytically from the point that we are receptive in cognition (i.e., that we are discursive rather than intuitive intellects). What Kant does rule out is the idea that there is fruitful metaphysical discussion to be had over, for example, whether this independent reality is composed of infinite monads, or whether we are all modes of an all-encompassing *Deus, sive Natura*. In this way, then, 'the proud name of an ontology . . . must give way to the modest one of a mere analytic of the pure understanding" (A247/B303) – for all such 'ontology' is nothing but groundless chatter and speculation. As Ralph Walker remarks, 'Beyond the limits of possible experience we can know nothing, we can only speculate: that is Kant's case against the dogmatic metaphysicians'.[40]

Although Kant can thus be defended against the charge of infringing his own anti-metaphysical strictures, a difficulty remains concerning how we are to make sense of this relation of 'grounding' or 'determining' that holds between the phenomenal world and the things-in-themselves, and which is 'causal' only in the most abstract (i.e., non-spatio-temporal) sense. Zeno Vendler, in a recent discussion of human agency, offers a very useful analogy, which I shall adopt and modify here for the purpose of making sense of this 'grounding' relation. Here is the relevant passage from Vendler.

Think of a writer seeking to 'eliminate' one of his characters in the novel he is composing. For reasons of his own he prefers a blameless way, death as a result of an accident, or 'act of God'. Shall it be an earthquake, storm, fire, or what? Well, he will choose one of these possibilities, and build it into his story. In doing so, however, he cannot just create, say, fire *ex nihilo*: he has to sketch, or at least allow for, the antecedents (e.g., how the house caught fire), and weave the whole sequence into the fabric of his story. Did *he*, the writer, cause the fire? Not at all, the heater's explosion caused it. Yet it was up to him whether there be a fire at all. His determination, moreover, that there be a fire at sometime in the story remains outside the temporal framework of the novel; one can write a story taking place in the nineteenth century now.[41]

I suggest that we think of the 'grounding' relation that holds between the phenomenal realm and the things-in-themselves on Vendler's analogy of the relation between the events in a story and the determinations of the writer. In other words, we can think of the independent reality (i.e., the things in themselves) as an author that is telling us (the subjects) a story. In order to make this analogy more accurate, it should really be said that the story (the phenomenal world) is the product of a joint authorship – a product of the interaction between the transcendental realm and the human subject,

---

[40] Walker, *Kant*, p. 130.
[41] Z. Vendler, *The Matter of Minds* (Oxford University Press, 1984), p. 119.

with its spatio-temporal forms of intuition, and spontaneously applied categories. This story (the phenomenal world) contains various characters and events within it (the appearances). The story is richly detailed and consistent, and we, the listeners, can thus trace causal relations within it (where I am using 'causal relation' in its ordinary, temporal sense). However, these causal relations are always from appearance to appearance, and never from appearance to thing in itself. Nonetheless, the things in themselves are the ultimate – and, to us, inaccessible – explanation or ground of just why the story unfolds the way it does.

This concludes my brief sketch of the interpretation of transcendental idealism that follows naturally from my claims about Kant's argument in the B-Deduction. All I have attempted to do here is to indicate that my views on Kant's notions of representation and cognition cannot be impugned on the basis that they entail an interpretation of transcendental idealism that is *obviously* indefensible. In the next chapter I return to the main theme of this book and discuss the crucial first premise of Kant's argument in the B-Deduction – his claim (α), that all our cognition must involve a spontaneous synthesis – and begin at last to provide some detailed textual support for my interpretation via a close examination of § 16 of the B-Deduction.

CHAPTER 3

The unity of consciousness

The previous chapter presented an overview of my interpretation of Kant's central argument in the B-Deduction. I have suggested that this argument is Kant's attempt to demonstrate the truth of his 'two-faculty' model of cognition – the claim that, in addition to receptivity, a category-governed spontaneity is essential to our cognition. My discussion in the previous chapter focused on Kant's reasoning for (β), the claim that if our cognition involves a spontaneous synthesis, then this synthesis must be governed by the categories. In this chapter I turn to examine Kant's reasoning for (α), the claim that all our cognition must involve a spontaneous synthesis. I argue that it is in § 16 of the B-Deduction that one finds what I shall call Kant's 'master argument' for this claim.

Kant's discussion in § 16 has been variously interpreted as concerned with the ontological unity of the mind, criteria of personal identity, or conditions for the 'ownership' of mental states. I shall argue in this chapter that all of these views are incorrect, and that Kant is in fact concerned with a problem that is the representationalist equivalent of the problem debated in the nineteenth and twentieth centuries as the problem of the 'unity of judgment' or the 'unity of the proposition'. Kant argues that if we are to make sense of the unity possessed by complex representations then we cannot think of representing objects as a purely passive, or receptive, affair, but as one that must also involve some element of spontaneity. This argument hinges on what Kant calls 'the unity of apperception', and I will thus begin my discussion with a consideration of the crucial and often misunderstood notion of apperception itself.

APPERCEPTION

The title of § 16 of the B-Deduction is 'On the original-synthetic unity of apperception', and, as this indicates, the notion of apperception is crucial to Kant's argument in this section. Hence, in order to understand that argument it is essential to have a clear grasp of the notion of appercep-tion, and of just what it is to apperceive something – or, as Kant also puts it, of what it is to 'accompany a representation with the *I think*'. In this section I argue that Kant's notion of apperception, despite initial ap-pearances, should not be assimilated to modern notions of 'self-awareness', 'self-consciousness', 'self-knowledge' or 'self-reference'. Rather, appercep-tion is the reflexive act whereby the mind grasps its own representations as representing, and is thus an essential part of all thought and cognition. In this section I give three arguments for the truth of this interpretation. Firstly, I present contextual evidence for it, via an examination of the role that the notion of apperception plays in Leibniz's epistemology. Secondly, I argue that my interpretation fits with Kant's own scattered comments on apperception in other parts of the *Critique*. Thirdly, I argue that my interpretation makes good sense of the opening of § 16. However, perhaps the most important evidence for the truth of my interpretation will come in the following sections, from the way in which it allows me to make good sense of Kant's argument in the B-Deduction as a whole.

The word *apperception* is a distinctive technical term of Leibniz's episte-mology, and was introduced by him in the *New Essays on Human Under-standing*, which Kant is known to have read soon after their publication; it is therefore reasonable to assume that Kant chose his terminology de-liberately to echo Leibniz.[1] Hence, attention to the role that the notion of apperception plays for Leibniz should help to shed light on the role that it plays for Kant. I will thus offer a brief sketch of the place of apperception in Leibniz's epistemology.[2] Leibniz originally coined the word *apperception* to translate the Scholastic Latin term *conscientia* – which referred to the soul's capacity to know itself and its operations.[3] Leibniz himself tends to talk of apperception as a reflexive awareness, or as an awareness of the self or 'the I'. However, I hope to show that this does not mean what it might at first suggest to a modern ear. The best way to begin demonstrating this is with a brief examination of the claim made by both Descartes and Locke that there is a necessary connection between (human) thought and self-consciousness.

Both Descartes and Locke hold that it is an obvious truth that in thinking or perceiving the (human) subject is always conscious that she herself is

---

[1] The term *apperception* was first introduced in the *New Essays*: see R. McRae, *Leibniz* (University of Toronto Press, 1976), p. 30; Kant read the *New Essays* in about 1769, as is noted by Bennett and Remnant in their introduction to Leibniz, *New Essays on Human Understanding*, p. x.

[2] This sketch is indebted to McRae, *Leibniz*, and M. Kulstad, *Leibniz on Apperception, Consciousness, and Reflection* (Munich: Philosophia, 1991).

[3] See G. Baker and K. J. Morris, *Descartes' Dualism* (London: Routledge, 1996), pp. 102f.

thinking or perceiving. Locke writes, for example, in the *Essay* that it is 'impossible for anyone to perceive without perceiving that he does perceive', and Descartes remarks in his correspondence that he does not 'think that animals see just as we do, i.e., being aware or thinking they see'.[4] Bernard Williams, after citing this latter remark from Descartes, makes what might seem to be a natural response to it – writing that it 'involves a confusion, between having conscious experiences in seeing, and having the reflexive consciousness that one is seeing'.[5] The accusation, in other words, is that Descartes (and no doubt Williams would extend this accusation to Locke as well) is confusing a situation in which the representational content of my consciousness is simply

(1) *p*

with the 'reflexive consciousness' in which the content of my consciousness is the much more complex

(2) I perceive *p*.

It may thus seem as if Descartes's and Locke's confusion of (1) and (2) leads them into making the dubious assumption that all my thoughts or perceptions incorporate some sort of reference to myself – as if I (myself) am always implicitly part of the subject matter of my thoughts (even when I am not explicitly thinking about, or aware of, myself).

Williams's accusation is, however, based upon a very uncharitable reading of what Descartes and Locke have said, and there is a better way of making sense of their claim that in thought or perception I (the subject) am always conscious of myself thinking or perceiving. I suggest that this claim is best construed as being, at least in part, an attempt to talk about what we would now refer to as the 'intentionality' of perception and thought.[6] The claim is, in other words, not a dubious piece of introspective reportage, but an attempt to make a conceptual point. As discussed in the first chapter above, a representation is not simply a mental state or thing which is in the subject and which happens to stand in a certain relation to its object, but is rather something more like the subject's perspective or point of view upon the object of the representation. To be conscious of my representation as representing is thus for it to come to function as a point of view *for me*,

---

[4] Locke, *Essay*, book 2, ch. 27, § 9; Descartes, Letter to Plempius for Fromondus (3 October 1637) in *Philosophical Writings*, vol. III, p. 61. I was led to this passage by the mention of it in B. Williams (see the following note).

[5] B. Williams, *Descartes* (Hamondsworth: Penguin, 1978), p. 226.

[6] See McRae, *Leibniz*, ch. 2.

or for it to become *my* view onto something. In this way a representation as it were intimates the 'point' from which that point of view is had – that is, the subject whose representation it is. But this does not mean that the subject is a further object within the field of the point of view. It is in this sense, I suggest, that Descartes and Locke claim that in perception we must be aware that we are perceiving. They are not claiming that we are always engaged in some sort of surreptitious introspection, but are instead attempting to capture the elusive sense in which conscious thought or perception involves a first-person perspective. This reading makes good sense of why Descartes, in the remark cited above, pointedly denies this accompanying self-consciousness to animals. For, notoriously, according to Descartes the 'perception' of animals is a mere physical mechanism.[7] A Cartesian animal can represent the world in much the same way as a computer or a camera can – that is, in the sense that it can be in a physical state that is related in certain systematic ways to external things – but it has, as it were, no first-person perspective on the world in the way that we do in our conscious experience. In the language used by Descartes and Locke, this is to say that a Cartesian animal perceives without perceiving (or, without the awareness) that it is perceiving.

In Leibniz's epistemology, this notion of 'perceiving that one perceives' or 'being aware that one sees' becomes the notion of *apperception*. Leibniz, unlike Locke and Descartes, is in a position to draw a clear distinction between apperception and perception. This is because, as is well known, Leibniz rejects the central Cartesian thesis that conscious thought is the essence, or primary attribute, of mind, and affirms the existence of unconscious ideas. For Descartes (and for Locke), an idea was, as it were, intrinsically self-revealing. As Descartes writes in the *Principles*, 'whatever we find in the mind is simply one of the various modes of thinking'[8] – that is, is a mode of conscious awareness. That Locke shares this commitment is shown by his use of the word *impossible* in the remark from the *Essay* quoted above (i.e., that it is '*impossible* for anyone to perceive without perceiving that he does perceive' – my emphasis), and is made completely explicit when he remarks that 'it is altogether as unintelligible to say that a body is extended without parts, as that anything *thinks without being conscious of it* or perceiving that it does so'.[9] Hence, whilst he may not share Descartes's

---

[7] This follows from his infamous doctrine of the '*bête-machine*'. For discussion, see J. Cottingham, 'Descartes' Treatment of Animals', in *Descartes*, ed. J. Cottingham (Oxford University Press, 1998), pp. 225–33.

[8] Descartes, *Principles of Philosophy*, art. 53, in *Philosophical Writings*, vol. I, p. 210.

[9] Locke, *Essay*, book 2, ch. 1, § 19.

claim to know the essence of mind, Locke is an orthodox Cartesian to the
extent of holding that an idea or a perception is essentially conscious.[10]
That is, simply in virtue of being a modification of the mind, an idea reveals or presents something to consciousness; hence, according to Descartes
and Locke, the notion of an 'unconscious idea' was self-contradictory or
'unintelligible'.

For Leibniz, on the other hand, the existence of unconscious ideas or
representations (the so-called *petites perceptions*) was a key part of his metaphysical and epistemological theories, and, as I shall show, his use of the
notion of apperception follows from this doctrine. Concerning the existence of unconscious ideas, Leibniz writes, for example, in the *New Essays*
that

at every moment there is in us an infinity of perceptions, unaccompanied by apperception or reflection [*mais sans apperception et sans reflexion*]; that is, of alterations
in the soul itself, of which we are unaware because these impressions are either
too minute [*petites*] and too numerous, or else too unvarying, so that they are not
sufficiently distinctive on their own.[11]

As this passage demonstrates, Leibniz holds that the difference between an
unconscious idea (or 'perception') and a conscious idea, is that the former
is 'unaccompanied by apperception or reflection', whilst the latter is so accompanied. The role that the notion of apperception is playing in Leibniz's
epistemology can thus be explained as follows. Leibniz holds that unconscious ideas are logically possible. If unconscious ideas are possible then the
mere existence of an idea in me (i.e., my faculty of representation being
modified or determined in a certain way) is not by itself sufficient for that
idea to present something to me, and thus to be part of my consciousness
or awareness. Therefore, for an idea to be conscious it must not only exist
in me, but must also meet some further condition. This further condition
is, according to Leibniz, that the idea must be *apperceived* by me – that is,
reflexively grasped by the mind. It is thus that Leibniz writes in § 4 of the
Principles of Nature and Grace that

it is well to make a distinction between perception, which is the inner state of the
monad representing external things, and *apperception*, which is consciousness or
the reflective knowledge of this inner state itself and which is not given to all souls
or to any soul all the time. It is for lack of this distinction that the Cartesians have

---

[10] For useful discussion of Locke's relation to the Cartesian theory of mind, see N. Jolley, *Locke* (Oxford
University Press, 1999), ch. 5.
[11] Leibniz, *New Essays*, p. 53; translation modified.

made the mistake of disregarding perceptions which are not themselves perceived, just as people commonly disregard imperceptible bodies.[12]

As this passage indicates, for Leibniz it is apperception that is the difference between simply being in a state that represents, 'expresses' or 'mirrors' external things – a state that, for example, a computer, a camera, or a thermometer can also be in – and genuine *conscious* experience – in which the state of the subject does not simply represent something, but represents something *to the subject*. As Leibniz notes, the epistemology of Descartes and Locke does not require this distinct act of apperception, precisely because those philosophers hold that an idea is necessarily conscious or self-revealing. For this Cartesian doctrine entails that the mere existence of an idea in the subject is by itself sufficient for that idea to present something to the subject's awareness. The contrast could thus be put as follows. For Descartes and Locke, ideas are, as it were, intrinsically luminescent, and they therefore necessarily reveal themselves to the mind's eye. But for Leibniz, ideas are in themselves dark, and must thus have a light shone on them to reveal them to the mind's eye – and the shining of this light is the act of apperception. In other words, because Leibniz rejects the Cartesian-Lockean thesis that ideas are essentially conscious, he analyses the proposition that

the idea (or 'perception') *i* presents something to the subject *S*

as the following conjunction:

i exists in *S* & *S* reflexively grasps (or 'apperceives') *i*.

As McRae puts this conclusion, for Leibniz 'the conjoining of apperception with perception provides the necessary and sufficient conditions of thought and understanding'.[13]

Given this understanding of the notion of apperception, it is not surprising that that notion should also feature in Kant's epistemology. I have argued that the notion of apperception is demanded by the conjunction of Leibniz's representationalism and his rejection of the Cartesian-Lockean thesis that ideas are necessarily conscious. Leibniz is a representationalist in that he holds that our awareness of the world is mediated by our internal representational states. However, unlike Descartes and Locke, Leibniz holds

---

[12] G. W. F. Leibniz, *Philosophical Papers and Letters*, ed. and trans. L. E. Loemker, 2nd edn (Dordrecht: D. Reidel, 1969), p. 637.

[13] McRae, *Leibniz*, p. 5. For further discussion see N. Jolley, *Leibniz and Locke* (Oxford University Press, 1984), pp. 106–10.

that these internal states do not present things to consciousness in their own right. It thus follows that in order for those states to present something to the subject, they need to be grasped via a special reflexive act of awareness – an act of apperception. Now, as was pointed out in the first chapter of this book, Kant shares Leibniz's commitment to representationalism. Kant also shares Leibniz's view that ideas are not necessarily conscious – that is, that unconscious representations are possible. An explicit acknowledgment of this possibility occurs in a well-known passage from a letter to Marcus Herz (26 May 1789).[14] Kant is discussing representations that did not meet the conditions for 'reaching the unity of consciousness', and says of them that

I would not even be able to know that I have them; consequently *for me*, as a cognising being, they would be absolutely nothing. They could still (if I imagine myself to be an animal) carry on their play in an orderly fashion, as representations connected according to empirical laws of association, and thus even have an influence on my feeling and desire, without my being aware of them . . . This might be so without my cognising the slightest thing thereby, not even what my own condition is. (11:52)

This passage makes it clear that Kant considers it logically possible for a subject to possess various representations that do not present anything to that subject's conscious awareness. Hence, like Leibniz, Kant is a representationalist and rejects the Cartesian-Lockean thesis that ideas are necessarily conscious. Kant's epistemology thus requires the notion of apperception.

So far I have argued for a certain interpretation of the Leibnizian roots of Kant's notion of apperception. I now want to show how this interpretation entails the conclusion that Kant's notion should not be assimilated to modern notions of self-awareness, self-consciousness, self-knowledge or self-reference. Let me begin by returning to Leibniz's definition of apperception, in the passage from the *Principles of Nature and Grace* quoted above, as the 'consciousness or the reflective knowledge of [our] inner state'. Apperception is thus, for Leibniz, a form of self-awareness or self-knowledge – that is, in which I (the subject) make myself and/or my inner states the object of my awareness or knowledge. Kant, however, because of his understanding of the notion of representation, is in a position to distinguish sharply between apperception, on the one hand, and (ordinary) self-awareness or self-knowledge, on the other. And therefore, as I will show, it is quite wrong to claim (e.g., as Derk Pereboom does) that 'Apperception . . . is the

---

[14] See also § 5 of Kant's *Anthropologie* (7:135–7), which is entitled 'Von den Vorstellungen, die wir haben, ohne uns ihrer bewußt zu sein'.

apprehension of a mental state as one's own'[15] – or, for that matter, that it is the 'consciousness of our activity, of what we are doing', as S. L. Hurley thinks.[16]

The best way to begin explaining this is by recalling my earlier discussion of pictorial representation and the ambiguity of the 'object of sight'. As mentioned before, when I see a smiling face in a picture there is a sense in which the 'object of sight' or 'what I see' is a certain spatial configuration of ink marks, and there is also a sense in which 'what I see' is a smiling face. In such a case the representational medium (i.e., the configuration of ink marks) is an object of awareness, but it is not thereby the object of my act of 'seeing in'. That is, what I see in the picture will be a face (for example) rather than a configuration of ink marks, but I see the face in the picture in virtue of having a certain sort of awareness of the configuration of ink marks. This ambiguity in the notion of the 'object of sight' could be cleared up by making a distinction between the sense in which I 'see' the face and the sense in which I 'see' the ink marks. We could do this by adopting Leibniz's terminology, and saying that I *perceive* the face in the picture in virtue of *apperceiving* the ink marks (as presenting the face). It is important to note that it is only a rich concept of pictorial representation that allows such 'perception' and 'apperception' to be clearly distinct from one another. For it is only if the face in the picture is not identical to the configuration of ink marks that it is possible to distinguish the two types of awareness. A reductive conception of pictures, in which they were *merely* configurations of ink marks, could not recognise two distinct 'objects of sight', and thus could not distinguish clearly between the awareness of one (the perception of the face) and the awareness of the other (the apperception of the ink marks as presenting the face).

This result can now be applied to the field of mental representations. In the discussion above, I argued that the notion of apperception features in Leibniz's and Kant's epistemologies because they both held that representations do not present something to the subject's consciousness by themselves (i.e., simply in virtue of their existence as a modification of the subject's faculty of representation), and therefore representations need to be brought to consciousness by apperception. In other words, it is in virtue of apperceiving a representation that I represent or perceive the object of that representation. Now, if one holds an indirect realist or idealist (i.e., Berkeleyan) model of cognition, then perception (of external things) is analysed

[15] D. Pereboom, 'Self-Understanding in Kant's Transcendental Deduction', *Synthese* 103 (1995), 8.
[16] Hurley, 'Kant on Spontaneity', 145.

as involving (a) the awareness of an idea or representation (thought of as simply a subjective mental state), and (b) an act of inference or construction on the basis of that representation. If Kant held a model of cognition like this, with its accompanying reductive conception of representation, then his notion of apperception would naturally play the role of (a). Apperception, in other words, would be simply the subject's awareness of its own subjective mental states. It was suggested in chapter 1 above, however, that Kant does not have this reductive understanding of representation. With the richer conception of representation that I have suggested is his, there is conceptual space for a notion of apperception that is quite distinct from ordinary notions of self-awareness, self-knowledge or self-consciousness. This is because, as in the case of pictorial representation discussed above, in Kant's model of cognition the notion of the 'object of awareness' is fundamentally ambiguous. In thought or cognition, I am aware of my representations, but I am not thereby thinking about or cognising my inner states. On the contrary, I am thinking about or cognising the objects presented by those inner states. I am, as it were, 'seeing' things *in* my inner states, and I do this in virtue of my awareness of those inner states. That is, to use the Leibnizian jargon, I perceive objects in virtue of apperceiving my representations.

There is thus an important distinction to be drawn between the object of apperception and the object of thought, cognition or 'perception'.[17] This in turn allows one to draw a distinction between apperception and ordinary self-awareness or self-consciousness. In being self-aware or self-conscious I make myself and/or my inner states the objects of thought or cognition. But in apperceiving I make my inner (representative) states the objects of apperception; the object of thought or cognition is the object presented by that inner state, and not the inner state itself. So, to apperceive a representation *R* is not to think about or to cognise *R* (to be 'self-aware'). Rather, the apperception of *R* is *that in virtue of which* I think about or cognise the *object represented by R*. Apperception is thus a special sort of self-awareness that is an essential component of all our conscious awareness; it is involved in bringing *any* representation to consciousness. The capacity of apperception is not a capacity for having a special class of representations or states of awareness, namely, those in which I (the subject) perceive, am aware of, think about, or refer to myself and/or my inner states. That is, apperception is not the species ('self-perception') of which perception is the genus, but a distinct notion. This distinction between apperception and ordinary

---

[17] Cf. McRae's discussion of the difference between 'thought' and 'consciousness' in *Leibniz*, ch. 2.

self-awareness is only possible because of Kant's model of cognition, in which the subject is not simply aware of its inner states ('the configuration of ink marks') but, in virtue of that apperceptive awareness, cognises things *in* them ('the smiling face'). All perception involves apperception, or all awareness a certain sort of self-awareness, just as seeing the depicted object involves seeing the representational medium.

To recapitulate: I have argued that the Leibnizian notion of apperception, in conjunction with Kant's rich conception of representation (as discussed above in chapter 1) allows Kant to distinguish between apperception and ordinary self-awareness. In his jargon, this distinction is that between *apperception* and *inner sense*. Kant defines inner sense as that faculty 'by means of which the mind intuits itself, or its inner state . . . represented in relations of time' (A22–3/B37). It is, in other words, the capacity to be self-aware or to introspect, and thus to become aware of one's own thoughts, feelings, sensations, and so forth – that is, to make them objects of cognition. Now, if the interpretation advanced here is correct, we would expect Kant to insist on the difference between this faculty of inner sense and the faculty of apperception, and this is indeed what we find. He writes, for example, in § 24 of the B-Deduction that 'it is customary in the systems of psychology to treat *inner sense* as the same as the faculty of *apperception* (which we carefully distinguish)' (B153). As was pointed out above, if one holds a reductive conception of representation then there is no conceptual room to distinguish between inner sense and apperception, and it is therefore not surprising that many 'systems of psychology' collapse those notions into one another. Kant, on the other hand, claims that 'we carefully distinguish' between them.

Kant does indeed 'carefully distinguish' between inner sense and apperception, as can be shown by examining the role that he assigns to apperception in his epistemology. Kant, it should be noted, although he does talk of 'apperception' and the 'faculty of apperception', does not talk (to the best of my knowledge) of 'apperceiving representations'. Rather, as shall be discussed below, he talks of what it is 'to accompany a representation with the *I think*'. And 'this representation [*sc.*, the *I think*] . . . I call . . . the *pure apperception*' (B132). Thus the 'faculty of apperception' is the capacity to 'accompany representations with the *I think*'. Perhaps the most informative discussion of 'the *I think*' occurs in the Paralogisms, where Kant tells us that it 'is the vehicle of *all* concepts whatever . . . [and] serves only to introduce *all* thinking as belonging to consciousness' (A341/B399; my emphasis in both cases). This passage fits with my interpretation, as presented above, for it makes it clear that apperception ('the *I think*') is necessarily involved in *all* conscious thought, and thus in the cases of both inner and outer cognition. Apperception is, in other words, not simply the capacity for introspection or self-awareness. That apperception is something quite different from inner sense is made even clearer by a remark in a footnote to § 16 of the B-Deduction, where Kant tells us that 'indeed, this faculty [*sc.*, of apperception] is the understanding itself' (B134n). As I have interpreted Kant, this remark makes good sense. Apperception is the reflexive awareness in virtue of which I (the subject) grasp my representations as presenting something to me. It is, in other words, that in virtue of which I have conscious thought or cognition, and is thus 'the faculty of understanding itself'.

My interpretation of Kant's notion of apperception or 'the *I think*' not only fits with his distinction between inner sense and apperception, it also allows me to make good sense of the famous opening sentence of § 16. This is as follows.

The *I think* must *be able* to accompany all my representations; for otherwise something would be represented in me that could not be thought at all, which is as much as to say that the representation would either be impossible or else at least would be nothing for me. (B131)

Let me begin with the opening clause: 'The *I think* must *be able* to accompany all my representations'. The first question this raises is just what it would be for 'the *I think*' to 'accompany' a certain representation, as this remark in itself is hardly pellucid. In my discussion above I have suggested a certain reading of this phrase. However, it is worth examining two other interpretations that this phrase naturally suggests to the modern ear – namely, that to 'accompany a representation with the *I think*' is:

(A) to think about a representation (perhaps: to be 'aware of it as mine' or to 'ascribe it to myself')
(B) to make a first-person propositional-attitude judgment ('I think *p*')

Both of these interpretations of 'the *I think*' claim are well represented in the secondary literature (not always clearly distinguished from one another), as a few examples will show. Two examples of the first interpretation (A), which probably deserves to be called the 'received' or 'textbook' reading, are provided by Henry Allison and Dieter Henrich. Allison glosses Kant's claim about 'the *I think*' as saying that in order for any of these [representations] to be anything to me, that is, to represent anything for me, it must be possible for me to be aware of it as mine. This is equivalent to the possibility of reflectively attaching the 'I think' to it.[18]

Henrich similarly claims that it means that 'a consciousness of the form "I think these thoughts" must be possible in relation to these thoughts'.[19] Both Allison and Henrich thus treat Kant as concerned with self-awareness or the capacity to think about my own thoughts – that is, they both hold to interpretation (A). A clear example of interpretation (B), on the other hand, is provided by Jonathan Bennett, who writes that 'the *I think*' claim expresses 'Kant's doctrine about self-consciousness'. Bennett explains this thus:

the self-consciousness doctrine does not say that all my judgments *are* of the form 'I think . . .', as though my judgment *that P* were really an ellipsis for my judgment *that I judge that P*. The doctrine makes no such absurd claim, but merely implies that given any judgment (*P*) which I make there is a *correlated* true judgment with myself as its subject matter (I judge that *P*).[20]

In other words, according to Bennett, 'to accompany a representation [*P*] with the *I think*' is simply to make the judgment *that I think P*. Patricia Kitcher follows Bennett's view closely, as her linguistic version of Kant's claim makes clear.

If and only if for any judgment J, it must belong to some subject, then it must be possible (for someone) to construct a true sentence 'I think (that) J'. That is, given that all judgments must belong to some subject, it must be possible for some 'I think' to be the subject of every judgment.[21]

Hence, both Bennett and Kitcher provide examples of what I have called interpretation (B) of Kant's notion of 'accompanying a representation with the *I think*'.

As my previous discussion of the origin of Kant's notion of apperception should have made clear, I reject both (A) and (B) as readings of Kant's claim about 'the *I think*', and I now want to show how a closer examination of the opening sentence of § 16 supports my own interpretation. That opening sentence contains a claim and a reason for that claim. The claim made in the first part of the sentence is

[18] Allison, *Kant's Transcendental Idealism*, p. 137.
[19] D. Henrich, 'The Identity of the Subject in the Transcendental Deduction', in *Reading Kant*, ed. E. Schaper and W. Vossenkuhl (Oxford: Blackwell, 1989), p. 268.
[20] J. Bennett, *Kant's Dialectic* (Cambridge University Press, 1974), p. 74.
[21] See P. Kitcher, *Kant's Transcendental Psychology* (Oxford University Press, 1990), p. 188.

(1) The *I think* must be able to accompany all my representations.

The reason for (1) is given in the second part, and is that (1) is true, 'for otherwise' the following claim would be true (changing from the subjunctive to the indicative mood):

(2) Something could be represented in me that could not be thought at all.

In other words, Kant tells us in the opening sentence of § 16 that (1) is true because (2) is false. Now, I propose that this opening sentence should be read in a very straightforward fashion – as being of the form 'P; for otherwise not-P'. This means, in other words, that (2) is the negation of (1). Hence, an understanding of (2) will give us an understanding of (1). Proceeding on this assumption, there are some simple but nonetheless important points that are worth making about (2). To begin with, (2) clearly states that it is *one and the same thing* that 'could be represented in me' and that 'could not be thought at all' – that is, the object of the representation is the object of thought. Now if, for example, I have the representation of a cat, then what is represented in me (by this representation) is a cat. In such a case, (2) would state that what 'could not be thought at all' would also be a cat. To make this sound more like English we could insert an 'of' or 'about' after the word 'thought' (as Guyer and Wood, for example, usually do when translating Kant's use of '*denken*' and its cognates), and we would then have the following as an amended version of (2):

(2′) Something [e.g., a cat] could be represented in me that could not be thought [about] at all.

Now, if (2) is the negation of (1), as I have claimed, then from the fact that (2) is equivalent in meaning to (2′) it follows that (1) must be equivalent in meaning to the following claim:

(1′) Everything that is represented in me must be able to be thought [about].

In other words, to 'accompany' a certain representation with 'the *I think*' is not for me to think about that representation but for me to think about what is represented by that representation. So, for example, when I 'accompany' my representation of a cat with 'the *I think*', I am thereby thinking about *a cat* (that its breath smells of fish, that it scratches, has dug up the agapanthus for the third time this week, and so forth). In such a case, I am *not* thereby thinking about *my representation of a cat* (that it is a mental state belonging to me, is indistinct, in need of further analysis, contains the predicate *mammal*, and so forth).

If this reading of 'the *I think*' is correct, then interpretations (A) and (B) are both incorrect. For my reading entails that 'accompanying a representation with the *I think*' means 'thinking about the object of that representation'. Hence, I 'accompany representations with the *I think*' whenever I engage in thought or cognition – it is, in other words, an essential component of *all* conscious awareness, whether of external objects or internal states. The rival interpretations, on the other hand, claim that to 'accompany a representation with the *I think*' is not to think or be consciously aware *per se*, but to have a particular class of thoughts or states of awareness. Interpretation (A) claims that it is to have thoughts about my own thoughts or representations (e.g., that they belong to me); interpretation (B) claims that it is to have first-person propositional-attitude thoughts. These interpretations are both natural ways of reading Kant's opening sentence, but a close examination of that sentence shows them to be mistaken. To 'accompany a representation with the *I think*' is neither for me to think about that representation nor for me to make a first-person propositional-attitude judgment. Rather, as I have suggested, it is for me to *apperceive* that representation.

My reading of the opening sentence of § 16 of the B-Deduction thus not only entails that the rival interpretations (A) and (B) are incorrect, but also supports the interpretation of apperception that I have argued for here. When Kant writes that 'the *I think* must be able to accompany all my representations', he is saying that I (the subject) must be able to think about (or cognise) the objects of those representations. Given his account of what is involved in conscious awareness, this means that I must be able to apperceive those representations. That is, for any representation that I have, I must be able to grasp that representation reflexively, so that it presents its object to my conscious awareness, for otherwise it could not contribute to my awareness. This reading thus makes good sense of the end of Kant's sentence. He writes that if I could not 'accompany' a representation with 'the *I think*' then this would be 'as much as to say that the representation would either be impossible or else at least would be nothing for me' (B131). That is, without the apperception of it, a representation, while still 'representing something in me' (i.e., existing as a modification of my faculty of representation), would remain unconscious and would not contribute to my conscious thought or cognition. In other words, it would never function to present an object to my conscious awareness. It would therefore be 'nothing *for me*', however much it might contribute to determining my behaviour in other ways. This, as should be clear, echoes Kant's remark in the letter to Marcus Herz quoted above, where he writes of unconscious representations that '*for me*, as a cognising being, they would be absolutely nothing' (11:52). Hence, Kant's claim at the opening of § 16 is simply as follows: any representation that is to be something 'for me' – that is, is to present something to my conscious awareness – must be able to be apperceived by me. And this claim, given my reading of the role that apperception plays in Kant's epistemology, is an analytic truth, for the apperception of a representation is a necessary and sufficient condition for bringing that representation to conscious awareness.

This interpretation of Kant's opening sentence of § 16 does depend, as I noted above, upon reading its first two clauses as being of the form 'P; for otherwise not-P'. This reading has the virtue of simplicity, it makes very clear the structure of the argument that Kant is using, and it makes his central claim an obvious conceptual truth (given his account of apperception). The rival interpretations (A) and (B) cannot read the sentence in this straightforward way, and must turn it into something much more complex and controversial. For it then becomes the claim that the capacity to be consciously aware of things presupposes the capacity (A) to think about or cognise one's own mental states, or (B) to make first-person propositional-attitude judgments. These readings thus turn the opening sentence of § 16 into a very rich and problematic claim. It is problematic because it seems, on the face of it, to be false. To be able to refer to or think about one's own mental states, or to make first-person propositional-attitude judgments, are both very sophisticated things to be able to do. So why must they be presupposed in the mere capacity to be aware of something? It seems perfectly plausible to imagine someone (e.g., a brain-damaged person) who was consciously aware of objects, but who lacked both the capacity to refer to herself or her own mental states, and the capacity to make first-person judgments. As Guyer remarks, 'there is no reason why I cannot *be* in a representational state which I cannot *say* I am in [or judge myself to be in]'.[22] If such a case were possible, then Kant's claim would be false. Obviously enough, just because a claim is false does not entail that Kant did not make it, but it is defeasible evidence for that. Furthermore, precisely because the claim (read in this way) is not obviously true (and, indeed, appears false), we would expect Kant to provide an argument for it – to show just why consciousness must presuppose these sophisticated capacities, in the face of the fact that 'there seems to be no good reasons for saying that . . . where there is consciousness there must be self-consciousness'.[23] But Kant's claim is the opening premise of § 16, not the conclusion of an

[22] Guyer, *Kant and the Claims of Knowledge*, p. 141.   [23] Bennett, *Kant's Analytic*, p. 105.

argument. Hence, interpretations (A) and (B) have to treat Kant's opening sentence as an enthymeme with a highly questionable conclusion, and all of its crucial premises omitted. This contrasts unfavourably with my own reading, which makes Kant's argument simple and his conclusion unproblematic.

In the following section I turn to consider how my interpretation of Kant's claim about 'the *I think*' and his notion of apperception makes good sense of the remainder of § 16; but before that it is worth summarising the results of the argument so far. From a consideration of the Leibnizian roots of the notion of apperception I have argued that Kant thinks of apperception as an essential component of all conscious awareness. Kant is a representationalist; that is, he holds that all our cognition is mediated by the modifications of our sensibility (our internal states). Kant also accepts the anti-Cartesian point that such modifications are not intrinsically available to conscious awareness; that is, that the existence of unconscious representations is logically possible. From these two doctrines it follows that conscious awareness (in thought and cognition) involves something over and above the mere existence of a representation. This extra component is the act of apperception. Apperception is thus the act whereby my internal states come to function as representations for me – as it were, as my point of view on the world. Apperception is a reflexive act, or an act of self-awareness (i.e., an awareness of the modifications of the self), but it is not therefore an act of thinking about or cognising the self or its internal states. It is rather the act whereby we grasp a representation as presenting something to us. I have argued that this act of apperception is what Kant means by his talk, in § 16 of the B-Deduction, of 'accompanying a representation with the *I think*'. Hence, in Kantian terminology we can say that to cognise an object O (i.e., to have the experience as of O being before me here and now) is (i) to have the intuition of O (i.e., to have my sensibility modified in such-and-such a way) and (ii) to apperceive the intuition of O, or, equivalently, to 'accompany' that intuition with 'the *I think*'.

Further support for this reading comes from an important passage that occurs later in the B-Deduction. But before quoting this passage, it is first necessary to touch on a point that will be discussed in detail in the following section of this chapter. This is the point that Kant holds that our intuitions are complex representations – in his terminology, they 'contain a manifold' – and that to apperceive an intuition will thus involve the grasp of that manifold as making up a single, complex representation. That is, it will involve a unified act of apperceiving the manifold, or, as Kant puts it, a 'unity of apperception'. Having noted this point, it can now be seen that the following remark from § 21 of the B-Deduction gives clear support to the interpretation of apperception defended here, for in § 21 Kant writes that we (human beings) have 'an understanding whose entire capacity consists in thinking, i.e., in the action of bringing the synthesis of the manifold that is given to it in intuition from elsewhere to the unity of apperception' (B145). Here the 'i.e.' ('*d.i.*') demonstrates unmistakably that, for Kant, the act of thinking just *is* the act of apperceiving the manifold in an intuition as a unity, and thus grasping the intuition as the complex representation of an object. If 'apperception' referred to ordinary self-awareness or introspection, then it would be very hard to see why Kant should define thought (in general) as essentially involving an act of apperception. On the interpretation that I have given in this section, on the other hand, this definition of thought makes perfectly good sense, and is precisely what one would expect a Leibnizian representationalist like Kant to say.

One of the few commentators on Kant to come close to agreeing with my reading of apperception is Andrew Brook in his recent work *Kant and the Mind*. He writes there that the 'process of forming objects of awareness is what Kant calls apperception'.[24] According to Brook, apperception is thus the capacity of the mind to bind together various of its perceptions simultaneously into the perception of a single object. So, for example, apperception is the act of binding together the perceptions of certain noises, textures, smells, and colours into the unified perception of a cat. Now, I think that Brook is correct insofar as he sees clearly that for Kant apperception is an essential component of *all* cognition, and therefore cannot be ordinary self-awareness or introspection. However, because he neglects the historical context of Kant's text, Brook thinks that this claim entails that apperception cannot be any kind of self-awareness at all. That is, writing as he is to demonstrate Kant's relevance to contemporary cognitive scientists and philosophers of mind, Brook fails to take Kant's representationalism seriously, and treats him as being some sort of direct realist. In other words, Brook thinks that for Kant representations are *states* of awareness, rather than the immediate *objects* of awareness.[25] Brook is thus not in a position to see that for Kant all cognition must involve the reflexive grasp of our own representations, and thus self-awareness of a special sort – namely, apperception. This in turn drives Brook to make the desperately unconvincing claim that apperception has nothing at all to do with self-awareness.

[24] A. Brook, *Kant and the Mind* (Cambridge University Press, 1994), p. 37.
[25] See ibid., pp. 47ff.

Unable to deny the obvious fact that Kant thought there was a close link between these two notions, Brook simply confesses to us that this fact 'leaves me bemused', and suggests that Kant is confused about the nature of his own argument.[26] My own interpretation of apperception does not suffer from these major flaws, for by taking Kant's representationalism seriously it becomes possible to see how apperception can be both an essential component of all cognition and a form of self-awareness.

If my interpretation of apperception is correct, it means that the topic of Kant's discussion in § 16 of the B-Deduction (the argument from the 'original-synthetic unity of apperception') is very distant from modern questions concerning self-knowledge, self-awareness, the reference of 'I', the semantics of first-person linguistic constructions and so forth. The word *apperception* does not refer to the capacity to think about or cognise oneself or one's own mental states; it is instead a technical term in Kant's representationalist epistemology referring to the reflexive grasp of one's own internal states as presenting something. Kant's discussion in § 16 is thus concerned not with self-knowledge, but with what is essentially involved in internal states functioning to present objects to the subject's awareness. Now, as is perhaps already clear, given my interpretation of the notion of apperception and my interpretation of the notion of synthesis, it follows that to apperceive a representation is to engage in a *synthesis*. The act of apperception is an act of synthesis – indeed, as I will argue below, it is an act of spontaneous synthesis. Kant's notion of apperception is thus the representationalist equivalent of the semantic notion of *understanding a sign*. The 'signs' in this case are the subject's internal states, so it is hardly surprising that apperception becomes a reflexive grasp of those states, or in other words, a special type of self-awareness. This thus suggests that Kant's discussion in § 16 of the 'original-synthetic unity of apperception' concerns the representationalist equivalent of the semantic problem of what it is to understand a complex unified sign – the problem of 'the unity of the proposition' or 'the unity of judgment'.

Hence, how one interprets Kant's notion of apperception plays a crucial role in determining how one interprets his argument in § 16, and thus the argument of the B-Deduction as a whole. If apperception is interpreted as the capacity to think about oneself or one's own mental states, or to make first-person propositional-attitude judgments, then Kant's argument in § 16 will tend to be read as concerned with questions about the unity of the mind, the ownership of mental states, and such like. I have

---

[26] See ibid., pp. 144–51. The 'bemused' remark is on p. 151.

argued here for an alternative conception of apperception, and thereby for an alternative reading of the argument in § 16. That argument I am calling Kant's 'master argument', and I turn to consider it in the following section of this chapter. I hope to show that the interpretation of apperception argued for here receives additional support from its capacity to make good sense of what Kant says in § 16, and from its capacity to shed light thereby into some of the darkest corners of the Transcendental Deduction in B.

SECTION 16: THE MASTER ARGUMENT

Kant's master argument in § 16 is his argument for premise (α) of the B-Deduction, the claim that all our cognition must involve a spontaneous synthesis. The discussion in § 16 is centrally concerned with the question of what apperception must be like in order for it to play the epistemological role demanded of it, and is thus part of the B-Deduction's analysis of the concept of (human) cognition. In more detail, the master argument concerns what Kant calls the 'original-synthetic unity of apperception', which is the question of just what is involved in the subject's grasping a variety of internal states as a unified presenting of something to consciousness. As I will show, Kant argues that for such unified complex representations to be possible, apperception cannot simply be a passive reception of data – as it were, the shining of a light on the modifications of the mind in order to reveal them to the mind's eye – but must instead be spontaneous – the mind's active application of a rule of projection. Kant's master argument in § 16 is thus an argument for what I have called his 'two-faculty' model of cognition, namely, the claim that all discursive cognition involves the contribution of both receptivity and spontaneity.

That § 16 will be concerned with the two-faculty model of cognition is shown by its opening passage (which contains the famous claim about 'the *I think*' discussed in the previous section). This passage is as follows.

The *I think* must *be able* to accompany all my representations; for otherwise something would be represented in me that could not be thought at all, which is as much as to say that the representation would either be impossible or else at least would be nothing for me. That representation that can be given prior to all thinking is called *intuition*. Thus all manifold of intuition has a necessary relation to the *I think* in the same subject in which this manifold is to be encountered. But this representation is an act of *spontaneity*, i.e., it cannot be regarded as belonging to sensibility. I call it the *pure apperception* . . . or also the *original apperception*. (B131–2)

There are no indications in this passage to support the idea that § 16 will be concerned with self-cognition, as opposed to cognition in general. For in this passage Kant introduces the distinction between intuition (or, sensibility) and thought, and claims that the apperception of an intuition is 'an act of spontaneity'. It is here, in other words, that Kant makes his crucial claim (α), that our cognition involves spontaneity. The opening of § 16 thus supports my interpretative claim that this section of the B-Deduction will be concerned with the two-faculty model of cognition and the demand for spontaneity.

So, in the first few sentences of the first paragraph of § 16 Kant has announced that our cognition demands 'an act of spontaneity'; in what follows he gives us his master argument for this crucial claim. He begins by claiming in the rest of that first paragraph that

> the manifold representations that are given in a certain intuition would not all together be *my* representations if they did not all together belong to a self-consciousness; i.e., as my representations (even if I am not conscious of them as such) they must yet necessarily be in accord with the condition under which alone they *can* stand together in a universal self-consciousness, because otherwise they would not throughout belong to me. From this original combination much may be inferred. (B132)

Although it may not be immediately obvious, this passage is essentially a lengthier restatement of Kant's initial claim about 'the *I think*', with the focus here particularly on the case of *complex* representations. As Kant tells us in this passage, his discussion in § 16 will concern not representations in general, but specifically the 'manifold representations' that are 'given in a certain intuition'. Now, an intuition, by definition, is a modification of my sensibility through which I (the subject) immediately cognise a particular object. Furthermore, Kant makes the implicit assumption that all the objects of cognition must be represented as being complex in some way – that it is impossible to cognise something *as* completely simple. In other words, he assumes that all sensible intuitions must be complex representations, that is, representations that each contain a variety or 'manifold' of component representations within themselves. The human form of intuition can be taken as an illustrative example of this point (although it should be noted that Kant's argument in § 16 does not rely on any premise about the particularly *spatio-temporal* character of our intuitions, but concerns simply complex unified intuitions in general). According to the doctrine of the Transcendental Aesthetic, all our (human) intuition is of spatial and/or temporal particulars. And if something is represented as extended in space and/or time, then it is thereby necessarily represented *as* complex (e.g., as potentially divisible into various parts). Therefore our (human) intuitions are essentially complex representations. As Kant puts this point in a footnote to § 17 of the B-Deduction, an intuition of a spatial and/or a temporal object consists of 'many representations that are contained in one and in the consciousness of it' (B136n).

Now, as I have argued in the previous section of this chapter, the consciousness or awareness of a representation demands apperception. That is, Kant's epistemology requires that in order for a representation to present an object to the subject, it must be apperceived by the subject – or 'belong to a self-consciousness', as he puts it in the passage quoted above. Hence, for an intuition to present a particular complex object to the subject in cognition, *all* of the representations that compose that intuition must be able to be apperceived by the subject; not only this, they must all be able to be apperceived *together* by the subject. That is, the subject must be able to grasp them all as hanging together to present a particular object, or as making up a unified complex representation. As Kant sometimes puts it, the subject's consciousness of an intuition is the 'representation of the *synthetic* unity of the manifold' (B130). Or, as he puts it in the quoted passage, the 'manifold' of representations in an apperceived intuition must '*all together* belong to a self-consciousness' or 'stand *together* in a universal self-consciousness'.

It may be objected that this reading of the passage from the first paragraph of § 16 is inadequate, for in that passage Kant seems to be concerned not with an epistemological question – namely, what conditions representations must meet in order to *present* to the subject – but with an ontological question – namely, what conditions representations must meet in order simply to *belong* to the subject. For, to quote the relevant part of that passage again, Kant writes there that

as my representations (even if I am not conscious of them as such) they must yet necessarily be in accord with the condition under which alone they *can* stand together in a universal self-consciousness, because otherwise they would not throughout belong to me. (B132)

Here Kant seems clearly to be saying that if 'self-consciousness' (i.e., the apperception) of the representations were not possible, then such representations 'would not all together be *my* representations' and 'would not throughout belong to me'. Indeed, this claim may seem inconsistent not only with my interpretation, but also with other things that Kant himself has said. For we know that Kant allows for the logical possibility of unconscious representations (i.e., representations that are not apperceived), and perhaps even of *essentially* unconscious representations (i.e., representations that cannot be apperceived). This is clear both from the passage in his letter to Marcus Herz (26 May 1789) quoted earlier, and from the final disjunctive clause of the opening sentence of § 16, namely, that an unconscious representation 'would either be impossible *or else at least* would be nothing for me' (B131; my emphasis). Here Kant seems to allow for the possibility that I could have representations which could not 'belong to a self-consciousness' or 'stand together in a universal self-consciousness' (and which would thus be 'nothing *for me*'), and yet which would still 'belong to me' in the ontological sense of existing as modifications of my mind. This seems to contradict the claim made in the passage above, that for a representation to belong to me it must be able to be apperceived.

In the face of this apparent inconsistency, it may be tempting to argue that by 'belongs to me' Kant must mean 'presents to me' or 'is something *for me*'. In this case, Kant would be saying that a representation that could not be apperceived would not be 'mine' simply in the sense that it would not contribute to my conscious awareness, or function to present an object to me. Pierre Keller, for example, thus writes that 'Kant understands mineness in a restrictive sense. What is mine is something for me, as opposed to something of which I might be an owner in a sense that is cognitively inaccessible to me'.[27] A closer reading of the passage from § 16 will, however, show that we do not need to reach for this saving interpretation, for the inconsistency is only apparent. As I have already noted, Kant announces at the beginning of the passage that he is concerned not with representations in general, but specifically with 'the manifold representations that are given in a certain intuition'. By definition, an intuition is a representation in virtue of which I cognise something. Kant's claim in the passage thus expressly concerns representations that function to present objects to my awareness, and which therefore must be able to be apperceived.[28] In other words, a *representation in an intuition* that could not be apperceived by me would not belong to me – in the ontological sense that it would not exist as a modification of my faculty of sensibility. It is thus that Kant concludes in the quoted passage that 'the manifold representations that are given in a certain intuition . . . must yet necessarily be in accord with the condition under which alone they *can* stand together in a universal self-consciousness'.

This interpretation of the starting point of Kant's master argument – the 'unity of apperception' – explains why he (notoriously) claims towards the

[27] P. Keller, *Kant and the Demands of Self-Consciousness* (Cambridge University Press, 1998), p. 67.
[28] Cf. Robert Howell, *Kant's Transcendental Deduction* (Dordrecht: Kluwer, 1992), pp. 132–4.

end of § 16 that 'this principle of the necessary unity of apperception is, to be sure, itself identical, thus an analytical proposition' (B135). This claim to analyticity is repeated and explained in § 17, where Kant writes that this

> last proposition is, as we said, itself analytic, although, to be sure, it makes synthetic unity into the conditions of all thinking; for it says nothing more than that all *my* representations in any given intuition must stand under the condition under which alone I can ascribe them to the identical self as *my* representations, and can thus grasp them together, as synthetically combined in an apperception, through the general expression *I think*. (B138)

At first reading, and without a correct understanding of the notion of apperception, this passage may give the impression that Kant is making the dubious claim that the proposition

If a representation is mine then I can ascribe it to myself.

is analytic. This proposition certainly does not look in the least analytic, involving as it does a leap from an ontological claim (that certain mental states *are* mine) to an epistemological one (that I can *recognise* those mental states *as* mine). This appears no more analytic than does the claim that, merely because all my relatives are mine, I can therefore recognise them as mine. Robert Howell, for example, reads the passage in this way and, unsurprisingly, convicts Kant of error.[29] Howell attempts to explain this mistake by suggesting that Kant has been beguiled by a simple *de dicto–de re* fallacy. In essence, his suggestion is that Kant slides illegitimately from the trivially true (and thus perhaps 'analytic') *de dicto* claim

I can know $\forall x$ (x is my representation $\rightarrow$ x is mine).

to the substantive *de re* claim

$\forall x$ (x is my representation $\rightarrow$ I can know x is mine).

Hence, if Kant were claiming that the proposition *If a representation is mine then I can ascribe it to myself* is analytic, then his claim would seem to be obviously false. Furthermore, even if it were not false, that claim would be inconsistent with the logical possibility of necessarily unconscious representations which we have already seen Kant is happy to admit.

In response to these problems, Henry Allison has argued that the 'principle of apperception' can be read in a weaker way, which allows both

---

[29] Ibid., p. 182.

its analyticity and its consistency with Kant's other doctrines to be maintained.[30] According to Allison, Kant's principle

asserts that in order for any of these [*sc.*, my representations] to be anything to me, that is, to represent anything for me, it must be possible for me to be aware of it as mine. This is equivalent to the possibility of reflectively attaching the 'I think' to it. Any representation for which this is not possible is *ipso facto* not a representation for me . . . [T]his principle . . . only affirms the necessity of this possibility if the representation is to function *as a* representation, that is, to represent some object. It therefore neither affirms nor implies that this is necessary in order for the representation to be 'mine' in any sense.[31]

In other words, Allison argues that Kant is not claiming analyticity for the very strong proposition

If a representation is mine then I can ascribe it to myself.

but for the weaker proposition

If a representation can be something for me (i.e., represent to me) then I can ascribe it to myself.

Allison thinks that Kant is correct to claim that this latter proposition is analytic, and defends this view as follows.

This necessity [*sc.*, of the possibility of self-ascription] is based on the premise that having a thought involves the capacity to recognise it as one's own. Since a thought which I (in principle) could not recognise as my own would *ipso facto* not be a thought *for* me, and since a thought which is not a thought for me could not enter into my cognition, I take this claim to be obviously analytic.[32]

However, Allison's argument here is fallacious, and trades on an ambiguity in the phrase 'for me', which occurs in the second sentence of the passage. A thought which I (in principle) could not recognise as my own would certainly not *be a thought for me* in the sense that that *thought* could not itself be an object of my own (self-)cognition. But perhaps that thought could still *be a thought for me* in the sense that, in virtue of having that thought, I could think about something (e.g., that a cat is black). In the latter sense of 'for me' the thought could thus 'enter into my cognition', although that thought would not itself be the object of that cognition. Hence, as was noted in the previous section, it seems logically possible that there

[30] Allison's view is also shared, e.g., by McCann in 'Skepticism and Kant's B Deduction', 73–4.
[31] Allison, *Kant's Transcendental Idealism*, p. 137.
[32] H. Allison, 'Apperception and Analyticity in the B–Deduction', in *Idealism and Freedom* (Cambridge University Press, 1996), p. 47.

could exist creatures with the capacity to have thoughts or representations, but who lacked the capacity to cognise (and thus 'self-ascribe') their own thoughts or representations. Such creatures would, for example, lack the linguistic capacity to use first-person propositional-attitude constructions. No doubt the understanding of such creatures would strike us as limited in important respects, but there seems no reason to say that they could not represent or think about things at all – at least, not without a good deal more argument, which Allison does not provide.[33] Hence, Allison gives us no good reason for thinking that the proposition

If a representation can be something for me (i.e., represent to me) then I can ascribe it to myself.

is analytic. The basic problem is that his interpretation of Kant's 'principle of apperception', although weaker than Howell's interpretation, still makes that principle too strong to have any obvious claim to analyticity.

It is my argument that both of these interpretations are incorrect, and that careful attention to the details and context of Kant's 'principle of the necessary unity of apperception' will show that it is not problematic, and that it has a good claim to analyticity. Firstly, it is important to be clear about the notion of 'ascribing a representation to myself'. Although Kant's verb *to ascribe* (*zählen zu*; more literally, 'to number among'), which he uses in the passage from B138 quoted earlier, may sound as if it refers to a capacity to know about or cognise one's own representations (e.g., to know that they are mine), from the rest of that passage it is clear that Kant is referring to apperception. And, as I have argued, apperception is not a capacity to cognise or think about one's own representations, but to grasp them as presenting something. Secondly, in their reading of the passage, both Howell and Allison neglect a crucial point that I have already emphasised. Whenever Kant states his 'principle of the necessary unity of apperception' he expressly qualifies it, so as to make clear that he is making a claim not about all representations in general, nor even about all representations that can be something 'for me', but only about a very specific class of representations: the 'manifold in an intuition'. With these two points in mind it is worth looking again at Kant's claim, in the passage previously quoted, that the 'principle of the necessary unity of apperception'

---

[33] Cf. Guyer's arguments that consciousness does not necessarily presuppose self-consciousness: *Kant and the Claims of Knowledge*, pp. 141ff.

says nothing more than that all *my* representations in any given intuition must stand under the condition under which alone I can ascribe them to the identical self, as *my* representations, and can thus grasp them together, as synthetically combined in an apperception, through the general expression *I think*. (B138)

This statement of the principle begins, as I have noted, with the qualification that it concerns only 'all my representations in any given intuition', and it says of those representations that they must be able to be 'ascribed to the identical self, as my representations'. As I have argued, this is not to 'introspect', via inner sense, and say of each one 'That's mine' – which would be a pointless and bizarre ceremony in any case. It is to say that the representations composing a certain intuition (a complex representation) of mine must be able to grasped by me (*i*) as representing, and (*ii*) as hanging together, so as to make up one and the same representation, or point of view on the world (i.e., *my* point of view). If this were not possible, then I would not be able to 'grasp them together, as synthetically combined in an apperception' – or, as hanging together as a complex unified representation. Hence, the proposition that Kant is claiming to be analytic – the principle of the unity of apperception – is neither

If a representation is mine then I can ascribe it to myself.

nor

If a representation can be something for me (i.e., represent to me) then I can ascribe it to myself.

but rather

All the representations composing an intuition of mine must be apperceivable by me as hanging together in a unity.

I think a good case can be made that this latter claim is indeed analytic, as follows. Firstly, as previously remarked, an intuition is, by definition, a representation in virtue of which I cognise something. Hence, all intuitions must be *apperceivable*, for otherwise they could not contribute to my conscious awareness as cognitions. Secondly, according to Kant, all intuitions are essentially complex, and therefore 'contain a manifold'. In other words, any intuitions that I (the subject) can have must be *complex unified* representations (i.e., many representations making up one representation). Hence, Kant's principle can be rewritten as follows:

All the representations composing an intuition (= a complex unified apperceivable representation) of mine must be apperceivable by me as making up a complex unified representation.

In other words, if I am able to apperceive complex unified representations, then I must be able to apperceive complex unified representations – which is, as I suggested previously, essentially a restatement of Kant's earlier claim about 'the *I think*'. Hence, my reading of the principle of the unity of apperception shows that Kant is correct to claim that it is analytic. But it might now be thought that I have rescued the analyticity of Kant's principle only at the cost of making it so trivial that it could lead to no interesting conclusions. However, Kant is correct to say that 'from this [principle] much may be inferred' (B132), as I now hope to show.

So far I have argued that Kant's discussion in § 16 concerns the condition under which the 'manifold' of representations composing an intuition can be apperceived – that is, grasped as hanging together to present an object. I have also suggested that this condition will be that such apperception can occur only through a spontaneous synthesis on the part of the subject, and that therefore (α) all our cognition involves a spontaneous synthesis. Kant gives his master argument for this claim in a difficult and crucially important passage (that follows the passage from § 16 that was quoted and discussed above). Here we are told that

this thoroughgoing identity of the apperception of a manifold given in the intuition [*diese durchgängige Identität der Apperception eines in der Anschauung gegebenen Mannigfaltigen*] contains a synthesis of the representations, and is possible only through the consciousness of this synthesis. For the empirical consciousness that accompanies different representations is by itself dispersed and without relation to the identity of the subject. The latter relation therefore does not yet come about by my accompanying each representation with consciousness, but rather by my *adding* one representation to the other and being conscious of their synthesis. (B133)

The 'thoroughgoing identity of the apperception of a manifold given in the intuition' refers to the unity possessed by a complex representation. That is, it refers to the fact that the component representations of an intuition must be apperceived as all hanging together so as to present a particular object – as the principle of the unity of apperception has told us. Now, Kant tells us that in order for this unity to be possible, the subject must perform a synthesis. His argument for this claim – the master argument – is worth laying out slightly more formally, as this will facilitate my discussion. Left in his own terminology, Kant's reasoning is as follows.

Premise   The empirical consciousness that accompanies different representations is by itself dispersed and without relation to the
identity of the subject.

Conclusion Therefore relation to the identity of the subject does not
come about by my accompanying each representation with
consciousness, but by my adding one representation to the
other and being conscious of their synthesis.

This argument thus concerns what Kant refers to as 'the relation of representations to the identity of the subject'. Now, my interpretative claim is
that this is the representationalist equivalent of the semantic problem of
the 'unity of the proposition' or the 'unity of judgment'. This may seem a
rather outlandish claim, for Kant's language appears to suggest an obvious
concern with questions about personal identity, mental unity or conditions
for the 'ownership' of mental states. This is how the argument of § 16 has
often been read (and some examples of this secondary literature will be discussed later), so justifying my own opposed interpretation will take some
discussion.

    The premise of Kant's master argument, in particular, may appear in-
compatible with my interpretation, for it sounds rather like Hume's claim
that he was unable to find within himself an impression of an enduring
self or mental substance. As Hume puts it in the famous passage from the
discussion of personal identity in the *Treatise*:

For my part, when I enter most intimately into what I call *myself*, I always stumble
on some particular perception or other, of heat or cold, light or shade, love or
hatred, pain or pleasure. I never can catch *myself* at any time without a perception,
and never can observe any thing but the perception ... If any one upon serious and
unprejudic'd reflexion, thinks he has a different notion of *himself*, I must confess
I can reason no longer with him.[34]

The view that Kant's argument in § 16 relies on a premise like this –
concerning the absence of a representation of the self in introspection –
is quite widespread in the literature. Guyer, for example, claims that 'Kant
clearly shares with Hume' the premise 'that there is no impression of self-
hood in any single representation',[35] and Kitcher remarks that 'in the Deduction, [Kant] points out in terms strikingly reminiscent of Hume's discussion, that inner sense does not reveal a self', and that these passages
thus 'fairly shout allusions to Hume'.[36] This view is, however, incorrect

---

[34] Hume, *Treatise*, book 1, part 4, § 6, p. 252.
[35] Guyer, *Kant and the Claims of Knowledge*, p. 137.
[36] Kitcher, *Kant's Transcendental Psychology*, p. 100.

and relies upon the assimilation of apperception to ordinary self-awareness that was criticised in the previous section of this chapter. Once the notion of apperception is understood, it should become clear that the premise of Kant's master argument resembles Hume's claim about the self in only a very superficial sense. As I have argued above, 'apperception' is not a fancy jargon term for 'introspection', but refers to the representationalist parallel of the semantic notion of understanding a sign. So when Kant talks (in the passage last quoted) of the 'thoroughgoing identity of the apperception of a manifold given in the intuition', he is not talking about how we come to find a unified conception of the self in introspection, but about how we come to have a unified grasp of a complex representation. Therefore the premise of the master argument – that 'the empirical consciousness that accompanies different representations is by itself dispersed and without relation to the identity of the subject' – is not a Hume-like claim that we fail to find a representation of the self in introspection.

What in fact this premise embodies is Kant's reason for claiming that the apperception of a unified complex representation cannot be purely receptive, but must involve an element of spontaneity. What is at stake in the master argument is the nature of apperception, or the question of what is necessarily involved in grasping an internal state as representing an object. Kant, by insisting on the importance of the subject's activity of 'adding', 'combining' or 'synthesising', is saying that apperception essentially involves a certain spontaneity. The apperception of an intuition is therefore not simply a question of my 'reading off' data that are already there, embodied in the modifications of my sensibility. If apperception were purely receptive in this way, then it would (in the logical terminology of Kant's day) simply be the faculty of making obscure representations clear. In that case, the function of thought (or, the faculty of understanding) in relation to the representations provided by sensibility could only be that of making distinct what is confused or indistinct in those representations. In other words, all the information would already be there in the representations of sensibility, with the only job thus left to the understanding being that of analysing, ordering, clarifying, classifying (etc.) that information. The understanding would thus be active in cognition, but it would not be *spontaneous* in the sense that, as explained in the previous chapter, is so important for Kant's philosophy. This 'one-faculty' model was a fairly standard account of human cognition. It is clearly to be found, for example, in Locke's *Essay*, and, according to Kant, in the 'Leibnizian-Wolffian philosophy', as his discussion at A44/B61 shows.

Now, as I have argued, Kant rejects this 'one-faculty' model of cognition in favour of a 'two-faculty' model, which brings with it a conception of apperception as spontaneous. To begin with, according to Kant the understanding does not serve simply to make distinct the confused representations of sensibility. As he writes in an important passage from the Second Analogy:

Understanding belongs to all experience and its possibility, and the first thing that it does for this is not to make the representation of the objects distinct, but rather to make the representation of an object possible at all. (A199/B244)

The understanding 'makes the representation of an object possible' because it does not simply reveal what is already given in sensibility, but plays an active role in constituting that representational content. This it does through the spontaneous synthesis that is the act of apperception – and thus, as quoted above, Kant remarks of the capacity to apperceive that 'indeed, this faculty is the understanding itself' (B134n). Apperception is not simply a faculty for making obscure representations clear – for revealing something that was already there, only hidden from consciousness. It is not, as it were, a light shone on my various internal states, which then reveal themselves and their contents to my mind's eye. If we are to compare apperception to a light then, to adopt a remark that Geach makes about Aquinas's doctrine of the 'agent intellect', we should be 'careful to add that this comparison goes on all fours only if we suppose that colours are generated by kindling the light – that the light is not just revealing colours that already existed in the dark'.[37] That is to say, in the act of apperception the subject is not simply determined (by the nature of the internal state or the modification of sensibility) but is also determining. This is to say that apperception is spontaneous – the spontaneous application of a rule of projection, in virtue of which the subject cognises appearances *in* the modifications of its sensibility.

Kant's master argument is an argument for this conception of apperception as spontaneous, and against the conception of apperception as simply the revelation of a content that is already given. He thus writes in the conclusion of that argument that the relation to the identity of the subject 'does not yet come about by my accompanying each representation with consciousness, but rather by my *adding* one representation to the other and being conscious of their synthesis' (B133). This is a rejection of the idea that

---

[37] Geach, *Mental Acts*, p. 130.

in order to have a unified grasp of a complex representation I simply have to shine the light of awareness, as it were, on each of the component representations, or 'accompany each representation with consciousness'. Kant is claiming that this conception of apperception as non-spontaneous cannot account for the relation of the representations (composing an intuition) to the 'identity of the subject' – that is, as I shall argue, for their hanging together as a unified point of view. In other words, Kant rejects the conception of apperception as non-spontaneous because of its inability to make sense of the unity possessed by complex representations. Hence, on my interpretation the master argument of § 16 is that apperception must be conceived of as a spontaneous synthesis because otherwise the unity of complex representations becomes unintelligible.

If it is correct to read Kant's argument in this way, then it means that the problem he is grappling with in § 16 of the B-Deduction is, as I have suggested, the representationalist equivalent of the problem that was discussed in later philosophy as the problem of the 'unity of judgment' or the 'unity of the proposition'. This latter problem (discussed by, among others, Bradley, Russell and Frege) is the question of how words, signs, ideas or meanings hang together in a proposition or judgment, so as to compose a unified meaning that is something more than a list or a mere aggregate of meanings.[38] Put in its simplest form, the problem is this: a proposition is a unity, not simply an aggregate of components. What makes this difference? Perhaps the most famous statement of the problem occurs in the following passage from Russell's *Principles of Mathematics*.

Consider, for example, the proposition 'A differs from B'. The constituents of this proposition, if we analyse it, appear to be only A, difference, B. Yet these constituents, thus placed side by side, do not reconstitute the proposition. The difference which occurs in the proposition actually relates A and B, whereas the difference after analysis is a notion which has no connection with A and B. It may be said that we ought, in the analysis, to mention the relations which difference has to A and B, relations which are expressed by *is* and *from* when we say 'A is different from B'. These relations consist in the fact that A is referent and B is relatum with respect to difference. But 'A, referent, difference, relatum, B' is still merely a list of terms, not a proposition. A proposition, in fact, is essentially a unity, and when analysis has destroyed the unity, no enumeration of constituents will restore the proposition.[39]

---

[38] For two useful discussions of the problem and its history see A. Palmer, *Concept and Object* (London: Routledge, 1988), and L. Linsky, 'The Unity of the Proposition', *Journal of the History of Philosophy* 30 (1992), 243–73.

[39] B. Russell, *The Principles of Mathematics* (London: Routledge, 1992), pp. 49–50.

Although this is a *locus classicus* of the problem, Russell's presentation of it is somewhat distorted by the rather peculiar view of propositions that he held at the time (in which they are complexes of the things they are about), which makes him treat the question of their unity as an ontological problem rather than a semantic one.[40] Considered in abstraction from this view, the problem of the unity of the proposition is, as much as anything, a way of putting questions about the nature of meaning, signification and understanding into dramatic form. Its central point is that understanding a proposition does not reduce to understanding each of its components. To use a clearer example than Russell's, take the sentence 'Jill loves Jack.' Understanding this sentence is not simply a question of understanding the three words of which it is composed, for then the sentence would be identical in meaning to the list 'Jill, loves, Jack' – which is clearly false. In response to this, it may be suggested that there is a further separable component that contributes to the meaning of the sentence, namely, the concatenation of the words. But in that case, the sentence would be identical in meaning to the longer list 'Jill, loves, Jack, concatenation' – which is both clearly false and an obvious first step on a vicious infinite regress. Hence, as Russell concludes, 'a proposition . . . is essentially a unity, and when analysis has destroyed the unity, no enumeration of constituents will restore the proposition'.

This may sound a long way from what Kant is discussing in § 16 of the B-Deduction, but the difference is largely one of terminology and of his representationalist (rather than semantic) starting point. As noted above, Kant's discussion concerns how the 'thoroughgoing identity of the apperception of a manifold given in the intuition' (B133) is possible. I have argued that Kant's notion of apperception is playing a role in his representationalist epistemology parallel to the semantic notion of understanding a sign. If this interpretation of apperception is correct, then 'the apperception of a manifold given in the intuition' possesses a 'thoroughgoing identity' in that all the 'manifold' representations hang together so as to compose one and the same unified complex representation (i.e., the intuition in question). That is, I (the subject) grasp the 'manifold' representations as hanging together *for me*, or as all together making up *my* point of view upon the (phenomenal) world. Hence, Kant's discussion concerns the question of how the component representations of a complex representation are grasped by the subject as the unified presenting of a complex object or state of affairs.

---

[40] See L. Linsky, 'Terms and Propositions in Russell's *Principles of Mathematics*', *Journal of the History of Philosophy* 26 (1988), 621–42.

This is the clear representationalist parallel to the problem of the unity of the proposition, which concerns the question of how the components of a proposition are grasped or understood as a unified proposing of something (that things are thus and so), rather than as a mere aggregate or collection of separate meanings.

This parallel becomes even clearer if the premise of Kant's master argument is examined. This premise is that 'the empirical consciousness that accompanies different representations is by itself dispersed and without relation to the identity of the subject' (B133). This, as I have suggested above, is the claim that the apperception or grasp of a complex representation does not reduce to the receptive awareness of each of its component representations. For Kant, the mere 'empirical awareness that accompanies different representations' is 'dispersed and without relation to the identity of the subject' in that it does not explain how the component representations hang together as *mine* (the subject's), or as composing one and the same point of view (i.e., *my* point of view). Now, put in its linguistic form, the problem of the unity of the proposition is that understanding a sentence (a unified complex sign) does not reduce to understanding a list of words (the signs that compose it). We could thus echo the premise of Kant's argument and say that in this case 'the understanding of each word is dispersed and without relation to the identity of the sentence as a whole'. That is, the understanding of each of the component signs is not sufficient to explain how they are grasped together as making up the linguistic expression of one and the same proposition. This further parallel between Kant's problem in § 16 and the problem of the unity of the proposition has, I hope, suggested that it may be profitable to pursue my interpretative suggestion further.

It should be pointed out here that I am not the first to note that there is a connection between Kant's argument in the Transcendental Deduction and the problem of the unity of the proposition. To the best of my knowledge, however, there is no detailed development of this claim (such development as I will provide in this book) in the secondary literature on Kant. Indeed, the connection has generally been noted not by Kant scholars, but by those working on figures such as Frege and Russell – who restrict themselves to a few suggestive remarks on the parallel with Kant. David Bell, for example, writes in his book on Frege that

just as a sentence possesses a unity quite absent from a mere list of words, so a thought (or judgment, or proposition) possesses a unity and completeness entirely absent from a mere medley or succession of images, impressions, ideas, concepts, or meanings . . . Kant [dubbed this] 'the synthetic unity of the manifold in representations in general'.[41]

Perhaps not surprisingly, as his book is not intended as a work on Kant, Bell does not go on to develop this point. Peter Hylton provides what, to my knowledge, is the longest and most explicit discussion of the parallel to be found in the literature, in four paragraphs of a paper discussing Russell's and Moore's attacks on idealism. He argues that the 'Kantian notion of synthesis can be thought of as providing a solution to a problem which structurally, at least, is very close to the Russellian problem [of the unity of the proposition]'.[42] Hylton and I thus both agree that Kant's problem is closely related to the problem of the unity of the proposition. However, as I shall discuss in a later section of this chapter, Hylton's (highly summarised) reading of Kant's solution to the problem differs crucially from my own reading. Hence, although there are some anticipations of aspects of my reading to be found in the secondary literature, there has been (again, to my knowledge) no detailed examination of the main argument of the B-Deduction in the light of the parallel between Kant's problem and the problem of the unity of the proposition.

The main reason for this is the fact that commentators have, in general, failed to see that Kant's notion of apperception (or 'the *I think*') is the representationalist equivalent of the semantic notion of understanding a sign. Once the role that the notion of apperception plays in Kant's epistemology is correctly interpreted in this way, then it becomes clear that his discussion in § 16 centrally concerns the unified grasp of complex representations (i.e., the unity of the 'manifold in an intuition'). A failure to understand the notion of apperception makes it tempting to interpret the argument of § 16 in two mistaken ways, which can be summarised as follows:

(1) Kant's talk of the 'unity of apperception' refers to the ontological unity possessed by a consciousness, mind, person or self. His discussion in § 16 thus concerns the criteria for thoughts or mental states *being mine*, in the sense of all together belonging to one and the same mind, or being episodes in the experience of one and the same person.

(2) Kant's talk of the 'unity of apperception' refers to the potential unity of self-consciousness (in the ordinary sense of that term). His discussion in § 16 thus concerns the criteria for my being able to cognise all my own thoughts or mental states *as mine*. In other words, it concerns what

---

[41] D. Bell, *Frege's Theory of Judgment* (Oxford University Press, 1979), p. 8.
[42] P. Hylton, 'The Nature of the Proposition and the Revolt against Idealism', in *Philosophy in History*, ed. R. Rorty, J. B. Schneewind and Q. Skinner (Cambridge University Press, 1984), p. 379.

else must be true of my thoughts or mental states if I am in a position to ascribe (potentially) all of them to one and the same self (i.e., to myself).

Approaches (1) and (2) certainly do not exhaust the range of alternative interpretations that can be found in the secondary literature, but they do represent two influential ways of making sense of Kant's argument in § 16. Before continuing with the details of my own reading of that section, it is worth looking briefly at some examples of (1) and (2) in order to compare and contrast them with my view. It should be noted that I do this in order to bring out what is distinctive about my own approach to § 16, rather than to offer detailed criticism of these alternative views. For such criticism would necessitate considering a commentator's interpretation of the B-Deduction as a whole – perhaps even of Kant's epistemology as a whole – and would thus be extremely lengthy.

An example of (1) can be found in Jonathan Bennett's work, *Kant's Analytic*, and this basic approach to Kant's argument in § 16 has also been extensively developed by Patricia Kitcher in her recent book, *Kant's Transcendental Psychology*. Bennett tells us that Kant's argument

has to do with the ownership of mental states. Kant says that mental states, or 'representations', can exist only as episodes in the history of minds. He expresses this by saying that representations must be subject to the 'unity of apperception' or 'unity of consciousness'.[43]

That is, according to Bennett the unity of apperception is simply the unity possessed by the class of thoughts belonging to one and the same mind. Kitcher holds a similar view, and reads Kant as being concerned with answering the question: 'What relation unites diverse states in one mind?'.[44] In a passage parallel to the one just quoted from Bennett, she writes that the

first edition [of the *Critique*] makes the claim that all judgments . . . must belong to a self in the material mode. In the second edition this claim is expressed by saying that the representation 'I think' can be attached to all my judgments. This manner of expression may court confusion, but the claims are materially equivalent: if and only if for any judgment J, it must belong to some subject, then it must be possible (for someone) to construct a true sentence 'I think that J'.[45]

Moving from this interpretation of the unity of apperception, Kitcher proceeds to argue that the Transcendental Deduction is, fundamentally, a

---

[43] Bennett, *Kant's Analytic*, p. 103.
[44] Kitcher, *Kant's Transcendental Psychology*, p. 123.   [45] Ibid., pp. 187–8.

response to Hume's famous sceptical treatment of the notion of the self (the so-called 'bundle theory'). The details of Kitcher's interpretation are complex and do not concern me here, but in essence she argues that Kant answers Hume by providing a sophisticated relational theory of the mind. According to this theory, mental states belong to one and the same mind in virtue of standing in certain dependency relations to one another – relations which hold between those states because they have been synthesised.[46]

Now, approach (1) has little in common with my own reading of Kant's concerns in § 16 of the B-Deduction, and it is worth trying to make the difference between them clear. As I read him, Kant is not concerned with the criteria for something's belonging to a complex entity (e.g., for a representation or 'mental state' to belong to one mind rather than another). For, according to my interpretation, the unity of apperception is not the ontological unity of a complex object, but rather the unity of our grasp or understanding (i.e., our apperception) of a complex representation. This is a crucial difference, which can be explained as follows. Suppose there is a complex object O composed of the two parts a and b. The ontological unity of O can easily be explained by saying that O exists as a unity in virtue of the fact that a relation R holds between a and b. So, for example, Kitcher is attempting to explain the ontological unity of the mind by saying that two mental states belong to one and the same mind in virtue of a certain dependency relation holding between those states. However, this appeal to the mere holding of a relation cannot solve Kant's problem, if his problem is indeed the parallel to the problem of the unity of the proposition. For in that case he is concerned with specifying the difference between (*i*) simply having a collection of separate representations in mind (e.g., the representation of a and the representation of b) and (*ii*) having a unified grasp (or apperception) of a complex representation composed of those representations (e.g., the representation of ab). The difference between (*i*) and (*ii*) is a difference in what the subject grasps or understands – that is, in the representational content of its thought. Hence, that difference cannot be explained simply by appealing to an ontological fact – simply by appealing, for example, to the fact that a relation (say, co-presence) holds between the representations in the case of (*ii*) but not in (*i*). For the holding of such a relation will help to solve Kant's problem only if the fact that that relation holds is something *for* the subject – that is, only if the holding of that relation contributes representational content to the content of the whole in

---

[46] See ibid., especially chs. 4 and 5. McCann has a similar view – see his 'Skepticism and Kant's B Deduction', 75.

(*ii*). But then the contribution made by the holding of that relation must simply be yet another representation, in which case we have taken the first step on a vicious infinite regress, with the unity of the apperception in the case of (*ii*) no closer to being explained.

In summary then, the difference between my interpretative approach to § 16 and the interpretative approach (1) of commentators like Bennett and Kitcher is as follows. Approach (1) reads Kant as being concerned with the unity of an object (e.g., a mind, person or consciousness) viewed as it were from *outside* – and thus with its ontological unity. I, on the other hand, read Kant as being concerned with the unity of the mind or consciousness viewed as it were from *inside* – that is, with the unity of the first-person point of view itself, or, equivalently, with the unity of our grasp (i.e., apperception) of our own representations. My reading thus explains why the argument of the B-Deduction is conducted largely in the first person (the word 'I' [*ich*], for example, occurs over a hundred times in §§ 15–27). Kitcher thinks that this grammatical fact is the result of a mere stylistic choice on Kant's part – a choice which 'may court confusion' as she complains in the passage quoted above. And this is not surprising, for its expression in the first person is completely irrelevant to the argument that she finds in Kant's text. On my reading, however, the first-person grammar of the text of the B-Deduction can be seen as an essential clue to what Kant is attempting to do there. For the unity of my apperception is a unity *for me* – that is, it makes a difference for me, in that it is in virtue of that unity (or that unified grasp) that I can have the conscious awareness as of a single complex object, rather than a mere aggregate of separated representations. Kant's problem – the parallel to the problem of the unity of the proposition – is to show how the difference made by the unity of apperception to the representational content of my experience can be specified or accounted for, and what such an account can tell us about the nature of representation in general.

Having explained the difference between my reading of § 16 and alternative approach (1), as exemplified by Bennett and Kitcher, I now turn to consider the difference between my reading and alternative approach (2) – in which the 'unity of apperception' is interpreted as a potential unity of self-consciousness or self-cognition. Since Strawson's seminal work, this has been perhaps the most popular interpretative approach in the literature.[47] An influential recent example of it can be found in Allison's book *Kant's Transcendental Idealism*. According to Allison, Kant's argument in the opening of the B-Deduction is that

---

[47] For Strawson's version of (2), see *The Bounds of Sense*, pp. 98ff.

since a single complex thought logically requires a single thinking subject, it fol-lows (1) that it must be a numerically identical 'I think' that can be reflectively attached to each of the component representations taken individually, and (2) it must (necessarily) be possible for this thinking subject to be aware of the numerical identity of the 'I think'.[48]

The conclusion of this argument is that all the representations that can re-present something to a subject must be able to be synthesised or combined together by that subject. Allison explains this conclusion with an example of

the simplest possible case: where a subject has two representations, *A* and *B*, each of which is accompanied by a distinct awareness or 'empirical consciousness'. In other words there is an 'I think' *A* and an 'I think' *B* pertaining to a single subject. Clearly, in order for the subject of both these thoughts to become reflectively aware of its identity, it must combine *A* and *B* in a single consciousness. Only by so combining *A* and *B* can it possibly become aware of the identity of the I that thinks *A* with the I that thinks *B*.[49]

The fundamental difference between Allison's reading of § 16 and my own reading lies in our very different views of apperception. As was pointed out above, Allison interprets apperception as ordinary self-consciousness – that is, as the subject's capacity to cognise its own representations or thoughts, and thereby recognise them as its own or 'ascribe' them to itself. This preoccupation with self-cognition rather than with cognition in general means that the problem I find in Kant (the parallel to the problem of the unity of the proposition) is not even visible to Allison. He notes above that 'a single complex thought logically requires a single thinking subject'. This is trivially true: S can have the complex representation of *ab* only if S has the representation of *a* and S has the representation of *b*. But Kant's problem of the unity of apperception concerns precisely the point that this, although necessary, is not sufficient to explain the possibility of our unified grasp of complex representations. Allison, however, takes this possibility of complex unified representations for granted. And this is why he thinks that Kant's aim is achieved when it has been shown, via the necessary possibility of self-consciousness, that all our representations can (potentially) be combined – that is, grasped together in one complex unified representation. But this is not a solution to Kant's problem in § 16 (if my interpretation is correct), for that problem cannot be solved by showing *that* certain representations are, or can be, unified, but only by giving an account (i.e., a conceptual analysis) of *how* such unity is possible.

[48] Allison, *Kant's Transcendental Idealism*, p. 138.   [49] Ibid., p. 142.

This comparison between my reading of § 16 and the two main alternative approaches to that section has, I hope, clarified the meaning of my claim that Kant's discussion concerns the representationalist parallel to the problem of the unity of the proposition. It is now necessary to consider in more detail what consequences this has for an understanding of his master argument. So far I have argued that Kant's master argument centrally involves the claim that the apperception of a complex representation does not reduce to the receptive awareness of each of its component representations (the 'manifold in an intuition'), for this does not account for the 'unity' or the 'thoroughgoing identity' of such apperception. As was stated above in the discussion of Kitcher, the problem is how to specify the difference made by the unity of my apperception to the representational content of my experience, without making that difference simply yet another representation and thus embarking on a vicious infinite regress. The reasoning behind this claim is thus much the same, *mutatis mutandis*, as in the case of the problem of the unity of the proposition.

It is worth spelling this problem of the unity of apperception out again, from a slightly different perspective. Imagine that I am conscious of a certain unified complex representation: a representation of *blue and red*. For simplicity's sake, I will abstract from any spatial arrangement of the colours and suppose that the phrase 'blue and red' exhaustively specifies the representational content of my awareness in this case. This complex awareness does not reduce to a grasp of the representation of blue and a grasp of the representation of red. For imagine an awareness of blue and an awareness of red, and occupy in imagination each of those points of view in turn. There would be a point of view on blue (where this exhausts the field of awareness) and a point of view on red (where this exhausts the field of awareness), but there would be no unified point of view on, or awareness of, blue and red *together*. That is, such a reduction would mean that *my* unified point of view (my apperception of a complex representation) would, as it were, fragment into the absurdity of a multiplicity of separate first-person points of view, each with its own independent object – just as a proposition collapses into a mere list if we try to conceive of it as composed of separable components. As Kant puts it in § 16, if I only had the receptive awareness of each component representation (without a spontaneous synthesis), then 'I would have as multicoloured, diverse a self as I have representations of which I am conscious' (B134). What more, then, have I grasped in grasping the representation of *blue and red* over and above the representation of blue and the representation of red? The problem is that whatever further representation we add is simply yet another separate point of view needing to be unified with the others – and we are thus started on a vicious infinite regress. To use an example mentioned earlier, let us suppose that, in addition to grasping the representation of blue and the representation of red, I also grasp the representation of the relation of co-presentation. But now I simply have a collection of three representations (of blue, red and co-presentation) and am no nearer to having a unified point of view – that is, the unity of my apperception has not been made intelligible.

The solution to (or, what is perhaps better, the dissolution of) this problem, as to the problem of the unity of the proposition, is to reject the presupposition that generates it – namely, the thought that the grasp of a complex representation is reducible to a grasp of each of its components. The problem of the 'unity of apperception' demonstrates that it is impossible to explain our grasp of a unified complex representation simply by appeal to our grasp of a collection of separable components. Therefore, we need to reverse the order of explanation and to explain our grasp of the components by appeal to our prior grasp of the unified complex representation. That is, instead of attempting (hopelessly) to take the atomistic route of explaining the properties of the whole by appeal to the properties of the parts, one must take the holistic route of explaining the properties of the parts by appeal to the properties of the whole. In other words, the problem of unity can only be resolved if the basic explanatory notion in an account of representation is that of a grasp of a unified complex representation as a whole, rather than that of a grasp of a part of that complex.

This is structurally the same solution as Frege's solution to the parallel problem of the unity of the proposition, and a brief examination of this will help to clarify what is at stake. Frege's solution is embodied in his famous distinction between object and function – between the 'complete' or 'saturated' components of a thought or proposition and the 'incomplete' or 'unsaturated' components. It is the 'unsaturated' component of the thought that holds the key to its unity. As Frege puts it, 'not all the parts of a thought can be complete; at least one must be unsaturated or predicative; otherwise they would not hold together'.[50] Now, Donald Davidson has written of this distinction between object and function as follows.

Frege sought to avoid the regress [*sc.*, the problem of the unity of the proposition] by saying that the entities corresponding to predicates (for example) are 'unsaturated' or 'incomplete' in contrast to the entities that correspond to names, but this doctrine seems to label a difficulty rather than solve it.[51]

---

[50] G. Frege, 'On Concept and Object', in *The Frege Reader*, ed. M. Beaney (Oxford: Blackwell, 1997), p. 193.

[51] D. Davidson, 'Truth and Meaning', in *Inquiries into Truth and Interpretation* (Oxford University Press, 1984), p. 17.

Davidson's objection is misplaced, because an 'unsaturated' component is not simply another separable component which has had bestowed on it (by fiat, as it were) the magical power of creating unity. If this were all Frege was saying, then his talk of 'unsaturated' components really would be a label for the problem, rather than a solution to it. However, this is not what Frege is saying. A function is 'unsaturated' precisely in that the contribution it makes to the sense of the proposition is not something that can be specified without appeal to the notion of a proposition or thought as a whole. For, Frege saw very clearly that avoiding the regress, and solving the problem of the unity of the proposition, was a matter of inverting one's explanatory priorities and insisting that the notion of a whole proposition is logically prior to the notion of a propositional component.

An example at the linguistic level may help to explain how Frege's doctrine resolves the problem of unity, for the same distinction between saturated and unsaturated components appears there as well.[52] In Frege's logic, the sentence 'Sooty is a cat' is analysed into two distinct logically relevant components: a component with a 'complete' or 'saturated' sense – the object expression 'Sooty' – and a component with an 'incomplete' or 'unsaturated' sense – the function expression 'ξ is a cat'. Now, it is obvious that the function expression 'ξ is a cat' does not literally occur as a physical component of the expression 'Sooty is a cat', for this latter expression contains no Greek letters. The point of writing the function expression with the letter ξ is to emphasise that what signifies the concept of being a cat is not the bare occurrence of the expression 'is a cat', but rather *the circumstance that* this expression is prefixed by a proper name (or quantified variable).[53] Hence, I understand the sense of the function expression 'ξ is a cat' if and only if I understand the *sentences* that would result from filling the argument place occupied by ξ with object expressions. In other words, for Frege a function expression is 'unsaturated' in that its sense can only be specified by appealing to the sense of the complete sentences in which it can feature. That is, the notion of the sense of a complete sentence (i.e., a thought) is logically prior to the notion of the sense of a function expression. This in turn means that my capacity to understand whole sentences (i.e., my capacity to grasp thoughts) cannot be reductively analysed in terms of a capacity to understand subsentential components and how they are put together. As Cora Diamond puts this point,

---

[52] In what follows I am drawing on Peter Geach's discussion in 'Saying and Showing in Frege and Wittgenstein', in *Essays on Wittgenstein in Honour of G. H. Von Wright*, ed. J. Hintikka (Amsterdam: North Holland Publishing, 1976), pp. 54–62.

[53] Here I am paraphrasing Geach, ibid., p. 60.

it is not possible on Frege's view to identify the parts of a sentence or other complex expression independently of each other as expressions with certain logical powers. A complete knowledge of the sense or reference or both of all the expressions forming a sentence is not what enables us to recognise them in the context, since what has sense and reference is only expressions recognisable through function-argument decomposition as having a certain role in the context.[54]

Hence, Frege's distinction between the 'saturated' and 'unsaturated' components of a thought or proposition resolves the problem of unity because it entails a rejection of the atomistic assumption that the properties of the proposition as a whole can be reductively explained in terms of the properties of its components. For every proposition must contain at least one 'unsaturated' component, and the specification of the properties of that component must make an irreducible reference to the notion of a proposition as a whole. In other words, as Linsky remarks, the notion of an 'unsaturated' component presupposes the notion of the unity of the proposition, and this just

is the way in which Frege deals with the problem of unity. Frege gives 'pride of place' to the whole thought. Any way of thinking about functions and objects which makes unity problematic or impossible is therefore mistaken, for functions and objects are only intelligible in terms of the prior notion. The dissolution of the problem [*sc.*, of the unity of the proposition] results from exhibiting the dependency.[55]

Or, as Frege himself put it, 'I do not begin with concepts and put them together to form a thought or judgment; I come by the parts of the thought by analysing the thought'.[56] Hence, the unity problem can be solved only by giving logical priority to the notion of the proposition (or the thought) as a whole – which in turn means giving logical priority to the notion of *understanding* the proposition as a whole.

This inversion of logical or explanatory priorities lies at the heart of Kant's solution to his own parallel problem of unity, and it has important consequences for his conception of apperception. For Kant, the apperception or grasp of a unified complex representation is not simply a question of becoming receptively aware of all its components (i.e., of the 'manifold in an intuition'). The subject cannot merely shine the light of awareness on each and every component – or 'accompany each representation with consciousness', as Kant puts it – and thereby generate a unified grasp of the

[54] C. Diamond, 'Frege and Nonsense', in *Realistic Spirit*, pp. 90–1.
[55] Linsky, 'Unity of the Proposition', p. 268.
[56] G. Frege, 'Notes for Ludwig Darmstaedter', in *Frege Reader*, ed. Beaney, p. 362.

whole. This is an inadequate conception of apperception, for it makes the 'unity' or 'thoroughgoing identity' of apperception unintelligible – that is, it does not explain how the component representations hang together as one and the same point of view on the world. The only solution to this problem is, as I have argued, to reverse the order of explanation and to take the notion of that unity or 'hanging-togetherness' as having logical priority. This entails that apperception must itself proceed in a holistic rather than an atomistic way. For my apperception of a unified complex representation cannot be 'built up' out of my apperception of the components of that representation. Rather, I must apperceive the representation as a whole, and thereby grasp it as an articulated, unified complex of representations. And thus, as with the capacity to grasp whole thoughts in Frege's account, for Kant the capacity to apperceive the 'manifold in an intuition' *as a unified whole* must be recognised as irreducible – that is, as not explicable in terms of the capacity to be aware of the content of individual component representations.

This holistic conception of apperception – a conception that is demanded by the fact of the 'original-synthetic unity of apperception' – entails that the apperception of the 'manifold in an intuition' must involve a spontaneous synthesis. The argument for this claim is as follows. Let us hypothesise, for the purposes of an indirect proof, that apperception is not spontaneous, but simply a matter of receptivity. In such a case, apperception would simply be the capacity to 'read off' the data that were given to us in the modifications of our sensibility. For such merely receptive 'reading off' to be possible, the modifications of sensibility would have to have, in themselves and prior to any act of (receptive) apperception, a fully determinate representational content. If that were the case, the modifications of sensibility would have to bring that fully determinate content into every possible context in which they occurred. But then the content of a unified complex of those representations would have to be fully determined by the content of the parts and the way they were combined. And therefore grasping a complex representation would simply be a matter of attending to all the components, recognising what they were and how they were combined, and thus building up a grasp of the whole. In other words, if apperception were simply a question of receptivity (i.e., if our cognition involved only one faculty rather than two), then this would entail that the grasp of a unified complex representation would be reducible to a grasp of a collection of separable components. As this is not the case, and unified complex representations are irreducible, then it follows that apperception must be spontaneous.

The apperception of an intuition is spontaneous in that it is a spontaneous synthesis, or the spontaneous application of a rule of projection. Through that synthesis, or by that application of the rule, the subject grasps the intuition as an articulated complex representation. The apperception is thus holistic rather than atomistic, in that the subject grasps the intuition as a whole, and spontaneously segments it into a determinate combination of representations. In doing so, the subject thereby grasps the intuition as presenting a particular object (in our case, a particular spatio-temporal object), that is, it cognises something *in* the modifications of its sensibility. It is thus that Kant writes in the master argument that the 'manifold in an intuition' is grasped 'by my *adding* one representation to the other and being conscious of their synthesis' (B133). For to be 'conscious of their synthesis' is precisely to grasp the modifications of my sensibility as a determinate combination of representations, and thereby to cognise a particular object (i.e., to have a particular object presented to my awareness). Of course, although the apperceptive act of segmenting the unified representation into its component representations is spontaneous, it is not therefore arbitrary – I do not segment it as I myself please. For, as was argued in the previous chapter, the segmentation or the synthesis (the act of 'articulating' the sign, as it were) is governed a priori by the categories.

Hence, Kant's master argument in § 16 of the B-Deduction is that if the 'original-synthetic unity of apperception' is to be possible, then apperception must be 'an act of spontaneity' (B132) – indeed, an act of spontaneous synthesis – and thus all (our) cognition must involve the two faculties of receptivity and spontaneity. All our cognition involves the apperception of intuitions (the representations given to us through our receptivity) as the unified complex representations of particular objects. That is, it involves a grasp of a 'manifold' of representations as the unified presenting of an object – or, as all hanging together as a unified point of view. And without spontaneity, the unity of a complex representation becomes unintelligible. It is thus that Kant writes as follows in a letter to J. S. Beck (20 January 1792).

> But one may also ask, how can a content that is a complex of representations be represented? Not just through the awareness that it is *given* to us; for such a content requires a *combining* (synthesis) of the manifold. It must thus (*qua* content) be *made*. (11:314)

Here Kant is repeating the conclusion of his master argument: a spontaneous synthesis or 'combination' is demanded as a necessary condition of grasping or apperceiving 'a content that is a *complex* of representations', for mere receptivity ('the awareness that it is given to us') is insufficient. Given that all our cognition involves the unified apperception of complex representations (namely, intuitions), it follows that (α) a spontaneous synthesis is a necessary condition of our cognition. Hence, as Kant writes, 'synthesis in general is . . . the mere effect of the imagination, of a blind though indispensable function of the soul, *without which we would have no cognition at all*' (A78/B103; my emphasis).

So far I have concentrated on Kant's initial statement of the master argument in the opening paragraphs of § 16; however, he restates that argument twice more in § 16 and it is important to show how my interpretation also makes good sense of these two further versions. The first is as follows.

The thought that these representations given in intuition all together belong *to me* means, accordingly, the same as that I unite them in a self-consciousness, or at least can unite them therein, and although it is itself not yet the consciousness of the *synthesis* of the representations, it still presupposes the possibility of the latter, i.e., only because I can comprehend their manifold in a consciousness do I call them all together *my* representations; for otherwise I would have as multi-coloured, diverse a self as I have representations. (B134)

As one would expect, this version of the master argument begins with Kant's claim about the unity of apperception. That is, he tells us that the component representations composing an intuition of mine must 'all together belong to me', in that they must all be able to hang together to present something to me, or to compose my unified point of view upon the world. Given Kant's representationalism, this means that the component representations must all be able to be apperceived as hanging together – or, in other words, I must be able to 'unite them in a self-consciousness'. And this 'presupposes the possibility' of a synthesis. For, as I have argued, if a synthesis were not possible, then the components of the intuition would (absurdly) not be able to hang together as a unified representation, and I would thus, as Kant puts it, have 'as multi-coloured, diverse a self as I have representations'. In summary: all the components of my intuitions must (by definition) be able to contribute to unified cognitions, and I must thus be able to 'comprehend their manifold' via a synthesis – for otherwise they would not 'all together' be '*my* representations'. My interpretation of the master argument in § 16 is thus compatible with Kant's first restatement of that argument.

I turn now to Kant's second restatement of the master argument, which occurs at the end of § 16 and is as follows.

I am therefore conscious of the identical self in regard to the manifold of the representations that are given to me in an intuition because I call them all together *my* representations, which constitute *one*. But that is as much as to say that I am conscious a priori of their necessary synthesis, which is called the original synthetic unity of apperception, under which all representations given to me stand, but under which they must also be brought by means of a synthesis. (B135–6)

Here Kant again makes clear that his concern in § 16 is not with representations in general, but specifically with 'the manifold of the representations that are given to me in an intuition', and how it is possible for me to 'call them all together *my* representations, which constitute *one*'. This passage thus supports my interpretative claim that the master argument is focused on the necessary condition for the subject being able to grasp (or apperceive) unified but complex representations. And, as Kant repeats in this passage, the necessary condition for that 'original synthetic unity of apperception' is that the component representations must be able to be apperceived 'by means of a synthesis'. Hence, Kant's second restatement of the master argument supports the interpretation that I have developed in this section – namely, that that argument proceeds from the possibility of unified complex representations to the conclusion that apperception (and thus cognition) must involve a spontaneous synthesis.

At this point it is necessary to deal with an important objection to my claim that Kant holds that apperception is holistic (and therefore spontaneous). This is the objection that my reading is inconsistent with the very way in which Kant first states his master argument. For, to repeat that earlier passage, the conclusion of the argument was that the 'relation to the identity of the subject' only comes about 'by my *adding* one representation to the other and being conscious of their synthesis' (B133). And surely, it might be objected, this language of 'adding one representation to the other' only makes sense on the presupposition of an atomistic rather than a holistic conception of representation. However, although this criticism may initially be tempting, it is very important to be clear about precisely what Kant is saying here. For there is a crucial difference between saying that various representations are 'added together' via the act of synthesis, and saying that my *understanding* of the whole representation is the result of 'adding together' my *understanding* of each of the components. Certainly Kant holds that there are a variety of representations – that is, modifications of the mind – that are 'added one to the other' via the act of synthesis. This is akin to saying that seeing something in a picture involves 'adding together' all the lines and patches of colour (i.e., grasping them as hanging together in a certain significant way, so as to represent something). But

Kant's holism is the point that these modifications of the mind do not function as representations *for* me – that is, they do not present anything to my conscious awareness – independently of, or prior to, the act of synthesis. This is why Kant says in the line quoted from B133 that I *first* add one representation to another, and *then* am 'conscious of their synthesis'. In other words, what I grasp in my conscious awareness (i.e., the representational content of my experience) is the *product* of that act of 'adding'. Kant is saying in the master argument that I do not apperceive each of the various parts ('accompany each with consciousness'), and then add up those atoms of understanding in order to build up my grasp of the whole. Rather, the starting point for my conscious experience is my consciousness of the synthesis – that is, of the complex unity as a whole. Hence, as Kant puts it in the so-called 'metaphysical deduction',

> the synthesis alone is that which properly collects the elements for cognitions and unifies them into a certain content; it is therefore the first thing to which we have to attend if we wish to judge about the first origin of our cognition. (A77–8/B103)

That is, independently of the act of synthesis, while there exists a variety of representations (in the sense of mere modifications of the mind) there is no conscious content at all. And for this reason, synthesis is the 'first origin of our cognition' and an 'indispensable function of the soul, without which we would have no cognition at all' (A78/B103).

As may already be obvious from this discussion, closely linked to the conclusion of the master argument is another important Kantian claim: that in themselves, independently of synthesis, the intuitions have no fully determinate representational content. As Kant famously puts it, 'intuitions without concepts are blind' (A51/B75). This point was made in a slightly different form in the previous chapter, where I argued that for Kant intuitions must be non-conceptual, for otherwise spontaneity would be impossible. If intuitions were not in themselves 'blind', and had a determinate content, then apperception would have to be merely receptive. For in such a case the data or content would already be there embodied, as it were, in the modifications of sensibility, and would thus only need to be 'read off' by the mind's awareness. If apperception is to proceed in a holistic way and thus be a spontaneous synthesis, then the representational content of the subject's conscious awareness (and thus cognition) must actually be generated through that synthesis. Independently of the synthesis there is no conscious content at all.

It is important to emphasise that this claim about intuitions and synthesis is not a claim about temporal psychological events – that intuitions need to be 'processed' by some sort of 'mental machinery'. It is a conceptual point about the nature of understanding and representation, and is comparable to saying that a certain number (our cognition) is the result of a mathematical function (synthesis) applied to an argument (the modifications of sensibility). Kant, because of his representationalist starting point, conceives of cognition as the mind grasping its internal states as representations of an objective world (and thus 'seeing' objects *in* those internal states). He has argued that this grasp – this understanding of complex signs, as it were – must be the spontaneous application of a rule of projection rather than simply the 'reading off' of pregiven data. Hence, the intuitions are 'blind' independently of that synthesis – as it were, the signs in themselves do not determine their own application. It is worth remarking here that, as I have argued in the previous chapter, this does not mean that the intuitions therefore play no role in determining the outcome of the synthesis. It simply means that they do not contribute a separately specifiable component to the representational content of the subject's awareness. The subject's awareness in cognition is instead the result of the inextricable contributions of both receptivity and spontaneity.

It might be objected at this point that Kant cannot consistently make knowledge claims about intuitions (e.g., that our intuitions represent spatio-temporal particulars) and simultaneously hold that without concepts they are 'blind'.[57] This objection is, however, based upon a serious misunderstanding of Kant's position. Obviously enough, the 'blindness' thesis entails that it is impossible for us to look within, inspect our intuitions, and thereby determine what properties they have independently of concepts. But Kant is basing his claims about intuitions upon a conceptual analysis of the notion of (discursive) cognition, and not on introspection. In summary form, this analysis goes as follows. In experiencing the world we are receptive to an independent reality – let us call the representations that are thus given to us 'intuitions'. The master argument has then shown that the apperception required for a unified awareness of these intuitions must be spontaneous, which in turn entails that the intuitions cannot have a fully determinate content independently of that synthesis. In other words, it has shown that 'intuitions without concepts are blind'.

This account of Kant's 'blindness' thesis allows me to clear away three potential confusions. Firstly, the 'blindness' thesis is not the absurd (because self-contradictory) claim that intuitions are ineffable, in that they

---

[57] Falkenstein, e.g., thinks that this is a major difficulty with Kant's position (see *Kant's Intuitionism*, pp. 54–9). This is because he mistakenly thinks that Kant is reliant upon introspection.

cannot be thought of as falling under any concepts.[58] This is to confuse a claim about the representational *content* of intuitions with a claim about intuitions themselves. Intuitions are 'blind' without concepts in that their representational content cannot be specified independently of a spontaneous synthesis (the application of a certain rule of projection). But this does not mean we cannot specify the properties of intuitions themselves – such as, for example, by pointing out that they have the property of being intuitions.

Secondly, the 'blindness' thesis is not the claim that intuitions contain a mysterious but determinate representational content that is essentially unconscious or hidden from our view. Rather, Kant means that if we consider intuitions independently of synthesis, they have no determinate representational content at all – that is, there is no fact of the matter about what they represent. Now, this may appear inconsistent with Kant's definition of intuition as the immediate representation *of an object* (see, e.g., A320/B377). J. S. Beck pointed this problem out in a letter to Kant (11 November 1791), writing that 'the *Critique* calls "intuition" a representation that relates immediately to an object. But, in fact, a representation does not become objective until it is subsumed under the categories'; hence, Beck concludes, 'I am in favour of leaving out that definition of "intuition"' (11:311). But this charge of inconsistency is confused, implicitly based as it is upon an argument like this:

Intuitions *qua* unsynthesised do not represent objects.
∴ Intuitions do not represent objects.

And this argument commits an obvious intensional fallacy – like the argument

Socrates *qua* animal is not rational.
∴ Socrates is not rational.

I suspect that the same mistaken reasoning underlies L. W. Beck's claim that the '*Critique* begins with an inspectional conception of intuition and ends with a functional conception'.[59] In fact, Kant neither contradicts himself (as the first Beck suggests), nor shifts between two incompatible conceptions of intuition (as the second Beck suggests). For an intuition is 'blind' *qua* unsynthesised, and 'a representation of an object' *qua* synthesised. And

[58] Wolff (*Kant's Theory*, p. 152n) suggests that this is a potential problem for Kant.
[59] L. W. Beck, 'Did the Sage of Königsberg Have No Dreams?', in *Essays on Kant and Hume* (New Haven: Yale University Press, 1978), p. 41.

this, it should be emphasised, is not to claim that there is first an unsyn-thesised 'proto-intuition', which then undergoes a certain temporal process and becomes a fully-fledged intuition.[60] Compare the following: an object considered in itself may be a mere metal rod – but considered in its rela-tion to a certain mechanism of which it is a part, it is a gear lever. So, for example, it is quite possible to say that when I cognise a cat, I have thereby had an intuition of a cat. But it must simply be remembered that this is shorthand for the claim that my faculty of sensibility has been modified in a certain way, which I have spontaneously apperceived as presenting a cat to me. It does not mean that the modifications of my mind, in themselves and independently of the synthesis, present a cat to me.[61]

Thirdly, and finally, the 'blindness' thesis does not entail that intuitions represent 'bare particulars'. This charge is made, for example, by Richard Rorty, who claims that 'the Kantian notion of intuition [is] the notion of something which we are aware of without being aware of it under any description' – a theory which leaves us 'saddled with awareness of bare par-ticulars'.[62] This charge is unfounded, because Rorty's initial assumption is simply wrong. An intuition, independently of synthesis, is not the con-scious awareness of anything at all, let alone of a 'bare particular'; and once grasped via a synthesis, an intuition is the awareness as of a determinate object, under various descriptions (e.g., as coloured, as extended, and so forth).

An analogy should help to make these points about the 'blindness' thesis clearer. Imagine a certain sequence of bits stored on a computer disk; a programme then reads these data and applies a certain rule of projection to them, thereby producing a certain image upon the monitor screen – a situation that is summed up in the following diagram.

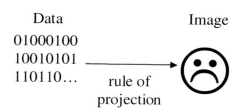

Data   Image

01000100
10010101
110110...   rule of
                  projection

[60] As is suggested in H. Robinson, 'Intuition and Manifold in the Transcendental Deduction', *Southern Journal of Philosophy* 22 (1984), 407f.
[61] Cf. Allison's response to the same problem, in *Kant's Transcendental Idealism*, pp. 67–8.
[62] R. Rorty, 'Strawson's Objectivity Argument', *Review of Metaphysics* 24 (1970), 218.

In this situation, the data are analogous to the modifications of our sensibility, and the images to the representational content of our conscious experience (i.e., our cognition). Now, the data in themselves – independently of the rule of projection that is to be applied to them – do not allow us to specify which particular image they have as their 'content'. The 'content' of the data in themselves is indeterminate, for any image one likes could be obtained from the data, depending upon which rule of projection one chooses to apply. It could thus be said, in echo of Kant, that 'data without a rule of projection are blind'. But this does not mean that therefore the data play no role at all in generating the image – that the rule of projection operates without any constraint – for 'a rule of projection without data is empty'.

One consequence of my interpretation of the 'blindness' of intuitions that I will note here is that our (human) intuitions *qua* unsynthesised do *not* represent anything spatio-temporal. For our intuitions, independently of synthesis (i.e., independently of the application of a rule of projection), do not have any determinate representational content at all – *a fortiori*, they do not represent anything spatio-temporal. Hence, Wayne Waxman is absolutely correct to argue that Kant denies 'not merely . . . super*sensible* reality to space and time, but super*imaginational* as well'; however, Waxman is wrong to conclude that therefore 'All spatial and temporal relations must then be supposed to exist only in and through imagination, and *in no way* to characterise sensations'.[63] That is, although our intuitions in themselves do not represent anything spatio-temporal, it can nonetheless be said that in themselves they do have a spatio-temporal form.

This claim may initially sound paradoxical, but it is simply an instance of the way in which intuitions can, in themselves, be 'blind' and yet function as a constraint on our experience (as explained above). As I have suggested in chapter 2, in the B-Deduction Kant argues that the cognition of all (discursive) minds must involve a category-governed synthesis. In the terms of the analogy used above, that is to say that all possible discursive minds must apply one and the same rule of projection to the data they receive. Now, Kant holds that our human cognition is essentially spatio-temporal – that is, the result of applying *the* rule of projection to *our* intuitions must be the cognition of a determinate spatial or temporal object. Furthermore, the proposition that *our cognition is essentially spatio-temporal* is true in virtue of the fact that we are human beings, and is not true in virtue of the fact that we are discursive minds. This is because other (non-spatio-temporal) modes

---

[63] W. Waxman, *Kant's Model of the Mind* (Oxford University Press, 1991), p. 14; my emphasis.

of discursive cognition are logically possible. That is, we can consistently conceive of other (non-human) cognising beings who apply *the* rule of projection to *their* intuitions, and who do not thereby cognise a spatio-temporal world. Hence, the fact that we must cognise a spatio-temporal world does not hold in virtue of the nature of the rule of projection (because that rule is one and the same for all possible discursive cognising minds); rather, that fact must hold in virtue of the particular nature of the data which we receive. That is, our experience is essentially spatio-temporal in virtue of the sort of intuitions which we are given. Now, as is well known, Kant argues in the Transcendental Aesthetic that the only possible way to explain the fact that our experience is essentially spatio-temporal is to argue that it is so in virtue of the *form* of our faculty of intuition (i.e., the mode in which we are receptive). In other words, there is something about the way in which human beings can receive data which entails that when *the* rule of projection is applied to those data, the cognition of a spatio-temporal world is always the result. It is in this sense that our intuitions in themselves are 'blind' yet also have a spatio-temporal form.

In conclusion, I have argued in this section that § 16 of the B-Deduction contains Kant's master argument for his claim (α), that all our cognition must involve a spontaneous synthesis. His argument concerns the representationalist parallel to the problem of the unity of the proposition, and is that the subject's unified grasp of a complex representation (i.e., the unity of apperception) would be impossible unless that grasp proceeded in a holistic rather than an atomistic fashion. This holistic conception of representation in turn entails that the apperception of intuitions, and thus all our cognition, must involve a spontaneous synthesis. I then argued that Kant's famous thesis that 'intuitions without concepts are blind' makes good sense, if it is seen as a further and crucial consequence of his representational holism.

SYNTHESIS, COMBINATION AND HOLISM

In this section I present two further pieces of evidence for my interpretative claim that Kant is a holist about representation, and then examine some of the further consequences this holism has for an understanding of his notion of synthesis or combination. The additional textual evidence for Kant's holism is, firstly, his Frege-like view that judgments are prior to concepts, and, secondly, the important footnote to § 16 of the B-Deduction, in which he claims that 'synthetic unities' (i.e., representations of objects as a whole) are prior to 'analytic unities' (i.e., concepts). I will discuss these doctrines in turn, and argue that they both support my claim that (*i*) apperception is the grasp of a unified complex representation (as presenting an object), and (*ii*) apperception proceeds in a holistic way – as the *segmentation* of a whole representation *into* its components – rather than an atomistic way – as the *building up* of a whole representation *out of* its components.

I begin with the Kantian thesis that judgments are prior to concepts.[64] The main textual evidence for attributing this view to Kant is as follows. To begin with, he tells us that every concept is 'the predicate for a possible judgment' (A69/B94). Now, if this statement simply meant that for every concept there could be a judgment in which that concept appeared in the predicate position, then it would say no more than what any traditional logician would agree with. For in Aristotelian logic there are no syntactic distinctions between concepts (i.e., terms) and thus any concept can appear in either the subject or predicate position of a categorical (this being demanded by the rules of the syllogistic). However, when this statement is read in conjunction with Kant's further claim that 'the understanding can make *no other use* of . . . concepts than that of judging by means of them' (A68/B93; my emphasis), then his position seems clear. If the *only* use of concepts is in judgments, then there is no separate act of conceptualisation. Hence Kant's claim that 'we can . . . trace all actions of the understanding back to judgments, so that the *understanding* in general can be represented as a *faculty for judging*' (A69/B94). This suggests that when Kant writes that every concept is the 'predicate for a possible judgment', he means that a concept is *essentially* predicative. This reading receives further support from Kant's tendency in the *Logic* (see 9:108, 111) to rewrite a categorical such as 'Every S is P' in a form something like 'Every *x*, which is S, is P' – in which both concepts have moved into predicative positions. If a concept is thus essentially predicative, it follows that the notion of a concept is only intelligible in terms of the prior notion of a judgment.

Like Frege, then, Kant is a holist about judgments. My discussion of the master argument shows that this doctrine is not an isolated theme of Kant's philosophy, but an expression of the representational holism that is a necessary condition of the unity of apperception. As I have argued, for Kant the apperception of an intuition is a spontaneous synthesis in virtue of which the subject grasps the intuition as a representation of a determinate object. And as discussed in chapter 1, this means that the synthesis of apperception results in a judgment – a cognition of the world as being thus and so. Because apperception is holistic rather than atomistic, judgments are

---

[64] This doctrine, and the parallel between Kant and Frege, is discussed by H. Sluga in *Gottlob Frege* (London: Routledge, 1980), pp. 90–5, and 'Frege against the Booleans', *Notre Dame Journal of Formal Logic* 28 (1987), 80–98.

therefore the basic units of cognition. As was also pointed out in chapter 1, this Kantian model is in distinct contrast to the Cartesian model of cognition, in which the subject begins with a conscious awareness of the content of its own ideas (an awareness which is not a judgment) and may then choose to proceed to judgment, by affirming or denying that content of the world. For Kant, on the other hand, the unity of apperception means that the minimum content of our conscious awareness is a judgment. He thus writes as follows in *Reflexion* no. 4634:

We are acquainted with each thing only through predicates which we think or say of it. Before this, any representations that are to be met with in us are to be counted merely as material [*sc.*, for cognition], not as cognition. (17:616)

That is to say, there is no determinate content available to our awareness until the synthesis of apperception. As Kant puts it here, there is no cognition until we 'think or say' certain predicates 'of an object' – that is, until we *judge*. The conclusion of Kant's master argument – that apperception must be holistic and thus spontaneous – therefore entails that he must also be a holist about judgments. For if concepts could be grasped independently of judging, then it would be possible for the subject to have conscious awareness with a determinate content that was not a judgment. And this in turn would mean that apperception could proceed in a receptive, atomistic fashion – which would make the unity of our awareness unintelligible. It is thus that the unity of apperception 'contains the ground of the unity of different concepts in judgment' (B131), for the holism that is the solution to the problem of the unity of apperception is simultaneously the solution to the problem of the unity of judgment.

The second piece of evidence for my thesis that Kant's master argument expresses his holism about representation is an important footnote to B133 – in the heart of the discussion in § 16 of the B-Deduction. This footnote is attached to Kant's remark that 'the *analytical* unity of apperception is only possible under the presupposition of some *synthetic* one', and is as follows.

The analytical unity of consciousness pertains to all common concepts as such, e.g., if I think *red* in general, I thereby represent to myself a feature that (as a mark) can be encountered in anything, or that can be combined with other representations; therefore only by means of an antecedently conceived possible synthetic unity can I represent to myself the analytical unity. A representation that is to be thought as common to *several* must be regarded as belonging to those that in addition to it also have something *different* in themselves; consequently they must antecedently be conceived in synthetic unity with other (even if only possible) representations before I can think the analytical unity of consciousness in it that makes it into a *conceptus communis*. And thus the synthetic unity of apperception is the highest point to which one must affix all use of the understanding, even the whole of logic and, after it, transcendental philosophy; indeed this faculty is the understanding itself. (B133–4n)

Here Kant tells us that one can represent to oneself an 'analytical unity' – that is, grasp a concept such as '*red* in general' – 'only by means of an antecedently conceived possible synthetic unity'. As I have argued, a 'synthetic unity' ('of consciousness' or 'of apperception') is the subject's grasp of an intuition as the unified complex representation of a particular object. Kant is thus claiming that concepts can only be grasped by seeing them as components of a representation of an object as a whole (a 'synthetic unity'). That is, concepts are not as it were independent building blocks, from which we construct complex representations. Rather, they are essentially an abstraction from complex representations of objects – that is, from cognitions and thus from judgments. In other words, for Kant (as was argued above) a concept is essentially the predicate of an object, and therefore, as he puts it in the quoted footnote, the concept 'must antecedently be conceived in synthetic unity with other (even if only possible) representations'. It is thus that Kant tells us that the synthetic unity of apperception is the 'highest point to which one must affix all use of the understanding' and that the faculty of apperception 'is the understanding itself', for it is our holistic capacity to grasp complex unified representations that makes cognition and thought possible.

At this point it may be objected that my view of Kant as a holist about representation is incompatible with the very notion of synthesis. For, it may be argued, the act of synthesis is precisely an act of building up a complex representation out of its parts, and thus presupposes an atomistic rather than a holistic account of representation. Kemp Smith, for example, thus writes that

a principle absolutely fundamental to the entire *Critique* is . . . that all analysis rests upon and presupposes a previously exercised synthesis. Synthesis or totality as such can never be given. Only in so far as a whole is synthetically constructed can it be apprehended by the mind. Representation of the parts precedes and renders possible representation of the whole.[65]

In the same discussion, Kemp Smith also argues that Kant is unable to keep consistently to this position, citing Kant's remark that 'the parts [of an appearance] are given for the very first time through the regress of the decomposing synthesis [*decomponirenden Synthesis*]' (A505/B533). According to Kemp Smith, the very phrase 'decomposing synthesis', which occurs

---

[65] Kemp Smith, *Commentary*, p. 95; italics omitted.

in this remark, is a contradiction in terms which Kant is forced to by an attempt to stitch together incompatible theses. For to talk of a 'decomposing synthesis' is as if one were to talk of an action that was simultaneously a taking-apart and a putting-together.

What lies at the heart of Kemp Smith's claims is a misunderstanding of the notion of synthesis. As I have argued throughout this book, synthesis ought to be interpreted as the act of cognising something *in* our representations. Hence, synthesis is not, as Kemp Smith is assuming, an act of constructing whole representations out of their parts, like Locke's act of 'combining several simple ideas into one compound one'[66] – as if the senses gave us the separated pieces of a jigsaw which the mind then puts together. Kemp Smith is not alone in holding this sort of conception of synthesis, as it is quite widespread even in recent secondary literature. Brook, for example, claims that Kant's notion of synthesis is primarily 'the tying of elements together into a single object or unified content of a representation' – such as occurs when the various 'dispersed representations' of a book (of its colour, shape, texture, etc.) are 'bound together' by a synthesis into a unified complex representation of the book as a whole.[67] And Howell also interprets the notion of synthesis in a similar fashion. He argues that, for Kant, an intuition of an object is a complex representation 'synthesised' by the subject from a 'manifold' of various component representations, each of which represents particular properties of that object (e.g., its colour, shape, and so forth).[68] Now, not only is this atomistic view of synthesis incorrect, but it must also be remembered that, as I have argued in the previous section, it is only via synthesis that there is any determinate representational content available to conscious awareness. That is, prior to (i.e., independently of) such synthesis, 'intuitions are blind'. Hence, it is not as if I am aware of each component as representing, and then assemble them together to form a cognition. Rather, I only grasp my inner states as representing something beyond themselves (i.e., cognise something *in* those states) via an act of apperceiving 'the manifold in an intuition' as a whole. Kemp Smith is thus wrong to say that for Kant 'representation of the parts precedes and renders possible representation of the whole'. This is to think of the relation between intuition and cognition as a relation between *parts* and *whole*, rather than as the relation between the *data* to which a rule of projection is applied (in synthesis) and the *result* of that application.

---

[66] Locke, *Essay*, book 2, ch. 12, § 1.
[67] See Brook, *Kant and the Mind*, pp. 35–7; the quotation is from p. 35.
[68] See Howell, *Kant's Transcendental Deduction*, especially pp. 214–15.

On my interpretation it is thus possible to explain both why Kant can consistently claim that synthesis is prior to analysis, and what he means by a 'decomposing synthesis'. Firstly, as Kemp Smith points out, it is indeed true that Kant holds that synthesis is (logically) prior to analysis. At the beginning of the B-Deduction, for example, Kant writes of synthesis (or 'combination') that 'the dissolution (*analysis*) that seems to be its opposite, in fact always presupposes it; for where the understanding has not previously combined anything, neither can it dissolve anything' (B130). But this is not the simple-minded thought that before we can disassemble a whole into its parts, we must have assembled that whole out of its parts. Analysis is the process by which we render the manifold of a representation more *distinct* – that is, become aware of the complexity of that representation. This is demonstrated by the 'i.e.' in the following remark: that in analytic judgments 'I need only to analyse that concept, i.e., become conscious of the manifold that I always think in it' (A7/B11).[69] Thus to analyse a representation is not to take it to pieces, but to acquire a clearer grasp of its complexity. Given Kant's holism, this presupposes a prior grasp of the complex representation as a whole – that is, analysis presupposes a synthesis.

Turning now to Kant's remark about the 'decomposing synthesis', it is clear on my interpretation that this is not, as Kemp Smith claims, a contradiction in terms. A synthesis can be 'decomposing' precisely in that it is via a synthesis that I grasp an intuition as an articulated complex of representations – that is, as segmented ('decomposed') into determinate components. For example, suppose that through a synthesis I grasp an intuition as the representation of a certain region of space. This does not mean that I have my representation of that spatial region in virtue of grasping and assembling a number of ultimate space-representing components (*minima visibilia*). Given the infinite divisibility of space, this is in any case an impossibility. Rather, I grasp the intuition as representing the region as a whole, and I simultaneously grasp that region as being potentially divisible into sub-regions *ad infinitum* (and as having a certain geometry, etc.). It is in this sense, then, that 'the [e.g., spatial] parts [of an appearance] are given for the very first time through the regress of the decomposing synthesis' (A505/B533).

Now, it might be thought that even if my interpretation is correct about this passage, it is contradicted by other remarks that Kant makes about our cognition of space, and which appear to demand an atomistic interpretation. And thus, it might be claimed, Kant is indeed guilty of the

---

[69] For further evidence, see Kant's discussion of distinctness and analysis in the *Logic* (9:35).

inconsistency that Kemp Smith charges him with. As a paradigm example of such remarks, take the following claim from the Axioms of Intuition: 'every appearance as intuition is an extensive magnitude, as it can only be cognised through successive synthesis (from part to part) in apprehension' (A163/B203–4). This remark may at first appear to suggest the atomistic picture of the mind assembling complex representations. However, to engage in a 'successive synthesis in apprehension' is to cognise the various parts of an object by scanning it, turning it over, walking around it, and so forth. And this is not to assemble a compound representation of that object in the mind as if one were putting a jigsaw together, it is rather to make a sequence of (increasingly complex) *judgments* about the object.[70] For Kant, as it were, the smallest mouthful that we can possibly bite off in conscious awareness is already the cognition *of an object* (and is thus a judgment). There is no conscious awareness of any representations that are logically prior to this, and from which the cognition of an object could thus be assembled. I thus conclude that Kemp Smith gives us no adequate reasons for doubting my interpretative claim that Kant is a holist about our grasp of complex representations.

There is one further important piece of text that may appear to be inconsistent with my interpretation of Kant as a holist about representation and which therefore requires attention: namely, his discussion of 'combination' (*Verbindung*) in the very first section (§ 15) of the B-Deduction. For it has often been thought that this discussion shows that the argument in § 16 relies ultimately on the premise that our sense-perception is 'atomistic'. For in § 15 Kant tells us that by 'combination' he means 'the representation of the *synthetic* unity of the manifold' (B130–1), and he states on a number of occasions that this representation 'cannot be given'. The relevant passages from § 15 are as follows.

(1) The *combination* (*conjunctio*) of a manifold in general can never come to us through the senses . . . for [*denn*] it is an act of the spontaneity of the power of representation. (B129–30)

(2) We can represent nothing as combined in the object without having previously combined it ourselves, and . . . among all representations *combination* is the only one that is not given through objects but can be executed only by the subject itself, because [*weil*] it is an act of its self-activity. (B130)

There is a further repetition of this claim in § 16, as follows.

---

[70] Cf. Wolff, *Kant's Theory of Mental Activity*, pp. 110–11, and Bennett, *Kant's Analytic*, p. 108.

(3) Combination does not lie in the objects, however, and cannot as it were be borrowed from them through perception and by that means first taken up into the understanding, but is rather only an operation of the understanding. (B134–5)

Perhaps not surprisingly, these passages have been interpreted by many commentators as expressing a dogmatic, quasi-empirical assumption about the limits of human cognitive powers. That is to say, they read Kant's claim that 'combination cannot be given' as the claim that human sense-perception is essentially atomistic, in that all that is given to us in sense-experience is an aggregate of isolated sensory qualities. And then, since combination is not given, it must be *made* – which thus explains Kant's demand that a synthesis is required for there to be unified complex representations. Hence, it is often suggested, the claim that combination cannot be given is one of the rock-bottom assumptions of the whole argument of the B-Deduction. Kemp Smith, for example, writes that it is 'a fundamental assumption which Kant does not dream of questioning and of which he nowhere attempts to offer proof'.[71] This assumption has then been explained (rather than justified) in terms of Kant's historical context. Henrich, for example, tells us that it is

one of the elementary assumptions that he shares with the theory of knowledge of his time, namely, that the primary occurrences of the real for cognition are presentations of simple qualities in diffuse spatial juxtaposition.[72]

And in his review of Henrich's book, A. Thomas reiterates that 'it must be born in mind that Kant's historical context is responsible for his assumption of . . . perceptual atomism'.[73] Similarly, Guyer tells us that

In both editions of the book, Kant makes it explicit that all aspects of his campaign are to be governed by the single underlying premise that any form of knowledge whatsoever involves a connection of diverse representations and that such a connection requires a mental act of combination.[74]

As their talk of 'elementary assumption', 'fundamental assumption' and 'underlying premise' makes clear, all of these commentators hold that some sort of perceptual atomism is a basic premise of the B-Deduction – 'basic' in the sense that it is not something for which Kant offers any arguments. If

[71] Kemp Smith, *Commentary*, p. 284.
[72] D. Henrich, 'Identity and Objectivity: An Inquiry into Kant's Transcendental Deduction', in *The Unity of Reason*, ed. R. L. Velkley, trans. J. Edwards (Cambridge, MA: Harvard University Press, 1994), p. 130.
[73] A. Thomas, 'Book Review: D. Henrich's *The Unity of Reason*', *Mind* 105 (1996), 707.
[74] Guyer, *Kant and the Claims of Knowledge*, p. 89.

this view is correct, then an obvious response to Kant's argument is simply to reject such a claim about human cognitive powers. As Julius Weinberg thus writes, 'an answer to Kant involves a reassessment of the "given" element in knowledge'.[75] For if combination *can* be given, then no mental act of synthesis would seem to be required, and therefore the argument of the B-Deduction would fall to the ground.

I think it is thus clear enough that if Kant's claim about combination were simply a dogmatic, question-begging assumption about the limits of human cognition, then this would make the argument of the B-Deduction much less interesting. However, this reading of Kant's claim that 'combination cannot be given' is not correct. For one thing, it relies precisely on the conception of synthesis as a compounding of parts into wholes that I criticised in the previous section. But it also has a more obvious flaw, in that it fails to make good sense of the very passages (1)–(3) in which Kant expresses his claim about combination. As I noted, the commentators cited above see Kant as simply *assuming* that combination cannot be given – of treating it as a basic, unargued premise. Their thought is then that because combination is not given, it must be constructed through a mental act (i.e., a synthesis). They thus read Kant to be arguing as follows:

Combination cannot be given – *therefore*, it must be an act.

In other words, if this representation of combination does not come in from 'outside', it must be something that the mind provides for itself, from 'inside', as it were. That this view is incorrect is shown by two little words in passages (1) and (2) quoted above: the words 'for' [*denn*] and 'because' [*weil*], respectively. That is, in these passages Kant in fact states the *converse* claim:

Combination cannot be given because it must be an act.

or, in other words,

Combination must be an act – *therefore*, it cannot be given.

Hence, Kemp Smith is simply wrong to say of the claim that combination cannot be given that it is 'a fundamental assumption . . . of which [Kant] nowhere attempts to offer proof'. A close reading of § 15 in fact reveals that Kant's claim about combination is not a basic premise or 'fundamental

---

[75] J. R. Weinberg, *Abstraction, Relation, and Induction* (Madison: University of Wisconsin Press, 1965), p. 116.

assumption', but the conclusion to an argument. Hence, the commentators that I have cited above all misread the opening of the B-Deduction, for that argument does not move from a dogmatic assumption about the limitations of our cognitive powers to the need for synthesis (if unified complex representations are to be possible).

I am not alone in rejecting the idea that Kant's claim about combination is merely a dogmatic assumption. Henry Allison also notes that this 'claim is frequently criticised on the grounds that it rests upon some dubious assumptions about what is actually given to the mind: an essentially Humean doctrine of psychological atomism or a "data sensualism" '. Allison argues that this criticism is 'misguided', because the demand for combination or synthesis in fact 'follows logically from the concept of a discursive understanding'. This is because

> even if we assume that the data is somehow given to the mind in an organised or unified fashion, the mind must still represent to itself or think, that is, conceptualise, this 'given' unity.[76]

Now, Allison is certainly correct insofar as he sees that the claim that combination cannot be given is not a basic premise of the B-Deduction. The problem is that his gloss on Kant's claim fails to explain why Kant holds this view. Kant is claiming that, unlike the grasp of a simple representation (e.g., the representation *a*), the grasp of a *complex* representation (e.g., the representation *a-in-R-to-b*) must involve a 'combination' or act of spontaneity. What thus needs to be explained is why a complex representation cannot be grasped in the same manner as a simple representation – through pure receptivity. Allison's appeal to the need for 'conceptualisation' is inadequate to account for this, because it does not explain why Kant thinks the grasp of complex representations is particularly problematic. For either Allison is claiming that the subject must conceptualise *all* of its representations – which obviously fails to explain what is special about complex representations – or he is claiming that the subject *only* needs to conceptualise its *complex* representations – which is simply a repetition of the very claim for which we wanted an explanation, only with Kant's jargon of 'combination' replaced with Allison's jargon of 'conceptualisation'. In either case, Allison fails to explain just why Kant should hold that our grasp of a complex representation must be an act of spontaneity, and thus why combination cannot be given.

[76] All quotes in this paragraph are from Allison, *Kant's Transcendental Idealism*, pp. 141–2.

In this chapter I, unlike Allison, have provided a detailed explanation of how Kant argues for his claim that combination cannot be given. For Kant's argument for this claim is precisely the master argument of § 16. This has shown that receptivity cannot account for our grasp of unified complex representations, and that therefore that grasp must be an act of spontaneity. Kant's argument does not rely on any ('atomistic') assumptions about what is given to us by our sense-perception, but reaches its conclusion simply on the basis of an analysis of the concept of what it is to grasp or apperceive the 'manifold given in an intuition'. The master argument thus concludes that 'combination' – that is, 'the representation of the *synthetic* unity of the manifold' (B130–1) or, in other words, our unified grasp of a complex representation – must be an act of spontaneity. From this it follows, as Kant has pointed out in § 15, that combination cannot be given, or, equivalently, is not the product of our receptivity.

The assumption that Kant is an atomist about representation – a view encouraged by the misreading of his discussion of 'combination' in § 15, as discussed above – is made by a number of commentators who otherwise share my general conception of the problem that Kant is addressing in § 16 of the B-Deduction. That is, such commentators share my view that Kant's discussion primarily concerns the problem of the unity of complex thoughts or representations. However, as I will show, because they all presuppose that Kant must have an atomistic conception of our grasp of representations, the 'solutions' to the unity problem that they find in Kant are no solutions at all – and their readings are thus, despite superficial similarities, quite distinct from the one that I have argued for in this chapter.

I begin with Dieter Henrich's influential discussion of the Transcendental Deduction in his book *Identität und Objektivität*, where he argues that Kant makes use of a number of distinct proof strategies in the Deduction. One of the proof strategies that Henrich finds in the Deduction bears some relation to my interpretation of the master argument, as the following passage indicates.

Now the conditions constituting complex thoughts must surely be distinguished from the conditions of the mere copresence of thoughts in the consciousness of one and the same subject. Otherwise the thought of a complex set of circumstances would be nothing other than an aggregate of thoughts – something which can well be counted as being clearly false. It follows, therefore, that a subject which becomes conscious of itself as a particular subject in relation to the elements of a complex thought must further be conscious of the way in which these elements are represented together within that complex thought. However, the way in which

elements such as these go to make up a complex thought can be properly compre-
hended only as a rule for the formation of complex thoughts. Consequently, the
consciousness that a subject has of itself appears also to include an awareness of
rules for the combination of thoughts, and it does not appear to be possible apart
from such awareness.[77]

Henrich thus suggests that Kant is arguing as follows: (1) we can become
conscious of our own thoughts (i.e., 'accompany them with the *I think*'); (2)
to be conscious of a complex thought is to be conscious of it as structured
(or synthesised) according to 'a rule for the formation of complex thoughts';
(3) consequently, self-consciousness must include an awareness of such rules
(which are, of course, the categories). Henrich, however, goes on to make
the obvious point that this proof strategy is a failure. This is because (3)
does not follow from premises (1) and (2) alone, but only if an additional
premise is added – such as that the consciousness of complex thoughts is a
necessary condition of self-consciousness.

Now, for the purposes of my discussion, the most interesting thing about
the passage from Henrich is its statement of something like the problem of
the unity of apperception. At the beginning of the passage, Henrich points
out (on Kant's behalf) that a complex thought is not merely 'an aggregate
of thoughts' that are co-present in consciousness, but that it has a certain
unity. Henrich then claims that therefore the subject thinking a complex
thought 'must further be conscious of the way in which these elements are
represented together within that complex thought' – and thus of 'a rule for
the formation of complex thoughts'. He seems to think that this response
to the unity problem is unproblematic, and this demonstrates his failure
to understand the real difficulty posed by that problem, and thus what a
solution to it must involve (i.e., holism). As I have repeatedly argued, the
unified grasp of a complex representation cannot possibly be explained by
saying that, in addition to the consciousness of its elements, the subject is
also conscious of 'the way in which these elements are represented together'.
For, no matter what special label this additional consciousness is given, it is
simply a further representation, and we are thus started on a vicious infinite
regress.

A similar blindness affects Peter Hylton's treatment of the unity problem
in Kant. As was pointed out earlier, Hylton shares my view that the Deduction concerns a problem that is structurally similar to the problem of
the unity of the proposition. According to Hylton, Kant argues in response
to this problem that

77 Henrich, 'Identity and Objectivity', pp. 171–2.

synthesis is the source of the unity and relatedness of these diverse elements [*sc.*, given in sensible intuition]. As Kant says at B130, the combination or unity of diverse representations is not something that can be 'given through objects'; the unity of representations cannot be just a further representation on a level with the others. This unity is rather the product of synthesis, which is our own *act* of combining the various representations.[78]

This is the same 'solution' to the unity problem that Henrich finds in Kant: the invocation of a special element that is not 'just a further representation on a level with the others', but something with the magical power of creating unity out of diversity. As should now be clear, this does not solve the unity problem, for what representational content does this special element – this 'act' – contribute to the unified whole? If that content is specifiable independently of the whole – as the presupposition of representational atomism demands – then this special element is simply a further representation (call it what you will) and we are started once again on the regress.

Another example of this sort of reading of Kant is provided by Robert Wolff in *Kant's Theory of Mental Activity*. Wolff argues there that synthesis is Kant's solution to the problem of the unity of diverse contents of consciousness – in particular, the diachronic unity possessed by our temporally extended experience. Like the other commentators I have discussed, Wolff thinks that Kant begins from an atomistic starting point, as the following passage makes clear.

The representation of Socrates, for example, contains the perceptions of his wit, his snub nose, his arms and legs and organs, the sharpness of his tongue, and so forth . . . Now, Hume had shown that such unities [of perceptions] can never be *given* as such to the understanding. Consequently, the mind must create them by a spontaneous act of unifying, an act to which Kant gives the title *synthesis*.[79]

He then proceeds to argue that this act of synthesis is 'a rule-directed reproduction in imagination', and that this suffices to solve the problem of unity.[80] However, his explicitly psychological approach to the argument of the Deduction means that he does not even consider the problem that I have argued is really the focus of Kant's discussion. Wolff thinks that the Deduction concerns the psychological mechanisms that must be involved in producing a current mental state that stands in the appropriate relation

---

[78] Hylton, 'Nature of the Proposition', p. 378. [79] Wolff, *Kant's Theory*, p. 68.

[80] See ibid., pp. 121–31; the quote is from p. 130. It should be noted that Wolff is in fact talking about the A-Deduction at this point, but as his later discussion makes clear, he thinks that the B-Deduction contains mainly a 'clarification of arguments already stated in the first edition' (p. 183; see also pp. 183–202).

to some set of previous mental states. But I have argued that Kant's problem does not concern such psychological machinery, but rather concerns the question of how one is to analyse the concept of representation, given that a unified grasp of complex representations is possible. And it should by now be clear that Wolff's appeal to 'rule-directed synthesis' is no solution to *this* problem. For suppose, as Wolff suggests, we have a mental state that contains the representational content of a previous set of states held together by a 'rule-directed synthesis'. The problem now, of course, is that it is impossible to specify what this synthesis adds to the representational content of the components (i.e., what difference their 'unity' makes to the subject) without falling into a vicious infinite regress. In other words, Wolff's 'solution' to the unity problem suffers from precisely the same problem as the 'solutions' that Henrich and Hylton find in Kant.[81]

Hence, whilst these three commentators share, in some respects, my interpretation of Kant's problem, none of them have a clear grasp of the real nature and difficulty of that problem, and thus none of them are in a position to see how Kant resolves it. They all presuppose that Kant starts from an atomistic view of representation, and that he then invokes the notion of synthesis in order to 'unify' these atoms. None of them sees clearly that 'synthesis' (understood in this fashion) cannot possibly solve the problem of the unity of apperception, and that indeed the whole problem is generated (and made insoluble) by the atomistic starting point. Thus, whilst these commentators share my view that Kant in § 16 is primarily concerned with the unity of complex representations (rather than with the unity of the mind or the unity of self-consciousness), the notion that the synthesis of apperception must be holistic and therefore spontaneous is completely absent from their accounts. Indeed, the very possibility that Kant might have a holistic conception of representation is not even considered. Of course, I am not saying that this fact entails that their interpretations of Kant are wrong. That is a judgment that depends upon the capacity of an interpretation to make good sense of Kant's argument in the B-Deduction as a whole. But I do hope that my discussion has helped to bring out more clearly what is distinctive about the reading of § 16 presented in this chapter. I certainly agree with these commentators that Kant's notion of synthesis is his solution to the problem of the unity of apperception. But the synthesis necessarily involved in cognition resolves that problem not by being some further 'atom', but by being a holistic grasp of a complex representation

---

[81] The same problem can also be found in Hoke Robinson's account of how one combines representations into a unity: see 'Transcendental Deduction from A to B', especially 56.

(an intuition) as a whole. It is thus the spontaneous application of a rule of projection to the modifications of the mind, or, equivalently, the segmentation of the intuition as a whole into a determinate combination of representations. And the consequence of this holistic conception of synthesis means that the representational content of our conscious experience must in fact be generated through the application of the rule of projection. Hence, if human cognition involves the apperception of complex unified representations (as Kant holds), then in our cognition we are not merely receptive but also spontaneous.

As a way of concluding this section, it is worth briefly comparing my interpretation of Kant's argument in § 16, as I have just summarised it, with Guyer's influential reading of it. Like Henrich, Guyer argues that in the Transcendental Deduction Kant pursues a number of different proof strategies. And according to Guyer, the argument of § 16 is a version of the proof strategy which runs as follows. It begins with the premise that

I . . . have *a priori* certainty of my numerical identity in all these states [*sc.*, my representations] . . . Then [Kant's] argument is that because (1) we are certain of such a connection – collective possession by a numerically identical self – among our representations, which is independent of their particular empirical content and thus of whatever particular empirical syntheses we may perform upon them, yet because (2) such a connection, like any other connection, presupposes a synthesis of its diverse elements, (3) there must therefore be a transcendental synthesis of all possible items of consciousness independent of all ordinary empirical cognition, indeed preceding all such experience.[82]

Guyer then proceeds to argue that this argument (and indeed the B-Deduction as a whole) is a failure. It is worth contrasting this reading with my own. To begin with, it is clear that, according to Guyer's interpretation, Kant's argument relies on two key premises: (1) that we know a priori that all our representations are combined as the representations of one and the same self; and (2) that any combination of representations presupposes a synthesis. Now, my reading of Kant's master argument does not saddle him with either of these extremely problematic premises. For, as I read it, that argument proceeds simply from a conceptual analysis of what our cognition must be like, if it is possible for us to have a unified grasp of complex representations. Hence, in this chapter I hope to have shown not only that my interpretation is well grounded in Kant's text, but also that

---

[82] Guyer, *Kant and the Claims of Knowledge*, p. 135. Guyer is in fact discussing the A-Deduction at this point, but his later discussion makes it clear that he finds the same argument in the opening of the B–Deduction as well. See his ch. 5, *passim*.

the argument that I find in § 16 of the B-Deduction is an *interesting* one (unlike, for example, that which Guyer finds there).

CONCLUSION

This concludes my discussion of Kant's master argument, but the argument of this chapter has been long and complex enough to warrant a summary. I have argued that § 16 of the B-Deduction contains Kant's central argument for the claim (α) that all our cognition must involve a spontaneous synthesis. Stated in his own terminology, this argument was as follows.

Premise   The empirical consciousness that accompanies different representations is by itself dispersed and without relation to the identity of the subject.

Conclusion   Therefore relation to the identity of the subject does not come about by my accompanying each representation with consciousness, but by my adding one representation to the other and being conscious of their synthesis.

In brief, this argument is that the unified apperception of a complex representation is not simply a question of being conscious of each component representation (i.e., 'accompanying each representation with consciousness'), for this does not account for how those components hang together as the subject's unified point of view. Such unity (or, the 'relation to the identity of the subject') is possible only if apperception involves a spontaneous synthesis of the various modifications of the mind. That is, it is possible only if my conscious experience is the result of spontaneously 'adding' or synthesising together various representations that are in themselves 'blind'. In other words, my cognition is not built up out of my awareness of various components; rather, the starting point for my conscious experience is the grasp of a synthetic unity as a whole (and thus the minimum representational content of my cognition is a judgment). This holism thus entails that the content of my conscious experience (i.e., my cognition) is the result of the interaction between receptivity and spontaneity. Kant's master argument is thus an argument for the truth of his 'two-faculty' model of cognition.

Laid out somewhat more formally, and put into a fuller context (although stripped of subsidiary discussion of such matters as the 'blindness' of intuitions and the priority of judgment), my reading of the master argument is as follows.

Kant's representationalist epistemology

1. Cognition occurs via the immediate awareness of internal states, or the 'modifications of sensibility'. (Kant's representationalist starting point.)
2. These internal states or representations are not intrinsically available to the subject's awareness; or, equivalently, unconscious representations are logically possible. (Leibnizian claim.)

∴ Cognition must involve the *apperception* of representations.

Complexity assumption

3. All objects of sensible intuition are represented *as* complex. (E.g., human beings must represent objects in space and/or time, and objects thus represented are represented as complex – e.g., as potentially divisible into parts.)

∴ Discursive cognition is the apperception of *unified complex* representations.

The master argument of § 16

4. If the subject can apperceive a unified complex representation, it must be able to apperceive all of the component representations as hanging together in a unity. (The 'principle of the necessary unity of apperception'.)
5. The apperception of a unified complex representation cannot be the mere receptive awareness of each component, for then the unity of that apprehension is incomprehensible. That is, it becomes impossible to understand how the component representations hang together as a single point of view upon the world.
6. This unity of apperception is only possible if the apperception of a unified complex representation is holistic rather than atomistic. That is, the subject must grasp the intuition as a unified complex whole, rather than build up that whole out of an awareness of its parts.
7. If the apperception of a unified complex representation must be holistic, then such apperception must involve a spontaneous synthesis – that is, the a priori application of a rule of projection, in virtue of which the subject grasps the whole representation as a determinate combination of component representations (e.g., in our human case, as the presentation of a certain spatio-temporal object).

∴ All apperception of a unified complex representation must involve a spontaneous synthesis.

Final conclusion (α)

∴ All discursive cognition must involve a spontaneous synthesis. QED.

This, then, is Kant's argument for (α), the first premise of the main argument of the Transcendental Deduction in B. In the following and final chapter of this book, I will give a close textual reading of the remaining important sections of the B-Deduction, in order to demonstrate how they support my overall interpretation of Kant's argument for the claim that the categories make our cognition possible.

CHAPTER 4

Judgment and the categories

In this book I have argued that Kant's central argument in the B-Deduction can be summarised in the form of two premises and a conclusion, as follows.

α. All our cognition must involve a spontaneous synthesis.

β. If our cognition involves a spontaneous synthesis then this synthesis must be governed by the categories.

$\therefore$ The categories make our cognition possible.

Or, as Kant himself puts this argument in a letter to J. S. Beck (20 January 1792): 'Since composition . . . cannot be *given* but must be *produced*, it must rest on the pure spontaneity of the understanding in concepts of objects in general' (11:315–16). In chapter 2 of this book I sketched out Kant's reasoning for his second premise (β), and in the previous chapter I argued that § 16 of the B-Deduction contains Kant's master argument for his first premise (α). This chapter continues with a reading of the remaining sections of the B-Deduction that contain Kant's main line of argument, namely, §§ 17–20 and § 26.

SECTION 17: SYNTHESIS AND OBJECTS

In § 17 of the B-Deduction, entitled 'The principle of the synthetic unity of apperception is the supreme principle of all use of the understanding', Kant discusses some of the further consequences of the conclusions reached in § 16. An examination of § 17 will provide further textual evidence for my interpretation of Kant's discussion in § 16 and, indeed, for my interpretation of the argument of the B-Deduction as a whole. This is because the text of § 17 reveals two things about how Kant conceives of his own argument. Firstly, it reveals that Kant thinks that the argument of § 16 concerns the necessary conditions of our being aware of an object in virtue of grasping an intuition – that that argument is, in other words, an analysis of the concept of discursive cognition. Secondly, it makes clear that Kant thinks that the argument of § 16 is an argument for his 'two-faculty' model of cognition – that is, for his claim that discursive cognition involves both receptivity and spontaneity.

At the beginning of § 17, Kant summarises the results of the master argument of the previous section. This first paragraph runs as follows.

> The supreme principle of the possibility of all intuition in relation to sensibility was, according to the Transcendental Aesthetic, that all the manifold of sensibility stand under the formal conditions of space and time. The supreme principle of all intuition in relation to the understanding is that all the manifold of the intuition [*alles Mannigfaltige der Anschauung*] stand under conditions of the original synthetic unity of apperception. All the manifold representations of the intuition stand under the first principle insofar as they are *given* to us, and under the second insofar as they must be capable of being *combined* in one consciousness; for without that nothing could be thought or cognised through them, since the given representations would not have in common the act of apperception, *I think*, and thereby would not be grasped together in a self-consciousness. (B136–7)

The argumentation of this paragraph is very dense, and it is important for an understanding of § 17 as a whole to be clear about the logical structure of what Kant is saying here. Hence, at the cost of some repetitiveness, it is worth rearranging the passage in a more formal way. I begin with Kant's 'supreme principle of all intuition in relation to the understanding', which states that

(1) All the manifold representations of the intuition must be capable of being combined in one consciousness.

This principle, he claims, holds because

(2) Without their being combined in one consciousness, nothing could be thought or cognised through the manifold representations of the intuition.

And this in turn is the case, because

(3) Without their being combined in one consciousness, the manifold representations of the intuition would not have in common the act of apperception, *I think*, and thereby would not be grasped together in a self-consciousness.

In other words, what Kant gives us in this opening passage is the argument:

(3) therefore (2), therefore (1).

An examination of Kant's reasoning here shows that the opening of § 17 is essentially a recapitulation of § 16's analysis of the notion of discursive cognition – of the 'principle of the unity of apperception' and the conclusion of the master argument. As was discussed in the previous chapter, an intuition is a unified complex representation in virtue of apperceiving which the subject cognises a particular object. An intuition thus contains a 'manifold' of component representations, and in apperceiving the intuition the subject thereby apperceives those components as hanging together so as to present an object. And, as the master argument concludes, this unified grasp of a complex representation is only possible via an act of spontaneous synthesis or 'combination'. Hence (3): without such a synthesis or combination, the components of an intuition cannot be apperceived as composing a unified representation – that is, cannot be 'grasped together in a self-consciousness'. Now, if the components of the intuition cannot be apperceived together in this way, then it is impossible for the subject to grasp the intuition as a unified representation of a particular object – that is, the subject cannot cognise anything through the manifold. We can thus add the following suppressed premise to Kant's enthymeme:

(4) If the manifold of an intuition cannot be grasped together in a self-consciousness, then nothing can be cognised through that manifold.

Premises (3) and (4) jointly entail (2): without a combination or synthesis, nothing can be cognised through the manifold of an intuition. Let us now add an additional suppressed premise (true in virtue of the definition of 'intuition' as a representation through which the subject is immediately aware of objects):

(5) Something must be able to be cognised through the manifold of an intuition.

Premises (2) and (5) jointly entail (1): the manifold of an intuition must be able to be combined in one consciousness. Hence, the full argument of the first paragraph of § 17 is as follows:

(3) If the manifold of an intuition cannot be combined in one consciousness, then that manifold cannot be grasped together in a self-consciousness.
(4) If the manifold of an intuition cannot be grasped together in a self-consciousness, then nothing can be cognised through that manifold.
∴ (2) If the manifold of an intuition cannot be combined in one consciousness, then nothing can be cognised through that manifold.

(5) Something must be able to be cognised through the manifold of an intuition.

∴ (1) The manifold of an intuition must be able to be combined in one consciousness.

That is to say, the component representations making up an intuition must be able to be apperceived as hanging together as a unified representation, via an act of spontaneous synthesis. For otherwise the subject would not be able to cognise an object through the intuition, which is a contradiction. This is, as I have claimed, essentially a summary of the discussion in § 16.

Kant's argument in the first paragraph of § 17 thus provides further textual support for both my reading of § 16 and for my reading of the strategy of the B-Deduction as a whole. To begin with, my reading of § 16 makes good sense of the structure of Kant's reasoning in the opening passage of § 17 – that is, of his arguing from (3) to (2), to (1). And this, in turn, is further evidence for my claim that the argument of the B-Deduction concerns the necessary conditions of our cognition – or that it is, in other words, an analysis of the concept of human cognition. As I have argued, given Kant's representationalist starting point, this is for him the question of what must be involved in our capacity to apperceive a complex intuition as the unified presentation of an object.

This interpretation of the opening arguments of the B-Deduction also makes good sense of Kant's argument in the second paragraph of § 17, which has been thought by many commentators to be problematic. This second paragraph, which is as densely argued as the previous one, is as follows.

Understanding is, generally speaking, the faculty of *cognitions*. These consist in the determinate relation of given representations to an object. An *object*, however, is that in the concept of which the manifold of a given intuition is *united*. Now, however, all unification of representations requires unity of consciousness in the synthesis of them. Consequently the unity of consciousness is that which alone constitutes the relation of representations to an object [*die Beziehung der Vorstellungen auf einen Gegenstand*], thus their objective validity, and consequently is that which makes them into cognitions and on which even the possibility of the understanding rests. (B137)

Now, there is no doubt that the argument in this passage at first gives the strong impression of committing a blatant fallacy – with its shift from the objectivity of representations *requiring* a unity of consciousness, to the unity of consciousness *constituting* such objectivity. That is, Kant may appear to be arguing as follows:

Representations relate to an object only if they have been unified.

Representations have been unified only if there is a unity of consciousness in the synthesis of them.

∴. Representations relate to an object *if and only if* there is a unity of consciousness.

And this argument certainly looks obviously invalid, for the premises only seem to license an 'only if' in the conclusion, rather than an 'if and only if'.

Several commentators have noted this apparent problem with Kant's argument in the second paragraph of § 17. For example, Henry Allison writes that in this passage

> it might seem that [Kant] is guilty of a gross non sequitur. The problem is that this principle is only strong enough to license the conclusion that the unity of consciousness is a *necessary* condition for the representation of an object; it is not strong enough to prove that this unity is also a *sufficient* condition.[1]

In order to rescue Kant from this apparent fallacy, Allison proposes that Kant is using the word object not in any 'weighty' sense, but in a merely 'logical' or 'judgmental' sense, in which 'any such synthetic unity counts as an object'.[2] As evidence for this interpretative hypothesis, over and above its capacity to rescue Kant's argument from an obvious fallacy, Allison points to the linguistic evidence

> that Kant uses the term 'Gegenstand' in the relevant passages in the First Edition, whereas, *with one exception*, he uses 'Objekt' [*sic*] in the first part of the Deduction in the Second Edition . . . [a] terminological difference [which] reflects a difference in the questions being addressed in the two texts.[3]

According to Allison, this 'difference in the questions being addressed' is, of course, that between objectivity in a 'weighty' sense and in a merely 'logical' sense. Now, what Allison omits to mention here is that the 'one exception' occurs in the second paragraph of § 17 – that is, in the very passage under consideration. Hence, Allison is suggesting that Kant, on this one occasion in § 17, is using the phrase 'the relation of representations to an object (*die Beziehung der Vorstellungen auf einen Gegenstand*)' simply as a synonym for 'the unity of representations in a consciousness' – despite the fact that, as Allison himself admits, Kant uses this phrase elsewhere to talk about objectivity in a 'weighty' sense. This fact alone makes Allison's interpretative hypothesis look extremely implausible, but another look at

---

[1] Allison, *Kant's Transcendental Idealism*, p. 146.
[2] See ibid., pp. 144–8; the quotation is from p. 146.   [3] Ibid., p. 147; my emphasis.

the final sentence of the second paragraph of § 17 makes its untenability clear. For Kant writes there that

the unity of consciousness is that which alone constitutes the relation of representations to an object [*Gegenstand*], thus their objective validity, and consequently is that which makes them into cognitions and on which even the possibility of the understanding rests. (B137)

That is, Kant does not simply say that the unity of consciousness constitutes the relation of representations to an object, for he also says that it constitutes (*ausmacht*) the *objective validity* of such representations and the fact that they are *cognitions*. Hence, Allison's reading of this passage would require us not only to reinterpret the term 'object' so as to remove any connotation of 'weighty' objectivity, but also the terms 'objective validity' and 'cognition' – despite the fact that these are precisely the terms which Kant uses in the rest of the *Critique* to talk about objectivity in the 'weighty' sense. It can thus be concluded that, *contra* Allison, the textual evidence demonstrates unmistakably that Kant is talking in the second paragraph of § 17 about genuine or 'weighty' objectivity, rather than about some ersatz or 'merely logical' objectivity. Hence, Allison's attempt to exculpate Kant from the charge of making a 'gross *non sequitur*' is a failure.

Paul Guyer is a commentator who would agree with this judgment about Allison's attempted rescuing interpretation, for he argues that Kant just does commit a gross *non sequitur* in the second paragraph of § 17. Guyer claims that there are two possible ways of interpreting the second paragraph of § 17, and that on both readings Kant's argument must be judged a failure. One can either find Kant 'guilty of mistaking a merely necessary for a sufficient condition', in which case his argument fails for obvious reasons, or, as Allison does, one can read Kant as relying on 'a stipulative redefinition of "object" which does away with its ordinary connotations of externality and independence'.[4] In this latter case, Kant's 'stipulative redefinition' either makes the categories part of the meaning of 'object', or it does not. Now, according to Guyer's reading, § 17 of the B-Deduction needs to show that the categories are necessary conditions of the unity of self-consciousness. Hence, either Kant begs the question by redefining 'object' to include the categories, or he needs to provide a separate argument to show that a consciousness of 'objects' (as he has redefined that term) entails the use of the categories – an argument which he does not provide. In either case, Guyer

---

[4] Guyer, *Kant and the Claims of Knowledge*, p. 117.

concludes, Kant's argument fails to demonstrate the required conclusion. Guyer thus writes that the B-Deduction 'sets out to derive the conditions for knowledge of objects from the conditions for self-consciousness, but instead just identifies the latter with the former', a fact which 'renders the argument of § 17, indeed the progress of the whole new deduction, circular'.[5]

I think that in fact both Allison and Guyer misread the second paragraph of § 17, and that my own interpretation of the B-Deduction can show that Kant's argument there is neither circular nor reliant upon dubious redefinitions of the word *object*. In order to understand the argument of this paragraph, it is crucial to bear in mind a point that I have repeatedly emphasised, but which both Allison and Guyer neglect. This is the point that Kant is not concerned in the opening arguments of the B-Deduction with representations in general, but specifically with the manifold of representations in an intuition. That is, he is concerned precisely with those very representations which are, by definition, those through which the subject cognises particular objects. Hence, the fundamental error about § 17 made by Allison and Guyer is that they think Kant is starting from a premise about representations in general (e.g., that we can unify them in a self-consciousness), and that he is then claiming to have *proved* the objectivity of our representations from this weak premise. When they find such an argument in § 17, it is not surprising that these commentators either attempt to weaken Kant's conclusion (by claiming, as Allison does, that Kant is concerned only with objectivity in a 'merely logical' sense) or find him guilty of a 'gross *non sequitur*' (as Guyer does). However, on my interpretation, the B-Deduction is an analysis of the concept of human cognition, or of objective experience. In other words, Kant is not attempting to prove *that* some set of representations is in fact objective; he is simply drawing out the necessary conditions of such objectivity. That is, he is analysing what else must be the case *if* we are able to grasp our internal modifications as presentations of an objective realm. As I shall demonstrate in what follows, by reading it as part of this overall project, it is possible to make good sense of § 17 without having to convict Kant of atrociously bad reasoning at a crucial point in his argument, and without having to assume that he is suddenly using old terminology (like 'object', 'objective validity' and 'cognition') in an entirely new and unexplained way. Now, this interpretation of the B-Deduction's project does raise important questions about

[5] Ibid., pp. 117–18.

the argument as a whole – in particular, about its relation to scepticism – but I will defer any discussion of such general issues until the end of this chapter, when my own reading is complete.

My claim is thus that the second paragraph of § 17 is best interpreted as a continuation of Kant's analysis of the concept of human cognition. In the light of my reading of the previous parts of the B-Deduction, what Kant is saying in this passage can be interpreted as follows. Given Kant's representationalist epistemology, I (the subject) cognise in virtue of ap-perceiving the manifold (or, component parts) of an intuition as hanging together as the unified presentation of a particular object. That is to say, as Kant puts it above, cognitions 'consist in the determinate relation of *given* representations [i.e., the manifold in an intuition] to an object'. The ob-ject of my cognition is precisely that which all the manifold of component representations hang together as representations of, and which I grasp as being presented to me by (or *in*) those representations. That is, the 'object [of a cognition] is that in the concept of which the manifold of a given intuition is united'. Now, as the master argument has shown, it is possible to grasp a manifold of given representations as a unified cognition only via a spontaneous synthesis. For without this synthesis there would be no unity of consciousness (i.e., no unified awareness of the representations), and therefore no cognition at all – that is, the unified grasp of complex rep-resentations, and thus the grasp of sensible intuitions, would be impossible. That is, the 'unification of representations requires unity of consciousness in the synthesis of them'. Now, as was discussed in the previous chapter, prior to this synthesis, and thus prior to this unified grasp of the manifold as a whole (i.e., as a complex unified representation), intuitions are 'blind'. That is, considered in themselves intuitions have no determinate repre-sentational content. Kant thus concludes that 'the unity of consciousness is that which alone constitutes the relation of [given] representations to an object'. For it is in virtue of the synthesis demanded by the unity of apperception that the manifold in an intuition becomes a cognition – or, hangs together in order to present a particular object to me.

Laid out somewhat more formally, my reading of Kant's argument in the second paragraph of § 17 is thus as follows.

1. An object is presented to the subject's awareness (i.e., the subject has a cognition) in virtue of the subject's having a unified apperception of a complex intuition. (Kant: 'an object is that in the concept of which the manifold of a given intuition is united'.)

2. This unified apperception of the manifold of an intuition is possible only if the intuition is grasped as a unified complex whole through a spontaneous synthesis. (Kant: 'all unification of representations requires unity of consciousness in the synthesis of them').

3. This spontaneity entails that an intuition is 'blind' – has no determinate representational content – independently of synthesis (i.e., independently of the manifold being grasped as composing a unified complex whole).

∴ The unified grasp (i.e., the synthesis) of an intuition constitutes it as a representation of an object. (Kant: 'the unity of consciousness is that which alone constitutes the relation of representations to an object'.)

This conclusion can also be put in terms of an analogy used in the previous chapter, in which the act of synthesis was compared to a piece of software applying a rule of projection to some data, in order to generate an image on a computer screen. In terms of this analogy, it could be said that the (potential) application of a rule of projection is that which alone constitutes the relation of the data to a particular image (as the 'content' of those data). For considered independently of a particular rule of projection, the data do not have any particular image as their 'content'.

This reading of Kant's argument explains his seemingly fallacious shift, as noted above, from the objectivity of representations *requiring* a unity of consciousness, to that unity of consciousness *constituting* the objectivity of representations. On my interpretation, this shift is not fallacious – or, at least, if it is, it is not in the trivially obvious way that the passage may at first suggest to the reader. This is because, as I have suggested, in drawing this conclusion Kant is implicitly relying on an important corollary of the master argument's conclusion. This corollary is listed above as the third (suppressed) premise, and is the point discussed in the previous chapter that, independently of their place in a synthetic unity – a unified consciousness – the manifold given representations have no determinate representational content and are thus 'blind' and without 'relation to an object'. That Kant should be relying on this claim in § 17 is hardly surprising. After all, the central conclusion of § 16 was that for the unity of experience to be possible, apperception must be an 'act of spontaneity'. And spontaneity means precisely that the subject is not only *determined in* experience, but also *determining of* its experience – that the subject plays a role in actually generating the content of its experience. Hence, as I read it, Kant's argument in the second paragraph of § 17 really does little more than emphasise the central implication of the master argument, namely, that our cognition involves spontaneity as well as receptivity.

Further evidence for this interpretation of Kant's argument comes in the following (i.e., third) paragraph of § 17. For in this passage Kant's crucial claim about the role of spontaneity, and the need for a 'two-faculty' model of human cognition, is given dramatic emphasis. Here he writes that

> the mere form of outer sensible intuition, space, is not yet cognition at all; it only gives the manifold of intuition a priori for a possible cognition. But in order to cognise something in space, e.g., a line, I must *draw* it, and thus synthetically bring about a determinate combination of the given manifold, so that the unity of this action is at the same time the unity of consciousness (in the concept of a line), and thereby is an object (a determinate space) first cognised. (B137–8)

The striking and provocative remark that 'in order to cognise . . . a line, I must *draw* it', makes it clear just how significant a result Kant thinks has been established by the argument of the B-Deduction at this point. Namely, that receptivity alone is not sufficient for the cognition of objects, because a spontaneous act of combining or synthesising is also required. For, as I have argued, if the subject is to cognise something through its internal states (i.e., if they are to function as representations for it) then this requires a spontaneous act of the imagination, an act of 'seeing in' or of applying a rule of projection, as I have put it. And this act is spontaneous precisely in that the subject's internal states do not, as it were, determine their own interpretation or projection – because if they did, the subject's unity of apperception or consciousness would be impossible. It is thus the cognising mind itself that 'synthetically bring[s] about a determinate combination of the given manifold', or, in other words, that spontaneously segments the intuition into a determinate complex of representations and thus grasps it as presenting a certain particular (e.g., a line). And therefore, as Kant writes, 'the unity of this action [of synthesis] is at the same time the unity of consciousness'. For the act of synthesis just is the act of grasping the intuition as a unified representation, and thus of having a unified consciousness or awareness (of an object).

After thus emphasising the role of spontaneity in human cognition, the third paragraph of § 17 goes on to repeat the point that this means the synthesis plays a role in constituting the representational content of our experience. Or, in other words, that the representational content of our experience (i.e., what is presented to us by our intuitions) is partly dependent upon the way in which we synthesise (or, which rule of projection we apply). For, continuing on from the passage previously quoted, Kant writes as follows.

The synthetic unity of consciousness is therefore an objective condition of all cognition, not merely something I myself need in order to cognise an object but rather something under which every intuition must stand *in order to become an object for me*, since in any other way, and without this synthesis, the manifold would *not* be united in one consciousness. (B138)

I suggest that in this passage – with its contrast between something being 'an objective condition of all cognition' and its being 'merely something I myself need in order to cognise an object' – Kant is attempting to rule out the following misunderstanding of his position. This is the view that receptivity alone (independently of spontaneity) provides fully determinate data, and that a synthesis is simply required in order for the subject to gain access to, or to be able to 'read off', these data. This would be to think of synthesis as being like the shining of a light in order to reveal colours in the dark – colours that were already there, independently of that light being shone. In such a case, synthesis, and thus the synthetic unity of consciousness, really would be merely something that 'I myself need in order to cognise an object' (or, in order to see the colours). But, as I have argued, this is not the correct understanding of Kant's doctrine of spontaneous synthesis. Synthesis is not simply a way of revealing or 'reading off' an already determinate representational content, for that content is in fact generated through the grasp of an intuition as a complex whole via a synthesis (and thus through having a synthetic unity of consciousness). Hence, the synthetic unity of consciousness is 'an objective condition of all cognition'. Kant also puts this point by saying that that unity is 'something under which every intuition must stand in order to become an object for me', a phrase which may at first seem puzzling. It might be thought that the only way to make sense of the idea of an intuition 'becoming an object for me' is to read Kant as talking here of the requirements for thinking *about* intuitions (i.e., of what is required for intuitions to become *objects of thought* for me). However, consider the following: when I grasp a spatial configuration of ink marks as the presentation of a face, it makes sense to say that that configuration 'becomes a face for me' – because I thereby come to see that the configuration *is* a face (where this is the 'is' of representation rather than the 'is' of identity). It is in this sense, I suggest, that Kant can say that when I (the subject) grasp an intuition as presenting something, the intuition thereby 'becomes an object for me'.

My interpretation of the opening arguments of the B-Deduction thus makes good sense of the text of § 17. As I have argued here, in this section Kant is primarily concerned to draw out the main idealist consequences of the master argument of the previous section. In § 16 he has argued that the unified apperception of a complex intuition (and thus a 'synthetic unity of consciousness') is only possible via a spontaneous act of synthesis. As he then makes clear in § 17, the spontaneity of this synthesis entails that the unified grasp of the manifold of the intuition constitutes the representational content of our cognition. Or, as Kant puts this point, 'the unity of consciousness is that which alone constitutes the relation of representations to an object, thus their objective validity, and consequently is that which makes them into cognitions' (B137).

INTERLUDE: SYNTHESIS AND THE INTUITIVE INTELLECT

Before proceeding to § 18 of the B-Deduction, it is worth briefly discussing Kant's notion of the intuitive intellect. This notion is mentioned in both § 16 and § 17, where Kant makes the interesting claim that the intuitive intellect, unlike our own intellect, would not require a synthesis – and, *a fortiori*, not require a category-governed synthesis – in order to cognise. By examining Kant's notion of the intuitive intellect, it will be possible to explain why he makes this claim, and therefore why he holds that our intellect does require such a synthesis in order to cognise. Hence, as well as explaining some Kantian claims that may seem obscure, such a discussion should help further to elucidate my interpretation of Kant's argument.

The notion of the intuitive intellect features in the *Critique* not as something of interest in its own right, but as a foil for the notion of the *discursive* intellect, and thus for the notion of the *human* intellect – for, as Kant writes, 'the cognition of every, at least human, understanding is a cognition through concepts, not intuitive but discursive' (A68/B93). We thus have the following taxonomy:

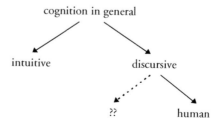

According to Kant, in other words, human cognition is a species of the genus *discursive cognition*, and this, in its turn, is a species of the genus *cognition in general*. Kant contrasts discursive cognition with another species of cognition in general, namely, *intuitive cognition*.

The essential features of Kant's conception of the intuitive intellect, and thus how this notion is differentiated from that of the discursive intellect, can be distilled through a brief survey of some relevant passages from the *Critique*. A good place to begin is with a remark in the chapter on 'Phenomena and noumena', where Kant writes that we can conceive without contradiction of an intellect that would cognise its objects 'not discursively through categories but intuitively in a non-sensible intuition' (A256/B311). Hence, the cognition of the intuitive intellect does not involve categories, but 'non-sensible' intuitions. What Kant means by a 'non-sensible' intuition is made clear by the following passage from the 'General remarks' appended to the Transcendental Aesthetic in B, where he writes that

> our kind of outer as well as inner intuition . . . is called sensible because it is *not original*, i.e., one through which the existence of the object of intuition is itself given (and that, so far as we can have insight, can only pertain to the original being [*Urwesen*]); rather it is dependent on the existence of the object, thus it is possible only insofar as the representational capacity of the subject is affected through that. (B72)

In other words, a sensible intuition occurs in virtue of the mind being modified, determined, or 'affected' by a reality *independent* of the mind. That is, to use another piece of Kantian terminology, the intuition of a discursive mind is 'sensible' in that it is a modification of that mind's faculty of *receptivity*. Hence, a non-sensible (or 'intellectual') intuition is one which is not grounded in receptivity. A non-sensible intuition is thus a representation in which the mind is not receiving data from an independent reality, but rather creating the data and thus creating that reality. Hence, as Kant writes in § 21 of the B-Deduction, an intuitive intellect would be 'a divine understanding, which would not represent given objects, but through whose representation the objects would themselves at the same time be given, or produced' (B145).

As already mentioned, Kant claims in the B-Deduction that the intuitive intellect would not require a synthesis or combination for cognition. The first mention of this claim is in the final paragraph of § 16, where Kant writes that we (discursive intellects) require a synthesis or combination because through the I, as a simple representation, nothing manifold is given; it can only be given in the intuition, which is distinct from it, and thought through *combination* in a consciousness. An understanding, in which through self-consciousness all the manifold would at the same time be given, would *intuit*; ours can only *think* and must seek the intuition in the senses. (B135)

This argument is repeated at somewhat greater length in the final paragraph of § 17, where Kant writes as follows.

This principle [*sc.*, of the necessary unity of apperception], however, is not a principle for every possible understanding, but only for one through whose pure apperception in the representation *I am* nothing manifold is given at all. That understanding through whose self-consciousness the manifold of intuition would at the same time be given, an understanding through whose representation the objects of this representation would at the same time exist, would not require a special act of the synthesis of the manifold for the unity of consciousness, which the human understanding, which merely thinks, but does not intuit, does require. (B138–9)

Kant's claim, in other words, is that we (discursive intellects) require a synthesis because through 'the I' or the 'pure apperception' alone we are not *given* any representations (i.e., any 'manifold'). An intuitive intellect, on the other hand, would not require a synthesis, precisely because through its 'self-consciousness the manifold of intuition would at the same time be given'.

From this brief overview of some of Kant's scattered references to the intuitive intellect it is possible to list the main characteristics of such an intellect, and how it differs from the discursive intellect. Left in Kant's terminology for the time being, in the passages cited above he has given us four main points of contrast:

1. The intuition of the intuitive intellect is non-sensible or intellectual; the intuition of the discursive intellect is sensible or receptive.
2. The intuitive intellect cognises objects solely through intuitions; the discursive intellect cognises only through the combination of intuitions and concepts.
3. For the intuitive intellect, mere self-consciousness suffices for a manifold to be given to it; for the discursive intellect, a manifold can only be given by the sensibility.
4. The intuitive intellect does not require a synthesis for cognition; the discursive intellect does require a synthesis for cognition.

This list of contrasts may appear to be a rather haphazard collection, which might suggest that Kant's text in fact contains no unitary doctrine of the intuitive intellect. Moltke S. Gram, for example, thus claims that 'Kant uses one *designation* to cover three very different issues, but historians of ideas have wrongly assumed that he is discussing only one doctrine'.[6] However, as I will now show, Gram's unnamed 'historians of ideas' are in fact correct, for the four points listed are not logically independent of one another, but very closely interrelated. The key to understanding them is provided by (1). As was noted above, the intuition of the intuitive intellect is non-sensible in that it is not receptive. That is, its intuition is not a representation that is dependent upon the object; instead, the object is dependent upon the representation. Hence, as Kant points out, the intuitive intellect's act of cognising actually *creates* the objects of its cognition. It should be noted that this is not the same as saying, as Gram claims, that the intuitive intellect's cognition 'is a kind of knowing in which cognitive acts and their objects are identical'.[7] As is clear from the passages quoted above, Kant does not say that a non-sensible intuition is identical to its object; rather, he says that such a representation produces or creates its object. Now, what this means is that whilst the cognition of the discursive intellect necessarily involves two faculties – receptivity and spontaneity – the cognition of the intuitive intellect involves only one faculty – spontaneity alone. To put this point another way, the intuitive intellect is purely *determining of* its experience, and never *determined by* its experience. From this defining property of the intuitive intellect, its three remaining characteristics can be explained.

I begin with (2), the point that the intuitive intellect cognises solely through intuitions, rather than through concepts and intuitions. This follows from the fact that the object of the intuitive intellect's cognition is dependent upon its representation, rather than vice versa. As was explained in chapter 2 above Kant holds the traditional view that a concept (i.e., an empirical concept) has generality precisely because it is founded on an act of abstraction. Therefore, any conceptual representation of an object is, to some degree, abstract. In other words, any conceptual representation of an object x will leave it undetermined, for some property ϕ, whether or not x is ϕ. Yet whatever exists must be completely concrete – that is, fully determinate. As Kant puts it, each thing must stand 'under the principle of *thoroughgoing determination*; according to which, among *all possible* predicates of *things*, insofar as they are compared with their opposites, one must apply to it' (A571/B599–A572/B600). This point can be illustrated

---

[6] M. S. Gram, 'Intellectual Intuition: The Continuity Thesis', *Journal of the History of Ideas* 42 (1981), 288.

[7] Ibid., 288.

by Anscombe's remark that 'I can think of a man without thinking of a man of any particular height; I cannot hit a man without hitting a man of some particular height, because there is no such thing as a man of no particular height'.[8] Hence, if the intuitive intellect could have a conceptual representation, then it would thereby have a representation that specified only certain properties of an object (i.e., would represent the object as falling under certain descriptions), and left it open what other properties that object had (i.e., which other descriptions the object could be truly represented as falling under). The object would therefore not be fully determined by the representation, and thus certain properties of that object would be independent of the representation. Yet this is a contradiction, for the object of the intuitive intellect's representation must, by definition, be dependent upon that representation. Hence, any possible representation of the intuitive intellect must fully determine its object and must therefore be an intuition rather than a concept – thus (1) entails (2). This argument can also proceed in the opposite direction: the intuitive intellect is 'intuitive' precisely in that it must represent objects under *all and only* the true descriptions of those objects, and must therefore have an infinitely detailed and complete knowledge of the objects. If error, misrepresentation or incomplete knowledge is thus logically impossible for the intuitive intellect, then the objects of its representations cannot be independent of those representations – thus (2) entails (1).

I turn now to look at (3), the rather obscure-sounding claim that for the intuitive intellect its mere self-consciousness suffices for a manifold to be given to it. To understand this claim it is first important to remember Kant's representationalism. On this epistemological view, conscious activity – that is, thought or cognition – is conceived of as primarily a type of self-consciousness (or 'apperception'), in that it is a reflexive awareness and manipulation of internal representational states. I thus suggest that what Kant means by (3) is that through the activity of its thought (its 'mere self-consciousness') the intuitive intellect generates its own data or produces its own manifold. A discursive intellect, on the other hand, can receive such data only from its sensibility or receptivity, that is, in virtue of being affected by an independent reality. Hence, Kant's claim (3) is in fact quite straightforward, and is little more than a repetition of (2).

Finally, I turn to discuss (4), the claim that the intuitive intellect, unlike the discursive intellect, would not require a synthesis for cognition. This claim also follows from (2). Kant has argued in the B-Deduction that we

---

[8] Anscombe, 'Intentionality of Sensation', p. 6.

require a spontaneous synthesis for cognition, because otherwise it would be impossible for us to grasp the manifold of representations given in an intuition as a unified presentation of an object (i.e., the unity of apperception would be impossible). Now, the intuitive intellect does not need a synthesis precisely because it is not receptive, and is thus never given a manifold by an independent reality. Therefore, its cognition is not the grasp or understanding of data that are presented to it, but rather the pure expression of an intention. In terms of the model used in my first chapter, the intuitive intellect's cognition is like the act of *drawing* a picture, rather than like the act of seeing something in an already given picture. Or, to use a semantic analogy, the apperception of the intuitive intellect is like an act of constructing a new sentence rather than an act of understanding a given sentence. Hence, as Kant puts it in a passage quoted above, through the intuitive intellect's 'self-consciousness the manifold of intuition would at the same time be given' (B138). That is, its grasp of its own internal states would not be a grasp of something independently there (the modifications of sensibility grounded in an independent reality), but rather the generation of that manifold and thus of its object. The cognition of such a being would thus be like the creation of a work of art through the power of thought alone, where its representation serves as the archetype or exemplar of the created object.

Kant's four main points of contrast (as listed above) thus express a unitary doctrine, and, as is probably already clear, his conception of the intuitive intellect corresponds to a very traditional theological conception of the divine intellect.[9] In a tradition of thought going back at least to Plato's *Timaeus*, the representations in God's mind (classically, 'ideas') were held to be 'the models of creation, themselves the primary reality, in imitation of which things are made'.[10] And God's cognition – indeed, His self-knowledge – was itself held to be an expression of His will, and thus an act of creation. That is, 'in God *seeing* and *willing* are one and the same thing' – as Descartes expresses the traditional Scholastic view.[11] And, furthermore, it was also held that '*scientia Dei, causa rerum*' – that is, that God's knowledge is the cause of things.[12] We thus reach the traditional conception of 'a simple divine nature whose unitary act of loving knowing of itself issues in a making (creating)

---

[9] As is pointed out in a useful discussion in A. W. Wood, *Kant's Rational Theology* (Ithaca, NY: Cornell University Press, 1978), pp. 84–6.

[10] R. Ariew and M. Grene, 'Ideas, in and before Descartes', *Journal of the History of Ideas* 56 (1995), 96.

[11] Descartes, letter to Mesland, 2 May 1644, in *Philosophical Writings*, vol. III, p. 235.

[12] P. T. Geach, 'God's Relation to the World', in *Logic Matters* (Berkeley: University of California Press, 1972), p. 324.

of the universe'.[13] This is essentially the same as Kant's conception of the intuitive intellect.

Hence, when Kant contrasts our discursive intellect with the logical possibility of an intuitive intellect, he is contrasting an intellect that is receptive to a mind-independent reality with one that is pure spontaneity, in that it creates the world through the act of cognition. Now, as I have explained, Kant argues that the discursive intellect must be not only receptive in cognition but also spontaneous. However, as was argued in chapter 2 in my discussion of Kant's premise (β), precisely because the discursive intellect is receptive to an independent reality, its spontaneity must be governed by the categories. For without the categories, the discursive intellect's spontaneous synthesis could not result in objective experience, and thus any sense of the discursive intellect's being determined in experience by something independent of it would be lost. The intuitive intellect, on the other hand, does not need its spontaneity to be constrained by any categories in this way, because it is not receptive. That is, the intuitive intellect's cognition creates its object, and its experience is thus objective simply in virtue of that fact alone. Hence, as Kant writes in § 21 of the B-Deduction,

if I wanted to think of an understanding that itself intuited (as, say, a divine understanding, which would not represent given objects, but through whose representation the objects would themselves at the same time be given, or produced), *then the categories would have no significance at all with regard to such a cognition.* They are only rules for an understanding whose entire capacity consists in thinking, i.e., in the action of bringing the synthesis of the manifold that is given to it in intuition from elsewhere to the unity of apperception, which therefore *cognises* nothing at all by itself, but only combines and orders the material for cognition, the intuition, which must be given to it through the object. (B145; my emphasis)

Our faculty of understanding 'cognises nothing at all by itself' because it is a spontaneity that cannot be exercised by itself, but only on what is given to it in receptivity (as I put this point in the previous chapter, 'a rule of projection without data is empty'). This difference between the intuitive intellect and our discursive intellect could thus be put in the following way. The intuitive intellect (i.e., God) *writes* the word of experience; we have to *read* it. And therefore God has a freedom in his writing that we do not have in our reading. Although our reading is like his writing insofar as it too is spontaneous, our spontaneity can be combined with receptivity (and thus remain a genuine 'reading' of what is given to us in experience) only if

---

[13] D. B. Burrell, 'Distinguishing God from the World', in *Language, Meaning and God*, ed. B. Davies (London: Geoffrey Chapman, 1987), p. 86.

that spontaneity is determined solely by the essential nature of the discursive cognising mind, and is therefore constrained by the categories. As Kant writes in the *Prolegomena*, 'the pure concepts of the understanding . . . serve as it were only to spell out appearances, so that they can be read as experience' (4:312). That is, the categories are the ways in which the discursive mind must articulate, or make intelligible to itself, the modifications of its sensibility.

It is worth emphasising at this point that Kant's claim that the discursive intellect must cognise via a category-governed spontaneity is something for which he *argues*, and not something that is simply 'built into' the definition of a discursive intellect from the outset of his discussion. Keller, for example, fails to recognise this. He thinks that the notion of a discursive intellect is defined from the beginning as something very rich and therefore problematic. Keller thus claims that 'the *Critique* as a whole can be regarded as a defence of the claim that ours is a discursive intellect', for Kant

cannot take the idea that ours is a discursive intellect in his sense as uncontested, for otherwise his philosophical critics can accept the conclusion that he draws from what is required for experience by a discursive understanding and simply deny that ours is a discursive intellect.[14]

Now, this is of course always possible, for no argument can compel the acceptance of its conclusion. However, as I have explained here, a discursive intellect is defined simply as a cognising mind that is receptive to an independent reality in its cognition, and the Transcendental Deduction is then Kant's argument that such receptivity entails a certain spontaneity (i.e., a category-governed synthesis). Hence, if Kant's 'philosophical critics' were to 'deny that ours is a discursive intellect', then this would be for them to deny that we are receptive in cognition to an independent reality – and they would thereby be committing themselves to an absolute idealism of some sort. The *Critique* is therefore not 'a defence of the claim that ours is a discursive intellect'; it is primarily an analysis of the concept of human cognition, and thus an analysis of the concept of a certain species of discursive cognition – a species differentiated by the fact that it has a spatio-temporal mode of receptivity rather than some other.

SECTION 18: APPERCEPTION AND OBJECTIVITY

I now return to my discussion of the main thread of the B-Deduction's argument, and thus to § 18, which is entitled 'What objective unity of

---

[14] Keller, *Kant and the Demands of Self-Consciousness*, p. 76.

self-consciousness is'. As the title indicates, Kant is concerned in this section with the notion of objectivity, and with clarifying the model of cognition that he has articulated in the previous sections (i.e., §§ 16–17). As I shall argue, in doing this Kant makes some important points about the nature of apperception and the nature of the spontaneous synthesis that, he has argued, makes the unity of apperception possible.

Kant begins § 18 with the statement that 'The *transcendental unity* of apperception is that unity through which all of the manifold given in an intuition is united in a concept of the object' (B139). As I hope is already clear, on my reading of the B-Deduction this is an unproblematic claim for Kant to make. For, given his representationalist epistemology, to cognise an object just is to apperceive an intuition. The unity of apperception is the unified grasp of the component representations making up a complex intuition (i.e., of 'the manifold given in an intuition'). And therefore this unity of apperception is the subject's grasp of the component representations as hanging together so as to make up the representation of a particular object (i.e., a grasp of the manifold as 'united in a concept of the object').

It is important to emphasise how different this reading of the opening statement of § 18 is from that given by two influential recent commentators – Allison and Guyer. I begin with Allison, who implies that that statement is the conclusion of Kant's attempt 'in the first part of the Deduction . . . to establish a reciprocal connection between the transcendental unity of apperception and the representation of objects'.[15] Allison's claim is incorrect because, as I have repeatedly argued, Kant is not attempting to *establish* any such thing. On the contrary, this 'reciprocal connection' is part of the starting point of the B-Deduction, for it is straightforwardly entailed by the facts that (*i*) apperception is, by definition, the subject's capacity to grasp its internal states as presentations of objects, and (*ii*) an intuition is, by definition, a representation through which the subject cognises a particular object. Allison holds that the Deduction needs to establish this 'reciprocal connection' because, as I have already noted, he makes two errors. Firstly, he neglects the point that Kant's argument is concerned specifically with the 'manifold representations in an intuition', and not with representations in general. Secondly, Allison mistakenly interprets 'apperception' as referring to the subject's capacity to make its own mental states objects of thought (i.e., the capacity to think about or cognise its own mental states). These two interpretative mistakes sever the analytic connection between the unity of apperception and the representation of objects. This in turn

---

[15] Allison, *Kant's Transcendental Idealism*, p. 144.

commits Allison to reading the first part of the B-Deduction as Kant's attempt to 'establish' that connection. On my reading, however, Kant is engaged in a rather different project, namely, an analysis of the concept of human cognition. He thus *begins* with human cognition – that is, with the unified apperception of the manifold in an intuition – and considers its necessary conditions. As I have argued, these necessary conditions are, according to Kant, (α) that our cognition must involve a spontaneous synthesis, and (β) that this spontaneous synthesis must be governed by the categories. It is the establishment of these two claims that is the focus of Kant's efforts in the B-Deduction, and not – as Allison suggests – the establishment of the 'reciprocal connection' between the unity of apperception and the representation of objects expressed in the opening claim of § 18, for that is an unproblematic consequence of Kant's representationalist starting point.

Whilst his interpretation of the B-Deduction differs in many ways from that of Allison, Guyer shares the latter's view that § 18 is the conclusion of Kant's attempt to establish such a 'reciprocal connection'. Guyer, however, has a much more critical view than Allison of Kant's tactics in attempting to establish this connection – and, ironically, Guyer thereby gets much closer to the truth than Allison does. For Guyer writes that 'in § 18 Kant just identifies the transcendental unity of apperception with knowledge of objects'; a little later, that he 'just equates the transcendental unity of apperception with knowledge of objects by fiat, instead of demonstrating a synthetic connection between them (in either direction)'.[16] Now, as should be clear, I think that these remarks are absolutely correct – Kant does just 'identify' or 'equate' the two, and does not attempt to 'demonstrate a synthetic connection between them'. Guyer, however, because he misreads the overall strategy of the B-Deduction, mistakenly thinks that this point constitutes a criticism of Kant. That is, Guyer (like Allison) holds that Kant is attempting to *prove* that there is a connection between the transcendental unity of apperception and knowledge of objects; therefore, if Kant 'just identifies' the two, then he is guilty of begging the question. On my reading of the B-Deduction, however, the transcendental unity of apperception (i.e., the unified grasp of the manifold in an intuition) just *is* the cognition of an object, and therefore Kant commits no fallacy in identifying the two. Hence, Guyer's remarks about § 18 are true, and yet their truth also constitutes (defeasible) evidence against his own interpretation of the B-Deduction, and in favour of my interpretation.

---

[16] Both quotes are from Guyer, *Kant and the Claims of Knowledge*, p. 118.

Having thus distinguished my reading of the opening statement of § 18 from those offered by Allison and Guyer, I now return to consider how Kant's argument continues. With the first sentence returned to its context, § 18 begins as follows.

The *transcendental unity* of apperception is that unity through which all of the manifold given in an intuition is united in a concept of the object. It is called *objective* on that account, and must be distinguished from the *subjective unity* of consciousness, which is a *determination of inner sense*. (B139)

The central feature of § 18 is the contrast drawn here between, on the one hand, the 'transcendental unity of apperception' or the 'objective unity of consciousness', and, on the other hand, the 'subjective' or 'empirical unity of consciousness'. Kant's discussion of this contrast is, it should be said, extraordinarily cryptic – even by his standards of obscurity. Nonetheless, it is possible to draw out the two main differences between the objective unity and the subjective unity. Firstly, as the quoted passage shows, the objective unity is a unity of apperception, whilst the subjective unity is a 'determination' of inner sense. Secondly, the objective unity is founded on a pure or a priori synthesis, and thus has necessary and universal validity, whilst the subjective unity is founded on contingent habits of association, and thus has only subjective validity.

These two characteristics of the contrast drawn in § 18 have suggested to some commentators that Kant is concerned in this section to distinguish the genuine representation of an object (an 'objective unity') from mere imaginative musing, reverie, or free association (a 'subjective unity'). According to Guyer, for example, Kant's 'subjective unity' is the unity of 'subjective states which are self-ascribed but which are not taken to represent an object, as in the case of a mere association of ideas or other idiosyncrasy'.[17] And, similarly, for Allison a 'subjective unity' is an 'imaginative association of . . . representations' through which 'nothing is represented, not even our subjective states'.[18]

This interpretation of Kant's contrast between the two unities may make some sense of what he says *within* § 18, but it fails to explain just why he bothers saying it at all at this point in the B-Deduction. As noted above, the title of § 18 is 'What objective unity of self-consciousness is'. This section can therefore be expected to consist of further clarification of the nature of such 'objective unity' – that is, of what the transcendental unity of apperception is like and what it is not like. But there seems no reason

---

[17] Ibid., p. 118.   [18] Allison, *Kant's Transcendental Idealism*, p. 154.

for Kant to take the trouble to inform us (as Guyer and Allison suggest) that the transcendental unity of apperception is not the same as a mere reverie or piece of free association. For *of course* the transcendental unity of apperception is not the same as this – and this fact would be clear on even the most superficial acquaintance with the text of the B-Deduction. Hence, the reading of the contrast in § 18 given by Guyer and Allison entails that Kant spends an entire section of the B-Deduction pointlessly insisting on a patently obvious difference.

A better interpretation of § 18 will be one that provides an adequate explanation of just why Kant should have felt it necessary to distinguish between the two different types of unity – 'objective' and 'subjective' – at this point in his argument, and explains how this distinction contributes to the overall project of the B-Deduction. Now, it seems reasonable to suggest that Kant draws this distinction because he believes that we (the readers) may be tempted to confuse the transcendental unity of apperception with the 'subjective unity of consciousness', and that it is important to forestall such a confusion. The precise nature of this potential confusion is, I shall argue, as follows. What Kant refers to as the 'subjective unity of consciousness' is something that, in a standard representationalist account of cognition, is supposed to be the representation of an object. Hence, in § 18 Kant is attempting to ensure that this standard view is not confused with the analysis of cognition and the representation of an object that he has articulated in the previous sections of the B-Deduction. As I shall now show, this interpretative suggestion makes good sense of much of what Kant says in § 18 about the distinction between the two unities.

I have suggested that what Kant calls the 'subjective unity of consciousness' is what one familiar representationalist account would consider to be the representation of an object. An example of such an account is provided by Locke, who writes in the *Essay* that the mind 'takes notice that a certain number of . . . simple *ideas* go constantly together; which, being presumed to belong to one thing, . . . are called, so united in one subject, by one name', and that the complex idea of a thing is thus 'the complication or collection of those several simple ideas of sensible qualities'.[19] The same essential thought, in an idealist setting, can also be found in Berkeley, who writes that 'for example, a certain colour, taste, smell, figure, and consistence having been observed to go together, are accounted one distinct thing, signified by the name *apple*'.[20] Now, despite their disagreements over

---

[19] Locke, *Essay*, book 2, ch. 23, §§ 1 and 4.
[20] G. Berkeley, *A Treatise Concerning the Principles of Human Knowledge*, § 1, in *New Theory of Vision and other Writings*, p. 113.

matters such as whether or not the complex idea of an object includes the idea of a 'substratum', Locke and Berkeley are thus proposing the same general analysis of what it is to represent an object. This analysis has two components: firstly, to represent an object is to be aware of a certain unified 'complication or collection' of ideas; secondly, the various ideas composing this collection hang together as the representation of a single object in virtue of the mind's past experience – that is, because the mind has 'taken notice' or 'observed' that those ideas 'go constantly together' in its experience. In a slight departure from the language used by Locke and Berkeley, this is effectively to say that the various ideas hang together as the complex idea of an object in virtue of the mind *associating* them with one another. So, Locke and Berkeley thus provide us with a familiar account of what it is to represent (or, have the idea of) an object: it is to be aware of a certain collection of associated ideas.

This account of what it is to represent an object corresponds closely with how Kant defines the notion of a subjective unity of consciousness in § 18. The first part of this definition is, as noted above, that the subjective unity of consciousness is a 'determination of inner sense'. Inner sense is that faculty of receptivity whereby the subject intuits its own mental states, and intuitions are those representations through which the subject cognises. Therefore the subjective unity of consciousness is the subject's unified cognition of a collection of its own internal perceptual states. Now, the second part of Kant's definition is that the subjective unity of consciousness is founded on habits of association. It thus follows that the subjective unity is the subject's unified cognition or awareness of a collection of associated perceptual states or ideas. Hence, all 'representations of objects' on the Locke–Berkeley model are what Kant refers to as 'subjective unities of consciousness'. This supports my interpretative hypothesis that Kant's primary concern in § 18 is to distinguish his own view of what it is to represent an object (as argued in §§ 16–17) from what I have called the 'Locke–Berkeley' view. This is not to suggest that Kant necessarily had Locke or Berkeley specifically in mind in § 18. For, given certain representationalist assumptions, their view is a very natural one to take. Perhaps more importantly, it is also a view which could be confused with Kant's own.

That such a confusion is a tempting one, and therefore one which Kant would be concerned to forestall in § 18, can be shown as follows. As I have argued, it follows from Kant's representationalist epistemology that to represent an object is, as he has repeated at the very beginning of § 18, to have a unified grasp or apperception of the manifold in an intuition – that is, it is to have a transcendental unity of apperception or an 'objective unity of consciousness'. Now, as I argued in my previous chapter, Kant holds (*i*) that there is an important distinction between inner sense and apperception, and (*ii*) that this distinction is often neglected. As he writes in § 24 of the B-Deduction, 'it is customary in the systems of psychology to treat *inner sense* as the same as the faculty of *apperception* (which we carefully distinguish)' (B153). Inner sense is the subject's capacity to intuit its own internal states, and thereby to make them objects of its self-cognition. Apperception, on the other hand, is the subject's reflexive grasp of an internal state as the presentation of something. That is, it is that act in virtue of which the internal state functions as the subject's point of view on the world. As I have previously discussed, Kant is in a position to make this distinction between inner sense and apperception – with its concomitant distinction between cognising one's inner states and cognising something *in* those states – because of his rich, non-reductive conception of representation. A reductive conception of representation leaves no room for this distinction, and one is thereby left with a standard form of representationalism in which all experience must begin with the cognition of one's internal perceptual states or 'ideas'. Hence, if one were to hold a reductive conception of representation, then one would collapse (the unity of) apperception into (the unity of) inner sense. One would thereby read Kant as saying in §§ 16–17 that to represent an object is to be aware of a certain collection of one's own perceptual states or ideas. In other words, there is a strong temptation to confuse Kant's position with the standard view held by representationalists such as Locke and Berkeley. That is, in Kant's terminology, there is a strong temptation to confuse the 'objective unity of consciousness' with the 'subjective unity of consciousness'. There is thus good reason for Kant to spend a section of the B-Deduction in clarifying the distinction between these two unities.

Further textual evidence for my reading of § 18 is provided by a closer examination of the two ways in which Kant distinguishes the objective from the subjective unity of consciousness. As was noted above, these two ways are as follows. Firstly, the objective unity is a unity of apperception, whilst the subjective unity is a unity of inner sense. Secondly, the objective unity is founded on a pure or a priori synthesis (and thus has necessary and universal validity), whilst the subjective unity is founded on contingent habits of association (and thus has only subjective validity). In other words, in order to distinguish his own account of what it is to represent an object from the 'Locke–Berkeley' view with which it could be confused, Kant is making two points. Firstly, the objective unity – unlike the subjective unity – is not the unified awareness of a collection of internal states (i.e., a unity of inner sense), but the awareness of something *in* those internal states (i.e., a unity of apperception). Secondly, the various representations hanging together in the objective unity – unlike the various ideas hanging together in the subjective unity – do not hang together in virtue of being associated with one another, but in virtue of being grasped via a synthesis that does not depend upon any contingent facts about the subject's psychology.

I begin with a consideration of Kant's first point, which is essentially an insistence that apperception not be confused with inner sense. The significance of this point – which was emphasised in my previous chapter – comes out in two remarks that Kant makes in § 18. Firstly, he writes there that, unlike the objective unity, 'the empirical [or "subjective"] unity of consciousness, through association of the representations, itself concerns an appearance' (B139–40). And secondly, he writes that the subjective (or 'empirical') unity of consciousness 'is also derived only from the former [*sc.*, the objective unity of consciousness], under given conditions *in concreto*' (B140). These two remarks can be explained as follows. The subjective unity of consciousness is the subject's cognition of its own internal states via its inner sense. As a species of cognition, that subjective unity thus presupposes the unified apperception of the manifold in an intuition (i.e., of the modifications of inner sense). As Kant thus writes in § 24:

Apperception and its synthetic unity is so far from being the same as the inner sense that the former, rather, as the source of all combination, applies to all sensible intuition of objects in general, to the manifold of *intuitions in general* [thus both inner and outer], under the name of the categories. (B154)

The subjective unity is thus 'derived only from' the objective unity. Furthermore, it also follows that the subjective unity (i.e., our inner experience) does not possess some special immediacy that outer experience lacks. That is, just like outer experience, inner experience 'itself concerns an appearance' – for it is, just like outer experience, mediated by our mode of intuition and by the categories applied in the act of apperception.

Hence, one of the central points that Kant is making in § 18 is that his analysis of human cognition entails that inner experience (or, the 'subjective unity of consciousness') does not in fact enjoy the kind of privileged position – the immediacy and the epistemological priority – that it enjoys according to standard representationalist accounts (such as the 'Locke–Berkeley' model). On Kant's view, inner experience is not the starting point for all cognition, but simply another species of cognition, with no more claim to priority than outer experience. (Indeed, in the Refutation of Idealism, Kant will argue that in fact outer experience possesses a kind of priority, but this later argument does not concern me here.) In § 18 Kant is thus clarifying his notion of apperception, by pointing out that although the unity of apperception is the starting point of all cognition, it is not to be confused with the conscious apprehension of a collection of private data or 'ideas'. That is, the transcendental unity of apperception is not to be confused with the subjective unity of consciousness. This in turn is preparing the ground for the deeply anti-Cartesian account of judgment that he gives in § 19. For there, as I will discuss in detail below, Kant claims that the unified grasp or apperception of the manifold in an intuition is not a representation or awareness that is prior to judgment, and upon which judgment is founded, but is itself an act of judging. That is, as I have argued in the previous chapter, Kant holds that our cognition does not begin with the conscious awareness of private data ('determinations of inner sense'), from which our cognition of the world is built up. Rather, his holism about representation entails that the starting point for conscious experience is with judgments about the objective realm (whether about things in space or about one's own psychological states). Or, as I have also put this point, our experience does not begin with the awareness of our own internal modifications (i.e., with the unity of inner sense), but with the awareness of things – appearances – *in* our internal modifications (i.e., with the unity of apperception).

I now turn to consider the second way in which Kant distinguishes the objective unity from the subjective unity – that is, his point that the objective unity must be founded on a pure synthesis rather than on contingent habits of association. In § 18 he writes, for example, that 'the empirical [or "subjective"] unity of consciousness, through association of the representations . . . is entirely contingent' whilst the manifold of an intuition is grasped in an objective unity 'solely . . . through the pure synthesis of the understanding' (B140). He thus concludes that the subjective unity, unlike the objective unity,

has merely subjective validity. One person combines the representation of a certain word with one thing, another with something else; and the unity of consciousness in that which is empirical is not, with regard to that which is given, necessarily and universally valid. (B140)

This last phrase echoes Kant's remark in the *Prolegomena* (discussed in chapter 2) that 'the objective validity of a judgment of experience means nothing other than its necessary universal validity' (4:298). Kant is insisting in § 18 that the spontaneous synthesis – through which an intuition is apperceived as the presentation of an *objective* world – cannot be based upon the habits of association appealed to in the empiricist (or 'Locke–Berkeley') model of representing objects. Instead, that synthesis must be pure or non-empirical. For only if it is thus 'necessarily and universally valid', rather than having 'merely subjective validity', can it generate genuine objective experience or cognition.

The reasoning that underlies this claim was discussed in chapter 2, but it is worth recapitulating it here. Habits of association are contingent psychological features of an individual cognising mind. If the spontaneous synthesis of apperception were based upon such contingent features of the subject, then the 'cognition' resulting from that synthesis would degenerate into mere fantasising or ego projection. That is, as Kant notes in the passage just quoted, such a unity of consciousness would have 'merely subjective validity'. To put this point another way, if the content of the subject's experience (which is generated by the synthesis) were dependent upon the personal psychology of the subject, then the subject's experience would no longer be a point of view upon an objective world – in which, for example, things stood in certain spatial relations to one another independently of what any particular perceiver happens to think, and independently of the past experience of any particular perceiver (etc.). Certainly, Kant holds that the objects of our experience are appearances or phenomena – that is, mind dependent – but they are dependent upon the nature of the human mind *in general*, not upon the nature of any *particular* human mind (or minds). Hence, as Kant puts it in § 18, the spontaneous synthesis required by his account of discursive cognition must be pure, or non-empirical, so that it generates a unity of consciousness that is 'necessarily and universally valid'. That is, the experience (i.e., the 'unity of consciousness') generated by the act of synthesis from the given data (i.e., the 'manifold in an intuition') is objective (i.e., 'necessarily and universally valid') only if the synthesis is determined solely by features common to *any possible* discursive mind. Hence, the spontaneous synthesis can produce objective experience or cognition from the given data only if that synthesis is grounded solely upon non-contingent – that is, essential – facts about the subject.

To conclude, I have argued that in § 18 of the B-Deduction Kant is primarily concerned to distinguish his account of human cognition (as given in §§ 16–17) from a familiar representationalist model with which it could be confused. In doing so, he makes two important claims. The first point he makes is that the notion of apperception is not to be confused with the notion of inner sense, and thus that cognition is not grounded upon a prior awareness of the mind's internal states. Hence, unlike standard forms of representationalism, Kant's own view does not treat inner experience as enjoying a special epistemological priority and immediacy over outer experience. For apperception, as I have argued, is not the awareness of a subjective realm of 'ideas' but rather the grasp of one's internal modifications as constituting a point of view upon an objective world (a world which includes both outer objects, i.e., things in space, and inner objects, i.e., psychological states). That is, apperception is the grasp of one's internal states as *Vorstellungen* – as functioning to put a world before the mind. The second point that Kant makes in § 18 is that there is an important criterion that must be met by the spontaneous synthesis of apperception if that synthesis is to generate that 'cognition of objects which is called experience' (B1) – that is, if it is to be possible for us to grasp our internal states as constituting a point of view on an objective world. This criterion is that that synthesis, although spontaneous – that is, grounded upon the nature of the subject rather than upon the nature of the given data – cannot be based upon contingent psychological features of the subject, but must instead be necessarily and universally valid. As should be clear from my discussion in chapter 2, this is a key step towards establishing Kant's premise (β), that if our cognition involves a spontaneous synthesis then this synthesis must be governed by the categories. The next step in Kant's argument is given in § 19 of the B-Deduction, to which I now turn.

SECTION 19: APPERCEPTION AND JUDGMENT

Section 19 of the B-Deduction is ponderously entitled 'The logical form of all judgments consists in the objective unity of the apperception of the concepts contained therein'. In this section, Kant tells us that the act of cognising is essentially an act of *judging*. In order to make clear the point and significance of this claim, it is worth briefly recalling the two main results that Kant believes himself to have established in §§ 16–18. Firstly, the cognising subject can grasp a complex of given representations (i.e., the manifold in an intuition) as the unified presentation of an object (i.e., in the transcendental unity of apperception) only via a spontaneous act of synthesis. Secondly, that act of spontaneity can produce the cognition of an objective (albeit phenomenal) realm only if the synthesis is necessarily and universally valid – that is, only if it is grounded solely on essential, rather than contingent, features of the cognising discursive mind. Now, up to this stage in Kant's analysis the cognising discursive mind has been characterised as a mind that spontaneously synthesises the manifold given in an intuition, and thereby apperceives that intuition as the presentation of an object. In § 19 Kant then makes the point that this act of cognition can also be characterised as an act of judging, and that therefore the cognising discursive mind is essentially a judging mind. Hence, as was noted in chapter 2, the essential features of the cognising discursive mind are given by the essential structure – that is, the logical form – of judgment. Kant's claim in § 19 is thus a crucial step towards demonstrating the truth of his premise (β), namely, that the categories – the possible logical forms of judgment – ground or determine the spontaneous synthesis involved in discursive cognition.

Having clarified the principal role of § 19 in the overall argument of the B-Deduction, I now turn to discuss the text in detail. Kant begins by asking what a judgment is, and, in particular, what relation holds between the representations composing a judgment. He then writes as follows.

> I find that a judgment is nothing other than the way to bring given cognitions to the *objective* unity of apperception. That is the aim of the copula *is* in them: to distinguish the objective unity of given representations from the subjective. For this word designates the relation of the representations to the original apperception and its *necessary unity*, even if the judgment itself is empirical, hence contingent, e.g., Bodies are heavy. By that, to be sure, I do not mean to say that these representations *necessarily* belong *to one another* in the empirical intuition, but rather that they belong to one another *in virtue of the necessary unity* of the apperception in the synthesis of intuitions, i.e., in accordance with principles of the objective determination of all representations insofar as cognition can come from them, which principles are all derived from the principle of the transcendental unity of apperception. Only in this way does there arise from this relation *a judgment*, i.e., a relation that is *objectively valid*, and that is sufficiently distinguished from the relation of these same representations in which there would be only subjective validity, e.g., in accordance with laws of association. In accordance with the latter I could only say: When I carry a body, I feel a pressure of weight; but not: It, the body, *is* heavy; which would be to say that these two representations are combined in the object, i.e., regardless of any difference in the condition of the subject, and are not merely found together in perception (however often as that might be repeated). (B141–2)

Three main features of this complex passage need to be discussed. Firstly, there is Kant's initial and fundamental claim that the act of judging just is the act of 'bringing given cognitions to the objective unity of apperception'. Secondly, there is his use of the notion of necessity, and, in particular, of the notion of 'necessary unity'. Thirdly, closely linked with the previous point, there is Kant's use of the contrast – which he introduced in § 18 – between the 'objective' and 'subjective' unity of consciousness. I will discuss these three points in turn.

I begin with the first point: Kant's opening statement that 'a judgment is nothing other than the way to bring given cognitions to the objective unity of apperception'. On my interpretation of the argument of the B-Deduction, this claim makes good sense, for it is already implicit in Kant's conception of representation and apperception. To bring given representations to the objective unity of apperception just is to grasp (i.e., apperceive) those representations as the unified presentation of an object. It is, in other words, the subject's act of cognising something *in* its internal modifications. Hence, through this act of bringing representations to the objective unity of apperception, the representations come to function as the subject's point of view on an objective world. That is, through this unified apperception the subject grasps the world as being thus and so – and thereby makes a judgment.

It is important to emphasise how this claim about judgment in § 19 supports my general interpretation of Kant's representationalism, and, in particular, my interpretation of his distinction between apperception and inner sense. As in § 18, what is under attack here is the familiar representationalist idea that cognition is ultimately founded upon an immediate awareness of one's own 'ideas'. An example of such a view is the 'two-stage' Cartesian model of cognition, which I discussed in chapter 1. In this model, the starting point for cognition is an immediate, indubitable awareness of the contents of one's own ideas – which are mental states, the *esse* of which is *percipi*. On the basis of such subjective awareness, one can then choose whether or not to proceed to make (potentially erroneous) judgments about the objective world – that is, the world of objects that are recognition transcendent, or independent of one's ideas. Hence, on the Cartesian model, our intentional awareness of the objective world via judgment is built upon a prior non-intentional awareness of our own ideas. Now, by equating the act of grasping representations in an objective unity of apperception with the act of judgment, Kant makes it clear that apperception is not to be identified with the immediate awareness of one's internal states or 'ideas', but with the cognition of an objective world *in* those internal states. Indeed, since apperception is a necessary precondition of all conscious experience, for Kant there can be no such immediate awareness of our ideas; as his holism about representation demands, all conscious awareness is in the form of judgments. Hence, the opening statement of § 19 represents a significant departure from Cartesian-style representationalism, namely, Kant's insistence that our conscious experience is intentional from the ground up.

I now turn to discuss the second feature of § 19 that requires explanation: Kant's claim that the objective unity of apperception has a *necessary* unity.

This has suggested to at least one commentator (namely, Guyer) that Kant is making the absurd claim in § 19, that every judgment is 'a claim to knowledge of *necessity*'.[21] It is clear that Kant himself saw the danger of being misinterpreted in this way, for he notes in the passage that his claim about necessary unity holds

> even if the judgment itself is empirical, hence contingent, e.g., Bodies are heavy. By that, to be sure, I do not mean to say that these representations *necessarily* belong *to one another* in the empirical intuition, but rather that they belong to one another *in virtue of the necessary unity* of the apperception in the synthesis of intuitions, i.e., in accordance with principles of the objective determination of all representations insofar as cognition can come from them, which principles are all derived from the principle of the transcendental unity of apperception. (B142)

Kant thus insists that his claim about the necessary unity of apperception is not to be confused with a claim about the modal status of the proposition asserted in an act of judgment. As Kant puts it in the quoted passage, he is not saying that the representations grasped together in a cognition 'necessarily belong to one another'. What he is instead saying is that they 'belong to one another in virtue of the necessary unity of the apperception in the synthesis of intuitions' – a phrase which makes it clear that what is under discussion is the problem of the unity of complex representations. That is, Kant is claiming that representations hang together as parts of a unified complex representation of an object (i.e., a cognition) in virtue of the 'necessary unity of apperception'.

This claim follows straightforwardly from Kant's argument in the B-Deduction. Firstly, he has argued that a manifold of internal states is grasped as (or, segmented into) a determinate complex of representations via a spontaneous synthesis. And secondly, he has argued that this synthesis can result in a representation of something objective only if the synthesis is necessarily and universally valid. That is to say, via an act of synthesis, the subject apperceives a certain 'manifold' of its internal states as a complex of representations that hang together in a unity to present an object to its awareness. Those representations therefore 'belong to one another', as parts of one and the same cognition, in virtue of the unity of apperception – that is, in virtue of the grasp of the manifold of internal states as a certain unified representation. This unity of apperception is necessary, not in that it is 'a claim to knowledge of necessity' (as Guyer suggests), but in that this is how the subject *must* apperceive its internal states, if its representation is not to degenerate into something merely personal and arbitrary, with no

---

[21] Guyer, *Kant and the Claims of Knowledge*, p. 119.

claim to objective validity. This thus explains why Kant also says in the passage quoted above that the representations in a cognition hang together 'in accordance with principles of the objective determination of all representations insofar as cognition can come from them'. For a cognition is the product of a spontaneous synthesis, and therefore the representational content of the cognition is in part determined by the nature of that synthesis – that is, by the method of projection applied to the intuitive data. If that synthesis is to produce genuine cognition (i.e., an objectively valid claim) then it must proceed 'in accordance with principles of the objective determination of all representations'. Hence, the representational content of the cognition (i.e., which representations it contains and how they hang together in a unity) will also be in accordance with such principles – in other words, with the categories.

This leads me to the third important feature of § 19: Kant's use of the contrast (introduced in § 18) between the objective and subjective unity of consciousness. I discussed this distinction above, where I argued that Kant is using it to contrast the following conceptions of representing an object. Firstly, there is his own view that to represent an object is to have an objective unity of consciousness – that is, to apperceive a manifold of internal states, and thus to cognise something *in* those states (i.e., to grasp them as presenting an object). Secondly, there is what I have called the 'Locke–Berkeley' view, that to represent an object is to have a subjective unity of consciousness – that is, to be aware of a collection of associated perceptual states. I hope to show how this interpretation of Kant's contrast receives further support from the text of § 19. In this section, Kant first tells us that 'the aim of the copula *is*' is 'to distinguish the objective unity of given representations from the subjective'. This contrast is then illustrated in the latter part of § 19, when he writes that only if representations are grasped as related together in a necessary unity of apperception (and thus 'in accordance with principles of the objective determination of all representations'),

does there arise from this relation *a judgment*, i.e., a relation that is *objectively valid*, and that is sufficiently distinguished from the relation of these same representations in which there would be only subjective validity, e.g., in accordance with laws of association. In accordance with the latter I could only say: When I carry a body, I feel a pressure of weight [*wenn ich einen Körper trage, so fühle ich einen Druck der Schwere*]; but not: It, the body, *is* heavy [*er, der Körper, ist schwer*]; which would be to say that these two representations are combined in the object, i.e., regardless of any difference in the condition of the subject, and are not merely found together in perception (however often as that might be repeated). (B142)

This passage is largely a repetition of what Kant has already told us both in § 18 and in the earlier part of § 19. Firstly, he is again emphasising the difference between his model of representing objects and the 'Locke–Berkeley' model. To grasp representations in an objective unity of consciousness is not simply to be aware of an associated collection of internal states – it is to cognise an object *in* one's internal states, and thus to make a *judgment* about that object. Secondly, Kant is also repeating his earlier point, that the unified apperception of representations (i.e., the objective unity of consciousness) cannot be grounded upon contingent psychological features of the cognising subject – such as habits of association founded upon the subject's particular course of past experience – if that unity of consciousness is to be a genuine cognition (i.e., an objectively valid claim). Any synthesis based upon such contingent features will generate a representation that has, as Kant notes in this passage, only subjective validity – that is, something which is personal and arbitrary, with no claim to constitute a point of view upon an objective world.

At this point it is worth responding to a criticism that has been made of Kant's definition of judgment in the above passage – namely, that that definition is inconsistent with the possibility of making judgments about our own mental states. This criticism has been made, for example, by Howell, who writes as follows.

If Kant takes a judgment to be an objectively valid relation of representations to an object distinct from any intuition-elements whatsoever, then he rules out the possibility of any judgment by *H* [i.e., the subject] that is about merely the (subjective) organisation of intuition-elements or other representations in *H*'s mind. But, as many readers have noticed, in his 'If I support a body' example he himself surely gives just such a judgment. And there are obviously many other such judgments, for we all can describe accurately much of the course of our own sequences of representations.[22]

This is not a valid criticism of Kant's position, because it presupposes precisely the (Cartesian) conception of inner, subjective experience that Kant has attacked in both § 18 and § 19 of the B-Deduction. Howell is assuming that Kantian phrases like 'object' and 'objectively valid' refer to external things distinct from the mind – as opposed to mental states, which are merely 'subjective' – and thus infers that Kant's definition of judgment (as a claim with 'objective validity') rules out the possibility of any judgments about mental states. But, as should be clear from my

22 Howell, *Kant's Transcendental Deduction*, p. 268.

previous discussions of this point, Howell's initial assumption is wrong. For Kant the contrast between subjective and objective does not line up with the contrast between inner and outer experience, as it does in the Cartesian model of cognition.[23] Rather, that which is subjective is that which is dependent upon contingent features of the individual cognising mind, whilst that which is objective is that which is independent of such contingent facts, and dependent only upon *essential* features of the cognising mind. Hence, for Kant, both psychological states (i.e., the objects of inner sense) and things in space (i.e., the objects of outer sense) are features of the objective world. That is, the subject's experience of those objects has objective validity, and is not something with merely subjective validity (i.e., a mere ego projection, spun out of the subject's own mind). Hence, Kant's definition of judgment in § 19 is perfectly compatible with the possibility of making judgments about our own mental states.

Although Howell's main criticism of the account of judgment in § 19 is thus mistaken, he does raise the more general question of just what the relation of the first example ('If I support a body . . .', as Howell renders it) is to Kant's account. To recall the passage from § 19 quoted above, Kant tells us there that if the relation of the representations to one another was merely 'subjectively valid' and 'in accordance with laws of association', then I (the subject) 'could only say'

(1) When I carry a body, I feel a pressure of weight.

and not

(2) It, the body, *is* heavy.

Now, it might seem that Kant intends this as an example of the contrast between a relation of representations that does not constitute a judgment, and one that does. And the obvious objection to this is that *both* are judgments – and that, in fact, (1) is a much more complex and sophisticated judgment than (2). It might thus be tempting to conclude, with Allison, that Kant's example is simply inept, for the 'difference between [(1) and (2)] is not relevant to the conception of judgment which Kant is here trying to explicate'.[24] This rejection is, however, too swift. One way to rescue Kant's example is to argue that (1) is intended merely as a way of illustrating or pointing to something that is not in fact a judgment (e.g., a mere *feeling* of

[23] Cf. M. D. Wilson, 'Kant and "the *Dogmatic* Idealism of Berkeley" ', in *Ideas and Mechanism* (Princeton University Press, 1999), pp. 280f.
[24] Allison, *Kant's Transcendental Idealism*, p. 158.

association).[25] However, as I now hope to show, it is possible to make better sense of Kant's example by reading it in terms of the dialectical context that I have explained in this chapter.[26]

Kant's example is an illustration of the contrast between the objective and the subjective unity of consciousness; it is thus part of his attempt clearly to distinguish the 'Locke–Berkeley' model from his own view of what it is to represent an object. As noted above, on that latter model, experience begins with an awareness of associated collections of one's own internal, perceptual states – that is, with a subjective unity of consciousness. On Kant's model, on the other hand, experience begins with a cognition of an object *in* one's internal states – that is, with an objective unity of consciousness. I thus suggest that the difference between (1) and (2) is an example of the difference between the representational content of a subjective unity of consciousness and an objective unity. What Kant is insisting on is that to apperceive the manifold in an intuition as an objective unity consisting of the representations *body* and *weight*, just is to have an awareness as of a heavy body being before one. It is, in other words, to be aware – or, to judge – that *it, the body, is heavy*. However, to have grasped those same representations in a subjective unity of consciousness amounts to something quite different. For that is merely to be aware that one associates the representations *body* and *heavy* with one another – or, as Kant puts it, that those representations are 'merely found together in perception'. Now, as I have previously discussed, on a standard (Cartesian-style) representationalist model of cognition, such an awareness or subjective unity of consciousness is thought to be an immediate or non-intentional awareness that is prior to judgment. On Kant's model, however, it is simply another sort of judgment – namely, a judgment about one's own perceptual states, such as the judgment that *when I carry a body, I feel a pressure of weight*. Hence, Kant's contrasting of (1) and (2) in § 19 becomes intelligible when it is read as a continuation of his attempt (begun in § 18) to make clear the way in which the representationalist model of cognition articulated in the B-Deduction differs from a superficially similar Cartesian-style model.

By the end of § 19, Kant has thus reached the following stage in the argument of the B-Deduction. He has argued that all our cognition must involve a spontaneous synthesis, and that that synthesis must be necessarily

---

[25] For an example of this interpretative manoeuvre, see R. E. Aquila, *Matter in Mind* (Bloomington: Indiana University Press, 1989), p. 138.

[26] For a very different reading from my own of this passage and its dialectical context, see B. Longuenesse, *Kant and the Capacity to Judge*, trans. C. T. Wolfe (Princeton University Press, 1998), ch. 7, especially pp. 186–7.

and universally valid if it is to generate a genuine cognition (i.e., a claim with objective validity). Furthermore, he has also argued that, from his representationalism, it follows that the cognising discursive mind is essentially a judging mind. Kant is now in a position to demonstrate that the categories play a constitutive role in the experience of any discursive cognising mind.

SECTION 20: JUDGMENT AND THE CATEGORIES

The title of § 20 of the B-Deduction is 'All sensible intuitions stand under the categories, as conditions under which alone their manifold can come together in one consciousness'. As this title makes clear, it is here that Kant at last links the categories to the argument developed in the previous sections. He argues in § 20 that the various representations that compose an intuition (i.e., the manifold in an intuition) can be apperceived as the unified awareness of an object (i.e., can come together in one consciousness) only through a *category-governed* synthesis. And therefore (β) the spontaneous synthesis that is essentially involved in discursive cognition is determined by the categories. Hence, by the end of § 20, Kant has completed his central argument for the claim that the categories make our cognition possible and are therefore both spontaneous and objective. The major remaining task of the B-Deduction is to link the results of this analysis of discursive cognition *in general* (as given in §§ 16–20) to the particular spatio-temporal nature of *human* cognition. This is a task which Kant carries out in § 26, and which I will discuss in the following section of this chapter.

In the single paragraph of § 20, Kant – first summarising the argument of §§ 16–19, and then concluding it – writes as follows.

The manifold that is given in a sensible intuition necessarily belongs under the original synthetic unity of apperception, since through this alone is the *unity* of the intuition possible (§ 17). That action of the understanding, however, through which the manifold of given representations (whether they be intuitions or concepts) is brought under an apperception in general, is the logical function of judgments (§ 19). Therefore all manifold, insofar as it is given in *one* [*Einer*] empirical intuition, is *determined* in regard to one of the logical functions for judgment, by means of which, namely, it is brought to a consciousness in general. But now the *categories* are nothing other than these very functions for judging, insofar as the manifold of a given intuition is determined with regard to them (§ 13). Thus the manifold in a given intuition also necessarily stands under categories. (B143)

That is to say, an intuition can be apperceived as a unified complex representation of an object only via a spontaneous synthesis – or, as Kant puts it here, the manifold in an intuition 'necessarily belongs under the original synthetic unity of apperception, since through this alone is the *unity* of the intuition possible'. However, if this spontaneous synthesis is to result in a cognition (i.e., a grasp of one's inner states as constituting a point of view on an objective world), then it must be necessarily and universally valid. Therefore, the synthesis must be grounded solely upon essential rather than contingent features of the cognising subject – that is, it must be grounded upon the nature of a discursive consciousness in general. Now, the cognising subject is essentially a judging subject. The essential structure of discursive cognition is thus given by the essential structure of judgment – that is, what Kant calls 'the logical function of judgments'. Hence, the synthesis of the manifold in an intuition – through which it is spontaneously grasped as, or segmented into, the determinate representation of a complex object – is grounded on the logical functions. As Kant puts it in the quoted passage, 'that action of the understanding through which the manifold of given representations is brought under an apperception in general, is the logical function of judgment'. And therefore the manifold in an intuition 'is *determined* in regard to one of the logical functions for judgment, by means of which, namely, it is brought to a consciousness in general'. As the italics emphasise, the logical functions thus play a role in determining the representational content of cognition – that is, they play a constitutive role in experience. 'Now', as Kant says, the categories just *are* 'these very functions for judging, insofar as the manifold of a given intuition is determined with regard to them' and therefore 'the manifold in a given intuition also necessarily stands under categories'. In other words, the representational content of the experience of a cognising discursive mind is, in part, determined by the categories.

The earlier parts of this argument have already been discussed; what needs particular attention here is Kant's notion of a 'logical function of judgment' and how this links with the notion of a category. As I have noted, by the end of § 19 Kant has argued that the cognising discursive mind is essentially a judging mind. That is to say, it is a mind that makes judgments – or performs mental acts of representing the world to itself as being thus and so. Hence, the spontaneous synthesis must be governed by the essential structure of judgment. Now, the essential structure of all judgments is given by their formal features, as studied by the logicians. Hence, the essential structure of judgment can be specified by an exhaustive categorisation of the possible logical forms that a judgment can have. As is well known, Kant claims to give such a categorisation in the so-called 'table of judgments', where he writes (at A70/B95) as follows.

If we abstract from all content of a judgment in general, and attend only to the mere form of the understanding in it, we find that the function of thinking in that can be brought under four titles, each of which contains under itself three moments. They can suitably be represented in the following table.

1. Quantity of Judgments
Universal
Particular
Singular

2. Quality	*3. Relation*
Affirmative	Categorical
Negative	Hypothetical
Infinite	Disjunctive

4. Modality
Problematic
Assertoric
Apodeictic

This table is thus Kant's way of specifying the general form of a judgment. It is, in other words, performing the job that in a more standard logic of categorical judgments would be performed by the following schema:

Every/Some (non-)**S** is/isn't (non-)**P**

For Kant, the table is thus a specification of all the possible logical forms of judgment, or the possible ways in which the mind can judge. This in turn means that the table is a specification of certain generic mental acts, or 'logical functions', such that to perform such-and-such a mental act is to make a judgment with such-and-such a logical form. Given Kant's argument in the previous sections of the B-Deduction, it follows that the spontaneous act of synthesis involved in discursive cognition must be performed via these mental acts. That is, the synthesis must be determined by the logical functions of judgment.

Now, it is clear that this part of Kant's argument in § 20 thus relies on two main assumptions: firstly, that there is such a thing as *the* essential structure, or *the* general form, of judgment; and secondly, that the quasi-Aristotelian logic of his time (i.e., the so-called 'traditional' logic) is *the* correct account of that general form. The first assumption would be false, for example, if judgments could be correctly analysed in a multiplicity of different and incompatible ways – which would thus entail that there is no clear distinction between the 'matter' and the 'form' of a judgment. The second assumption was famously attacked by Frege, and by now most logicians would consider it to be clearly false. These two assumptions are not, however, defended anywhere in the *Critique* – which is not surprising, for they were basic presuppositions of Kant's time. Kant in fact claims in

§ 21 of the B-Deduction that no ground 'can be offered for why we have precisely these and no other functions for judgment' (B146). In other words, according to Kant, the fact that judgment has the general form given in the table of judgments is (for us) an inexplicable, brute fact. Hence, as this book is an essay in exegesis and not a 'rational reconstruction', rather than attempting either to defend or attack these rock-bottom assumptions of Kant's argument, I will simply note them and pass on.

In any case, the precise details of the table of judgments are not relevant to the argument of the B-Deduction, for all Kant has argued in § 20 is that the logical functions (i.e., the basic ways of making judgments) – whatever they may be – play a determining or constitutive role in the experience of a discursive mind. That is, a manifold of internal states can be grasped as hanging together to present an object to the mind (i.e., as an intuition), only if they are grasped together through a spontaneous synthesis; and this synthesis can produce cognition only if it is grounded in the essential structure of judgment. Hence, as Kant writes in the 'metaphysical deduction':

The same function that gives unity to the different representations *in a judgment* also gives unity to the mere synthesis of different representations *in an intuition*, which, expressed generally, is called the pure concept of the understanding. (A79/B104–5)

For a logical function is the mental act of representing the world to oneself as being thus and so (i.e., of making a judgment with a certain logical form), and thus a way of grasping certain representations as a complex unity. It is, as Kant puts it here, a way of giving 'unity to the different representations in a judgment'. And from the argument of the B-Deduction it follows that this act is also the way in which the manifold in an intuition is grasped or apperceived as a unified representation of an object. That is, the logical function 'also gives unity to the mere synthesis of different representations in an intuition'. It is, in other words, the act through which the intuition is spontaneously grasped as, or segmented into, a determinate combination of representations. Or, equivalently, the logical function is the act of applying a method of projection to the 'blind' data given in intuition, and through which the subject thus cognises something *in* its internal states. Hence, the logical functions partially determine the representational content of experience.

Kant now claims that insofar as the logical functions play this constitutive role, they are the categories. That is, the categories are the logical functions insofar as those functions determine the representational content of experience – or, are the expression of the *spontaneity* of the discursive subject – as the way in which an intuition is apperceived as a unified complex representation. As Kant puts it in § 20, 'the *categories* are nothing other than these very functions for judging, insofar as the manifold of a given intuition is determined with regard to them' (B143). Hence, as he writes in the 'metaphysical deduction', 'there arise exactly as many pure concepts of the understanding [i.e., categories], which apply to objects of intuition in general a priori, as there were logical functions of all possible judgments' (A79/B105). A systematic enumeration of the categories can thus be given in a 'table of categories' that is parallel to the 'table of judgments' – and this Kant gives (at A80/B106), as follows:

1. Of Quantity
Unity
Plurality
Totality

2. Of Quality
Reality
Negation
Limitation

3. Of Relation
Of Inherence and Subsistence
Of Causality and Dependence
Of Community

4. Of Modality
Possibility – Impossibility
Existence – Non-existence
Necessity – Contingency

Kant's argument to this point can be explained as follows. Cognition is essentially the act of grasping an intuition as the unified presentation of an object, and thereby making a judgment. This judgment will have a particular logical form, and will thus involve a characteristic mental act – that is, the application of a particular logical function. This mental act, however, not only determines the logical form of the judgment but also partially determines the actual representational content of the intuition grasped in the judgment. Insofar as it does the former, the mental act is the application of a 'logical function'; insofar as it does the latter, this mental act is the application of a 'category' or 'pure concept of the understanding'.

Kant's central point is thus that there are not *two* distinct activities – the making of a certain type of judgment and the application of a category – but only *one*, namely, the act of spontaneously grasping the manifold in an intuition as the presentation of an object. To take what is perhaps the most plausible example, to grasp an intuition as the unified presentation of a single complex object just *is* to grasp the intuition as the presentation of a multiplicity of properties inhering in a substance (i.e., to apply the category of inherence and subsistence), and this just *is* to make a certain categorical judgment (i.e., to judge that an *x*, that is S, is P – as Kant would put it). To take another example, to grasp an intuition as the presentation of something that exists (and thus to apply the category of existence – non-existence) is not to predicate an additional concept of that object, but simply to make an assertoric judgment about it. To take a third and somewhat less plausible example, Kant is suggesting that to grasp an intuition as the unified presentation of one object standing in a dependency relation to another object (i.e., as linked as cause and effect in the most abstract sense) just *is* to make a certain hypothetical judgment (i.e., to link two categorical judgments with an 'If . . . then – ').

Kant's conception of the categories can be made clearer by a brief consideration of a remark made by Bennett, who thinks it a criticism of Kant to point out that

> it is just not true that the only task of categorical judgments is to attribute properties to substances. Again, causal judgments are only a sub-class of hypotheticals, and the concept of cause is therefore not just the ability to handle hypotheticals.[27]

This remark is largely correct, but it does not affect Kant's point, for he is not claiming that every categorical judgment is the attribution of a property to a substance, nor that every hypothetical judgment is the cognition of a cause – effect relation. Rather, he is claiming the converse of this: every attribution of a property to a substance (i.e., the application of the category of inherence and subsistence) is a categorical judgment, and every cognition of two objects in a dependency relation (i.e., the application of the category of cause and effect) is a hypothetical judgment. In other words, Kant is not saying, as Bennett thinks, that every use of the logical functions is (identical to) an application of the categories; he is saying that every use of the logical functions to grasp the manifold in an intuition as the immediate presentation of a particular state of affairs is (identical to) an application of the categories.

Although Kant's argument can thus be defended against certain criticisms, it is nonetheless true that many of the details of the metaphysical deduction – that is, the derivation of the categories from the table of judgments – do not appear very persuasive. As I have noted, some of the parallels that Kant draws between logical function and category are plausible (e.g., the parallel between the categorical function and the category of subsistence and inherence); however, many others seem arbitrary. Perhaps we should

---

[27] Bennett, *Kant's Analytic*, p. 92.

thus agree with Strawson that the 'meagreness' of the argument 'is such as to render almost pointless any critical consideration of the detail of Kant's derivation of the categories from the Table of Judgments'.[28] On the other hand, Béatrice Longuenesse has recently written an interesting defence of Kant that takes very seriously his claim that the table of judgments provides the 'guiding thread' (*Leitfaden*) to the system of categories.[29] However, just as in the case of the table of judgments, the precise details of the table of categories are not directly relevant to Kant's general argument in the B-Deduction – which is the focus of my concern in this book – and thus I will not attempt to evaluate the argument of the metaphysical deduction. For in § 20 Kant has simply argued for the general claim that the essential structure of judgment determines the representational content of the experience of a discursive mind, and that therefore any possible cognition of such a mind must exhibit a certain category-determined structure (whatever the precise nature of those categories may be).

In general, it can thus be said that the categories are the most abstract, fundamental ways in which a discursive cognising mind can grasp its internal modifications as hanging together to compose a point of view upon an objective world. Another way of putting this point is to say that the categories are the essential resources of the (productive) imagination, whereby the discursive mind is able to cognise objects *in* its internal states – for, after all, 'the imagination is a necessary ingredient of perception itself' (A120n). And, because of the spontaneity of the discursive mind, these basic imaginative ways of cognising things in the manifold also play a role in determining just *what* is cognised in the manifold. Kant thus writes in § 24 of the B-Deduction that 'insofar as the imagination is spontaneity, I also call it the *productive* imagination' (B152), and that the

> synthesis of intuitions, *in accordance with the categories*, must be the transcendental synthesis of the *imagination*, which is an effect of the understanding on sensibility and its first application (and at the same time the ground of all others) to objects of the intuition that is possible for us. (B151)

If this spontaneous synthesis of the productive imagination were not thereby grounded in the essential structure of judgment, and thus 'in accordance with the categories' – in virtue of which the synthesis is necessarily and universally valid – it would not produce any representations deserving to be called 'cognition'. In other words, any objective (i.e., cognition-generating) synthesis must be performed via an application of the categories. Now, the

---

[28] Strawson, *Bounds of Sense*, p. 82. [29] See Longuenesse, *Kant and the Capacity to Judge.*

categories do not completely determine how any particular synthesis is to be performed. They specify only the (abstract) structure of an objective synthesis in general – just as the rules of chess specify only how chess in general is to be played, and not how any particular game of chess must be played. That is, the particular judgments that would be made in grasping the same intuitive input will vary from subject to subject (depending upon contingent psychological features of the subjects, such as habits, interests and capacities), and some of these judgments will be true and others false (e.g., because they involve perceptual errors, misjudgments, hallucinations or dreams mistaken for reality, etc.). However, if the varied experiences of the possible subjects are all to be genuine cognitions (whether veridical or non-veridical) at all, then they must all share the same category-determined structure – just as every game of chess must be played in accordance with the rules of chess in general, if it is to be a genuine game of chess. In Kant's terminology, the categories thus specify only the *transcendental* synthesis and not the *empirical* synthesis. These syntheses, it should be noted, are therefore related not as two distinct events (the first being the mysterious precursor of the second), but simply as abstract (determinable) and concrete (determination).

It is worth emphasising at this point that Kant's argument in § 20 has not simply been for the claim that all experience involves making judgments (and that these judgments must involve the logical functions, and thus the categories, etc.). Walker, for example, reads the argument in this way, as his summary of the B-Deduction makes clear:

in its late form, the transcendental deduction turns entirely on the notion of a judgment. All experience . . . involves making judgments, for the data that are given to us in intuition must be classified and subsumed under concepts. And (as has been shown in the metaphysical deduction) there are only twelve fundamental forms of judgment. But the categories can be identified with these twelve forms of judgment, at least so far as they are employed in judging about what is empirically given; to make such a judgment is the same thing as to apply the relevant category. Hence all experience involves the categories.[30]

This reading completely fails to explain why Kant should think that a crucially important idealist consequence follows from the argument of the B-Deduction – namely, that the logical functions of judgment play a role in determining the representational content of our experience. For merely showing that experience must involve the 'classification' and 'subsumption'

---

[30] Walker, *Kant*, p. 77.

of data under concepts, and thus judgment, does not explain why cognition cannot simply be receptive – a question of 'reading off' determinate data given in intuition. Furthermore, such an interpretation of Kant's argument immediately invites Guyer's criticism that it

is hard to see why we should be able to make hypothetical . . . judgments only if we can detect *causal* connections among objects, and disjunctive . . . judgments only if objects *interact*.[31]

But Kant's reasoning in the B-Deduction is much more interesting than the simple interpretation given by Walker – that is, it is not merely the argument that we are able to make judgments and that therefore objects must exhibit a category-determined structure. As I have explained here, the logical forms of judgment come to play such a vitally important role for Kant, not simply because all cognition involves judgment, but because all cognition necessarily involves not only receptivity but also *spontaneity*, and this spontaneity can be objective only if it is grounded in the essential structure of judgment.

In § 20, then, Kant has argued that all discursive cognition must involve a category-governed spontaneous synthesis. However, this conclusion does not yet complete the main project of the B-Deduction. For, according to Kant, human cognition is not merely essentially discursive, it is also essentially cognition as of a spatio-temporal world. That is to say, human cognition is not simply *receptive* to an independent reality, but – at a less abstract level – is receptive in a certain *way*, namely, spatio-temporally. Hence, the final task of the B-Deduction is to relate the very abstract results reached in § 20, which concern discursive cognition in general, to Kant's overall project in the *Critique*, namely, the clarification of the nature of our (human) cognition. This is done in § 26 of the B-Deduction, to which I now turn.

SECTION 26: SPACE, TIME AND THE CATEGORIES

Kant makes it clear that the project of the B-Deduction is not completed by the argument of § 20, when he announces in § 21 that a '*beginning* of a deduction of the pure concepts of the understanding has been made' (B144; my emphasis). Kant then tells us that his argument to this point is incomplete, because he has

---

[31] Guyer, *Kant and the Claims of Knowledge*, p. 99.

abstract[ed] from the way in which the manifold for an empirical intuition is given, in order to attend only to the unity that is added to the intuition through the understanding by means of the category. In the sequel (§ 26) it will be shown from the way in which the empirical intuition is given in sensibility that its unity can be none other than the one the category prescribes to the manifold of an intuition in general according to the preceding § 20; thus by the explanation of its a priori validity in regard to all objects of *our* senses the aim of the deduction will first be fully attained. (B144–5; my emphasis)

This passage thus makes two points clear. Firstly, the argument of the B-Deduction will be completed in § 26. Secondly, Kant holds that the argument concluded in § 20 is incomplete because it is still too abstract – that is, it concerns only discursive cognition in general, and sensible (i.e., receptive or non-intellectual) intuition in general. As Kant notes in the paragraph following the quoted passage:

In the above proof [*sc.*, §§ 16–20], however, I still could not abstract from one point, namely, from the fact that the manifold for intuition must already be *given* prior to the synthesis of understanding and independently from it; how, however, is here left undetermined. (B145)

In other words, as I have discussed previously, Kant's argument in §§ 16–20 deals only with the essential conditions for being a receptive (or 'discursive') mind, rather than a purely spontaneous (or 'intuitive') mind. However, his analysis up to this point has concerned only discursive cognition *in general*, for it does not depend upon any assumptions about the nature of the data given by receptivity (i.e., 'how the manifold for intuition is given'). That is, as my reading has emphasised, Kant has simply dealt with the necessary conditions for grasping a given collection of internal modifications as constituting a point of view upon an objective world. As yet, there has therefore been no discussion of what implications the results of this analysis have for the human form of cognition – which involves the grasp of intuitions as a point of view upon a unified spatio-temporal world. It can thus be expected that the completion of Kant's argument in § 26 will involve the application of the conclusion of § 20 to the nature of *human* cognition in general. As Kant puts it in the passage quoted above, § 26 will concern what it means for the categories to have 'a priori validity in regard to all objects of *our* senses' – that is, in regard to all possible spatio-temporal objects.

The fact that the argument of the B-Deduction thus proceeds in two separate stages (one from §§ 16–20, and the other concluded in § 26), has often been noted in the secondary literature, and various interpretations have been proposed in order to make sense of this two-part structure.[32] A well-known attempt to solve this 'problem of the two-steps-in-one-proof' is given by Henrich, who argues that § 20 has established only the restricted conclusion 'that intuitions are subject to the categories *insofar* as they, as intuitions, already possess unity', and that § 26 is thus required to show that our spatio-temporal intuitions all meet this condition of possessing unity.[33] Allison argues against this view and offers an alternative interpretation of the 'two-steps-in-one-proof'. He suggests that the first part of the B-Deduction merely 'establishes the necessity of the categories for representing an object in the judgmental or logical sense', whilst the second part attempts to establish that the categories make experience possible, where 'by "experience" is meant empirical knowledge of objects in the "weighty" sense'.[34] A third alternative interpretation is offered by Howell, who argues that because the '§ 15 to § 20 argument has concerned only the objects of sensible intuitions in general, it has not shown that the categories apply to the objects of our own human empirical knowledge' – and this conclusion is thus demonstrated in § 26.[35]

These three interpretations of the two-part structure of the B-Deduction all fail adequately to explain the details of Kant's text. The problem is that they all assume that the task of § 26 is to prove that the conclusion reached in § 20 also applies to human cognition, and they are thus committed to the claim that the conclusion of § 20 is restricted in some way. But it is clear from Kant's text that, as I have shown, § 20 reaches an unrestricted conclusion about discursive cognition in general, so *of course* this conclusion also applies to human cognition, for that is a species of discursive cognition.[36] After all, the conclusion of § 20 is that 'the manifold in a given intuition also necessarily stands under categories' (B143) – that is, it applies to all given (i.e., sensible) intuitions. Human intuition is a species of sensible intuition, so it too necessarily stands under categories. It would thus be absurd for Kant to spend § 26 proving the trivially obvious point that the result of § 20 also applies to human cognition – it would be as if one had shown that chess games in general began with a move by white, and then took pains to show that all chess games played in Sydney also began the same

[32] A useful summary of the literature on this topic is given by Keller, *Kant and the Demands of Self-Consciousness*, pp. 89–90.

[33] D. Henrich, 'The Proof-Structure of Kant's Transcendental Deduction', *Review of Metaphysics* 22 (1969), 640–59; the 'two-steps-in-one-proof' quote is from p. 642, the other quote is from p. 645.

[34] Allison, *Kant's Transcendental Idealism*, p. 159; see also H. E. Allison, 'Reflections on the B-Deduction', in *Idealism and Freedom*, pp. 32–9.

[35] Howell, *Kant's Transcendental Deduction*, pp. 131–2.

[36] Robinson makes this point in criticising Henrich's view – see 'Intuition and Manifold', 404–5.

way. In other words, Kant's text clearly shows that the conclusion of § 20 is unrestricted, and therefore the task of § 26 cannot be to prove that the categories also apply to human cognition – as Henrich, Allison and Howell all assume.

This result thus raises the question of just what § 26 of the B-Deduction is supposed to show. In the passage from § 21 quoted above, Kant answers this question by stating that § 26 will show 'from the way in which the empirical intuition is given in [our] sensibility that its unity [i.e., the unity of our intuition] can be none other than the one the category prescribes to the manifold of an intuition in general' (B144–5). The 'unity of our (human) intuition' is, as Kant has emphasised in the Transcendental Aesthetic, a spatio-temporal unity. That is to say, in cognition we grasp our outer intuitions as representations of spatial parts of a single space, and we grasp our inner intuitions as representations of temporal parts of a single time. Hence, according to Kant, the task of § 26 is to show that the spatio-temporal unity of our intuition 'is none other than' the unity which 'the category prescribes to the manifold of an intuition in general'. The meaning of this is as follows. As explained above, Kant's argument from §§ 16–20 concluded with the claim that all discursive cognition must exhibit a category-determined structure. In the Aesthetic, Kant has also claimed that all human cognition must exhibit a spatio-temporal structure. Now, as I will show below, in § 26 Kant argues that the spatio-temporal structure of human cognition is not *independent* of its category-determined structure. Rather, the spatio-temporal structure of all possible human cognition is a particular *determination* of the abstract (i.e., determinable) category-determined structure, which is common to all possible discursive cognition.

This interpretation accounts for how the argument in § 26 of the B-Deduction completes a project that is still incomplete at the end of § 20, despite the unrestricted nature of the conclusion in that latter section. This can be explained as follows. As everyone knows, a (perhaps *the*) central task of the *Critique* is to explain our possession of synthetic a priori knowledge. Kant holds, in particular, that we need to explain our synthetic a priori knowledge of the spatio-temporal structure of experience – the fact that, for example, we know a priori that geometry and mathematics (e.g., the infinitesimal calculus) can be validly applied to space and time. In the Aesthetic, he has argued that, in virtue of our mode of receptivity (or form of intuition), all the objects of our experience must exhibit a spatio-temporal structure. However, although this conclusion thus 'makes the *possibility* of geometry [etc.] as a synthetic a priori cognition comprehensible' (B41), it does not yet explain precisely *what* synthetic truths we can know a priori about space and time, nor precisely *how* we can know them. Now, the argument of the B-Deduction has concluded in § 20 with the claim that all objects of discursive experience must exhibit a category-determined structure, and in the 'metaphysical deduction' it was argued that a precise list of twelve categories can be given. Hence, by the end of § 20 Kant has provided the resources for explaining how we can know a priori a determinate range of synthetic truths about our experience – insofar as it is simply a species of discursive experience in general. However, the conclusion of § 20 does not yet suffice to explain how we can know anything a priori about the *spatio-temporal* structure of our (human) experience. For if that spatio-temporal structure were independent of the category-determined structure of our experience, then from the fact that we could know certain truths a priori about the latter, nothing would follow concerning what we could know a priori about the former. Kant thus argues in § 26 that the spatio-temporal structure of experience is not independent of its category-determined structure, but is instead a particular determination of it – and that therefore we can know a priori a particular range of truths about space and time.

In other words, the purpose of § 26 of the B-Deduction is to show how the very abstract claim made about the categories in § 20 provides an explanation of our capacity to make synthetic a priori judgments about the structure of space and time. It is thus that Kant writes as follows in the first paragraph of § 26.

Now the possibility of cognising a priori *through categories* whatever objects *may come before our senses*, not as far as the form of their intuition but rather as far as the laws of their combination are concerned, thus the possibility of as it were prescribing the law to nature and even making the latter possible, is to be explained. (B159)

That is to say, the task of § 26 is to explain how our a priori knowledge of the category-determined structure of our experience is at the same time an a priori knowledge of the 'laws of combination' of 'whatever objects may come before our senses' – that is, the ways in which those objects can be related (or 'combined') in space and time.

In order to justify this interpretation of § 26, I now turn to examine the details of Kant's text. The essential part of his argument in that section runs as follows.

We have *forms* of outer as well as inner sensible intuition a priori in the representations of space and time, and the synthesis of the apprehension of the manifold of appearance must always be in agreement with the latter, since it can only occur in accordance with this form. But space and time are represented a priori not merely as *forms* of sensible intuition, but also as *intuitions* themselves (which contain a manifold), and thus with the determination of the *unity* of this manifold in them (see the Transcendental Aesthetic). Thus even *unity of the synthesis* of the manifold, outside or within us, hence also a *combination* with which everything that is to be represented as determined in space or time must agree, is already given a priori along with (not in) these intuitions, as conditions of the synthesis of all *apprehension*. But this synthetic unity can be none other than that of the combination of the manifold of a given *intuition in general* in an original consciousness, in agreement with the categories, only applied to our *sensible intuition*. Consequently all synthesis, through which even perception itself becomes possible, stands under the categories, and since experience is cognition through connected perceptions, the categories are conditions of the possibility of experience, and are thus also valid a priori of all objects of experience. (B160–1)

The crucial premise of this argument is Kant's claim that 'space and time are represented a priori not merely as *forms* of intuition, but as *intuitions* themselves (which contain a manifold), and thus with the determination of the *unity* of this manifold in them'. In a footnote to this claim, Kant makes its meaning clearer by writing that

Space, represented as *object* (as is really required in geometry), contains more than the mere form of intuition, namely the *comprehension* of the manifold given in accordance with the form of sensibility in an *intuitive* representation, so that the *form of intuition* merely gives the manifold, but the *formal intuition* gives unity of the representation. (B160n)

This thus suggests that the crucial premise of § 26 is Kant's claim from the Aesthetic that space and time are themselves represented as objects – that is, as complex particulars.[37]

What is perhaps Kant's clearest exposition of this claim that space and time are themselves represented as objects occurs in the third argument of the 'Metaphysical Exposition' of the concept of space, in the Transcendental Aesthetic. He writes here that

one can only represent a single space, and if one speaks of many spaces, one understands by that only parts of one and the same unique space. And these parts cannot as it were precede the single all-encompassing space as its components (from which its composition would be possible), but rather are only thought *in it*. (A25/B39)

In other words, in representing things as spatial (or temporal), one is not merely representing a class of objects that happen to share some general

---

[37] The importance of this point is also emphasised by M. Baum, 'The B-Deduction and the Refutation of Idealism', *Southern Journal of Philosophy (Supplement)* 25 (1986), 104.

characteristic, such as the colour blue.[38] That is, in experience one cognises particular spaces and times (e.g., the inside of a room, the duration of a conversation, etc.), but these particular spaces and times are not represented as standing to space and time in general as a particular blue thing is represented as standing to the class of blue things in general. Rather, when we represent a particular space or time, we represent it as a *part* of a single (spatial or temporal) system – that is, as a part of 'the single all-encompassing space (or time)' – and as individuated by its position within that overall system. Hence, space and time are themselves represented as complex particulars. Or, as Kant puts it in § 26, space and time are represented 'as intuitions themselves (which contain a manifold)'. It should be noted that these intuitions of space and time in general are, as he insists in the footnote at B160, *formal* intuitions. That is, they are representations of space and time not as containing particular empirical objects and events, but simply as pure structures – intuitive representations that, for Kant, lie at the heart of a priori disciplines such as geometry.

The significance of this premise for Kant's argument in § 26 is that, in conjunction with the conclusion of § 20, it entails that space and time are themselves grasped through a category-governed synthesis, and that therefore they will possess a category-determined structure. In §§ 16–20 it was argued that the manifold in an intuition could only be grasped as the unified presentation of a complex object via a category-governed spontaneous synthesis. In § 26 Kant has claimed that space and time are themselves cognised as complex objects, via the unified grasp of a manifold in an intuition. As he writes in the passage quoted above 'space and time are represented a priori . . . as *intuitions* themselves (which contain a manifold), and thus with the determination of the *unity* of this manifold in them' (B160). From the conclusion of § 20 it therefore follows that the representations of space and time are grasped via a category-governed spontaneous synthesis. Or, as Kant himself puts it:

Thus even *unity of the synthesis* of the manifold, outside or within us, hence also a *combination* with which everything that is to be represented as determined in space or time must agree, is already given a priori along with (not in) these intuitions, as conditions of the synthesis of all *apprehension*. But this synthetic unity can be none other than that of the combination of the manifold of a given *intuition in general* in an original consciousness, in agreement with the categories, only applied to our *sensible intuition*. (B161)

---

[38] Cf. Falkenstein's discussion of the third exposition in *Kant's Intuitionism*, pp. 219–22.

That is, the representations of space ('the manifold outside us') and time ('the manifold within us') are complex unified representations (or, synthetic unities); therefore, a grasp of those representations must involve a synthesis or 'combination with which everything that is to be represented as determined in space or time must agree'. But, as § 20 has shown, the unified grasp of the manifold in an intuition as the presentation of an object 'can be none other than that of the combination of the manifold of a given *intuition in general* in an original consciousness, in agreement with the categories'.

It thus follows that the structures of space and time in general are particular determinations of the more abstract category-determined structure that is common to all possible discursive experience. Kant makes this conclusion clear in the paragraphs following the main argument of § 26 (i.e., those following the first row of asterisks), where he writes as follows.

Thus if, e.g., I make the empirical intuition of a house into perception through apprehension of its manifold, my ground is the *necessary unity* of space and of outer sensible intuition in general, and I as it were draw its shape in agreement with this synthetic unity of the manifold in space. This very same synthetic unity, however, if I abstract from the form of space, has its seat in the understanding, and is the category of . . . *quantity*, with which that synthesis of apprehension, i.e., the perception, must therefore be in thoroughgoing agreement. (B162)

Similarly, Kant writes, the synthetic unity of time is, 'if I abstract from the constant form of my inner intuition . . . the category of *cause*' (B163). That is, the spatio-temporal structure of our (human) experience is the particular *way* in which our experience is structured by the categories. Or, the structures of space and time are, in a sense, the human expression of the discursive categories.

What Kant's argument in § 26 thus rules out is the possibility that space and time might have a structure that is independent of the category-governed structure of experience. This would be the case, for example, if the structures of space and time were not grasped as complex particulars, but instead propositions about those structures supervened on the set of empirical propositions about existing objects and their intrinsic properties. From the argument of §§ 16–20, it would still follow that our experience would have a category-determined structure. However, our a priori knowledge of that category-determined structure would, in such a case, provide no a priori knowledge of the structure of space and time – for that would depend simply upon the empirical (a posteriori) facts about experience.

The earlier sections of the B-Deduction would thus fail to provide any explanation of our a priori knowledge of space and time.

The argument of § 26 thus links the analysis of cognition given in the earlier parts of the B-Deduction to the more general project of the *Critique* – the explanation of our a priori knowledge of synthetic truths about space and time – and thus prepares the way for the particular proofs of those truths that Kant gives in the following Analytic of Principles. In §§ 16–20 of the B-Deduction he has provided an argument to show that we can know a priori that our experience – as a species of discursive cognition in general – must exhibit a certain category-determined structure. In § 26 Kant has then argued that space as a whole and time as a whole must both exhibit that very same structure. That is, he shows 'from the way in which the empirical intuition is given in [our] sensibility that its unity can be none other than the one the category prescribes to the manifold of an intuition in general' (B144–5). Hence, our a priori knowledge of the category-governed structure of discursive experience in general explains our a priori knowledge of the spatio-temporal structure of our (human) experience.

SUMMARY OF THE B-DEDUCTION

The above discussion of § 26 completes my reading of the main sections of the B-Deduction. In order to draw together the results of that reading, I will now give in summary form my interpretation of the central argument of the B-Deduction – that is, of Kant's analysis of the concept of human cognition.

The representationalist background

1. All cognition occurs via the mind's immediate awareness of its own internal representational states. (Kant's representationalist starting point.)
2. These representations are not intrinsically available to the subject's awareness; that is, unconscious representations are logically possible. (Leibnizian claim.)
3. Therefore, cognition must involve a special reflexive act of bringing representations to awareness – that is, it must involve the *apperception* of representations. (From 1 and 2.)
4. A discursive mind is a mind that is *receptive* in cognition to an independent reality. (Definition of 'discursive'.)
5. Therefore, in cognition the discursive mind apperceives its own internal states as presenting an independent, objective world to itself. (From 3 and 4.)

6. This is to say that discursive cognition is the apperception of sensible intuitions. (From 5 and the definition of 'sensible intuition' – as a determination of the faculty of receptivity (or sensibility) which the subject grasps as presenting an object.)
7. All objects of sensible intuitions are represented *as* complex. (Implicit assumption – certainly valid in the case of human cognition; for in representing objects in space and/or time one thereby represents them as complex (e.g., as potentially divisible into parts).)
8. Therefore, discursive cognition is the apperception of unified complex representations. (From 6 and 7.)

The master argument (§ 16)

9. To apperceive unified complex representations is to apperceive all of the component representations as hanging together in a unity. (The 'principle of the necessary unity of apperception' – an analytic truth.)
10. Such 'unity of apperception' is possible only if the apperception of a unified complex representation is holistic rather than atomistic, and therefore involves a spontaneous synthesis. (The master argument of § 16.)
11. Therefore, all apperception of unified complex representations must involve a spontaneous synthesis. (From 9 and 10.)
12. Therefore, (α) all discursive cognition must involve a spontaneous synthesis. (From 8 and 11.)

The objectivity criterion (§§ 17–18)

13. The discursive subject's spontaneous synthesis can result in an objectively valid representation (i.e., a cognition) only if that synthesis is necessarily and universally valid (i.e., would be performed the same way by all logically possible discursive cognisers). (From analysis of concept of objectivity.)
14. Therefore, the discursive subject's spontaneous synthesis can result in a cognition only if it is 'pure' or non-empirical – that is, grounded solely upon essential features of the discursive cognising subject. (From 13.)

Judgment (§ 19)

15. The act of discursive cognition (the act of cognising an object *in* one's internal states) is a judgment. (Kant's analysis of the concept of judgment.)
16. Therefore, the discursive cognising mind is essentially a judging mind. (From 15.)

The categories (§ 20)

17. Therefore, the discursive subject's spontaneous synthesis can result in a cognition only if that synthesis is grounded solely upon the essential features of the act of judgment. (From 14 and 16.)
18. The essential features of the act of judgment are the logical functions listed in the 'table of judgments'. (From the 'metaphysical deduction'.)
19. Therefore, the discursive subject's spontaneous act of synthesis can result in a cognition only if that synthesis is governed by the logical functions. (From 17 and 18.)
20. The logical functions, insofar as they govern the spontaneous synthesis of intuitions involved in discursive cognition, are the categories. (From the 'metaphysical deduction'.)
21. Therefore, (β) if discursive cognition involves a spontaneous synthesis, then this synthesis must be governed by the categories. (From 19 and 20.)

The conclusion of § 20

22. Therefore, discursive cognition must involve a category-governed spontaneous synthesis (and thus the representational content of that cognition is, in part, determined by the categories). (From 12 and 21.)

Our a priori knowledge of space and time (§ 26)

23. Space and time in general are represented by us (human beings) as objects (rather than as common properties of objects); and thus the representations of space and time in general (i.e., our 'formal intuitions') are themselves unified complex representations. (From the Transcendental Aesthetic.)
24. Therefore, we cognise space and time in general via a category-governed synthesis. (From 22 and 23.)
25. Therefore, the structure of space and time in general is a determination of the category-governed structure of discursive experience in general. (From 24.)
26. Therefore, our a priori knowledge of that category-governed structure (which we have via the arguments of the *Critique*) is a source of a priori knowledge of the structure of space and time in general (and therefore a potential means of explaining our a priori knowledge of synthetic principles of geometry, mechanics, etc.). (From 25.)

The diagram below of the argument's structure may assist in making this summary of my reading of the B-Deduction clearer.

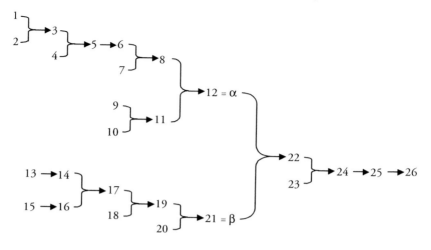

The argument summarised here fulfils the aim that Kant announced in the introductory part of the Transcendental Deduction, and follows the strategy that he outlined there. As I argued in chapter 2, according to Kant, the central aim of the Deduction was to show how the *spontaneity* of the categories was compatible with their *objectivity*. That is, we make synthetic a priori judgments, and therefore use certain concepts spontaneously. In other words, we use those concepts (i.e., the categories) in a way that is not grounded upon a recognition of features of that which is given to us by our receptivity. This immediately raises the question of how it is possible for the categories to be objective. For if their use is thus not constrained by the nature of independent reality, then their use seems to collapse into mere fantasising or the imaginative projection of psychological habits of association. In the face of this difficulty, Kant suggested that the spontaneity of the categories could be shown to be compatible with their objectivity, if the categories could be shown to be 'a priori conditions of the possibility of experiences' (A94/B126). Kant attempts to show this in the B-Deduction via an analysis of the concept of human cognition. This analysis entails that if we are *receptive* in cognition then we must also be *spontaneous* in a way that is grounded on a priori concepts derived from the logical forms of judgment in general – that is, the categories. That is, Kant argues that if we are responsive in cognition to a world that is in some way independent of us, and therefore not something that we have simply spun out of our own heads, then an act of the mind – a category-governed synthesis – must play a role in actually generating the representational content of our experience.

This conclusion can be put in the terms of the mathematical analogy of function and argument that I have used previously. The *arguments* are the modifications of our (human) sensibility. These data are, in themselves, 'blind' or of indeterminate representational content – in that various contents can be generated, depending upon which function is applied to the data. The form of these data is, according to the argument of the Aesthetic, grounded upon our mode of receptivity (i.e., the way in which the human faculty of sensibility is determinable); its matter (i.e., the way our faculty of sensibility is determined) is grounded upon things as they are in themselves. The categories are then the *function* (or rule of projection), which is grounded upon our nature *qua* cognising discursive mind, and is applied to those data in the transcendental synthesis. The result of applying the function to the arguments is our experience (or cognition) of the phenomenal world of space and time. Hence, as Kant promised at the beginning of the Deduction, the categories have turned out to be essential to the objectivity of our cognition, for it is 'through them alone that it is possible for us to cognise something as an object' (see A92/B125). That is, it is only by applying the categories in a transcendental synthesis that we can have experience that is genuinely receptive to an independent reality – in other words, that is genuinely objective.

The category-governed synthesis (i.e., the 'transcendental synthesis of the imagination') is thus Kant's answer to the problem of how the discursive subject can grasp its 'manifold' of private, internal modifications as constituting its point of view on an objective world. The fact that the categories constitute experience means that the world we cognise is not independent of our mind. In Kant's jargon, that is to say that it is the world of appearances rather than of things in themselves. But our phenomenal world is transcendentally ideal, rather than empirically ideal, in that it is dependent only upon *essential* features of our mind, and is thus independent of any contingent, psychological facts about the individual cognising subject. Hence, despite the subjective differences between the ways in which different human beings experience the world, all our experience has, nonetheless, an objective, category-determined core. It thus makes sense for us to talk of, and make claims about, the way in which the phenomenal world is, independently of any particular human observer (as we do, most systematically, in natural science). So Kant is saying, for example, *contra* Hume, that I (the subject) can claim that As cause Bs, and thereby mean *more* than that A and B have been constantly conjoined in my experience and that therefore I (personally) associate their ideas with one another. Rather, the judgment that I thus make – whether it is veridical or non-veridical – has a representational content that reaches beyond facts about my personal psychology and makes a claim about how appearances are connected in a world that is common to all possible human cognisers.

If this analysis of the concept of human cognition given in the B-Deduction is correct, then it is a major step towards explaining how synthetic a priori judgments are possible. For Kant claims to have proven in his analysis that all of our experience must have a category-determined structure. On the basis of that argument, we can thus know a priori that the categories – because of the role they play in constituting the representational content of cognition – will apply to all possible objects of our experience. Of course, the categories only play a constitutive role with regard to the objects that we cognise *in* our internal modifications – that is, the appearances. Therefore, the categories can only be known a priori to be essential features of the phenomenal world, and not of the realm of things as they are in themselves. Hence, the only valid synthetic a priori judgments that we can make with the categories concern the appearances. As Kant puts it in § 22 of the B-Deduction, 'the categories have no other use for the cognition of things except insofar as these are taken as objects of possible experience' (B147–8).

CONCLUDING REMARKS: THE B-DEDUCTION AND SCEPTICISM

In this book I have argued that the B-Deduction should be read as being primarily an analysis of the concept of human cognition. As I noted in my discussion of § 17, this raises a question about the relation of Kant's argument to scepticism. The problem is obvious enough. If the B-Deduction is simply an analysis of cognition, then the most it can achieve is a proof of what else must be the case *if* we have cognition or objective experience. (It is worth noting that this is therefore not the same as saying that it is a 'regressive' argument which begins with the premise *that* we have objective cognition.[39]) Hence, it would be possible for a sceptic to accept all of Kant's conclusions about the necessary conditions of objective experience, yet also to deny that the B-Deduction proves anything about the necessary conditions of *our* experience, for it does not prove that our experience is objective. It might thus be objected that my interpretation of Kant's argument must be wrong, because it renders the B-Deduction totally ineffective against such a sceptical challenge. A lot could be said about this topic, but

---

[39] As Karl Ameriks argues in an important paper – 'Kant's Transcendental Deduction as a Regressive Argument', *Kant Studien* 69 (1978), 273–87.

I only have the space here to make two brief responses to this potential objection – one textual and the other philosophical. The textual response is simply that the interpretation of the B-Deduction as an anti-sceptical argument does not fit Kant's text as well as my own interpretation. The philosophical response is that Kant's argument is nonetheless philosophically interesting, because it moves in a way that is not obviously fallacious from something fairly weak (i.e., receptivity) to something very strong (i.e., category-governed spontaneity).

If the B-Deduction is to have any chance of success as an anti-sceptical argument, then it must not presuppose that our experience is objective, but must attempt to prove that objectivity from some weaker premise. The obvious candidate for that weaker starting point is Kant's claim about the unity of apperception in § 16. As I have argued, if Kant's notion of apperception is read as being much like the ordinary notion of introspection or self-consciousness, then it is initially very tempting to think that the B-Deduction is an anti-sceptical argument that moves from some weak premise about mere self-conscious experience to the strong conclusion that we have genuinely objective cognition. However, as I also pointed out in my discussion of § 17, it is very difficult to reconcile this reading with the fact that Kant appears simply to *identify* the unified apperception of the manifold in an intuition with the cognition of an object. In other words, according to the anti-sceptical reading, the heart of the B-Deduction must be an argument from self-consciousness to objectivity – but such an argument appears to be absent from Kant's text. Hence, if one wishes to read the B-Deduction as an anti-sceptical argument, then one must either conclude (as, for example, Guyer does) that it is grossly question-begging, or one must engage in some extensive reconstructive surgery, in order to make Kant's text fit the interpretation. As I have argued in this chapter, my own reading of the B-Deduction avoids these problems.

There is a revealing passage in Keller's recent book which provides an instructive example of just what is involved in attempting to read the B-Deduction as an anti-sceptical argument. Discussing the early sections of the B-Deduction, Keller writes as follows.

Initially, we expect to see Kant derive the conditions for concept use, judgment, and knowledge from the conditions governing self-consciousness; he seems instead merely to shift from talking about conditions on self-consciousness to talk of conditions on conceptual cognition and judgment without clarifying how concepts or judgments depend on self-consciousness.[40]

---

[40] Keller, *Kant and the Demands of Self-Consciousness*, p. 78; all the other quotes from Keller in this paragraph are from the same page.

In this passage Keller is expressing puzzlement that, whilst § 16 begins with 'self-consciousness' (i.e., apperception), §§ 17–20 'merely shift' to talking about objectivity, cognition and judgment. That is, as I have said, Kant's text appears simply to identify the unity of apperception (of the manifold in an intuition) with the cognition of an object. Clearly enough, this is incompatible with Kant's argument being an adequate response to scepticism. What we then get in Keller's text are the usual warning signals that an outbreak of interpretative violence is about to occur: 'Initial appearances to the contrary, Kant really wants to argue' and 'His line of thought . . . may be reconstructed as follows'. In other words, Keller is saying that an argument that *should* be there – that is, an argument from self-consciousness to objectivity – is *not* there, so we must 'reconstruct' what Kant 'really wants to argue'. Now, Keller's *sole* reason for being so confident that he knows what Kant 'really wanted to argue' (but, unaccountably, did not argue) is this: 'An argument to a priori enabling conditions for self-consciousness based on the existence of knowledge will only be convincing to the reader who is already prepared to accept the existence of knowledge as given'. This last statement is perfectly correct. However, it only constitutes a reason for 'reconstructing what Kant really wanted to argue' if one is already convinced that the B-Deduction is intended as an anti-sceptical argument. And the very fact that reading the B-Deduction in this way entails that one must 'reconstruct' it at the crucial point – as Keller himself admits – is strong evidence that Kant's argument is not in fact intended as an anti-sceptical argument.

This denial that the B-Deduction is aimed at a sceptic (i.e., one who doubts the objectivity of our experience) does not empty Kant's argument, as I read it, of any philosophical interest or value (unless one holds that the only interesting kind of argument is one that attempts to refute radical scepticism – in which case one would find most of the history of philosophy uninteresting). To begin with, as I noted above, it is true that a sceptic could accept Kant's analysis of cognition, and yet deny that this proves anything about our own experience. It is, however, worth emphasising just what that sceptic would thereby be doubting, as this will show just how much Kant's argument claims to prove. As I have argued, the most important part of the B-Deduction (i.e., §§ 16–20) is an analysis of the concept of discursive cognition. Now, a discursive mind is one that is *receptive* in cognition – that is, its conscious experience is constrained by an independent reality. Hence, to accept Kant's analysis whilst simultaneously denying that it shows us anything about our experience, would be to doubt that we are receptive in cognition. And this would be to suggest that, for all we know, our experience might not be a contact with an independent reality, but instead spun entirely out of our own heads – and, as Kant writes in another context, that the objects of our experience might be 'mere self-produced fantasies' (4:292). Hence, if Kant's analysis is correct, then anyone other than the most radical of sceptics must accept his conclusion that our cognition involves a category-governed spontaneous synthesis. In other words, Kant has argued in the B-Deduction that denying the objective validity of the a priori categories is inconsistent with holding that we are receptive in cognition to an independent reality (and that therefore, e.g., any thoroughgoing empiricism is false). This, it seems to me, is an interesting argument, despite its failure to make any attempt to refute a radical sceptic.

There is one final question that I will now briefly discuss: the relation of the argument of the B-Deduction to so-called 'Cartesian scepticism', or 'problematic idealism', as Kant himself called it. A Cartesian sceptic might suggest that although our experience is receptive – in that we have one stream of perceptual states rather than another in virtue of an independent reality – perhaps we never successfully get 'out of our own heads' and cognise the 'real' objects beyond our ideas. It has been suggested by some commentators that a refutation of this sort of scepticism is one of Kant's major aims in the B-Deduction – or at least that the 'Deduction plays an important role in [the] internal refutation of Cartesian scepticism'.[41] They suggest that, in order to refute Cartesian scepticism, Kant would need to prove that we are conscious of, or cognise, something over and above our subjective, perceptual states. In other words, Kant would need to prove that there are 'external things which we perceive but which exist independently of our perceiving them'.[42] Howell, for example, thus writes that

in the Deduction Kant ultimately needs to establish in a non-question-begging manner the conclusion that what *H* [i.e., the cognising subject] knows through *i*'s elements [i.e., the manifold in an intuition] is a category-subsumed object distinct from those elements as they are presented to the mind.[43]

And Bennett claims that 'what Kant . . . repeatedly offers to prove in the Transcendental Deduction, is that all experience must be of a realm of items which are objective in the sense that they can be distinguished from oneself and one's inner states'.[44]

---

[41] McCann, 'Skepticism and Kant's B Deduction', 71.
[42] T. E. Wilkerson, *Kant's Critique of Pure Reason*, 2nd edn (Bristol: Thoemmes Press, 1998), p. 48.
[43] Howell, *Kant's Transcendental Deduction*, p. 151.
[44] Bennett, *Kant's Analytic*, p. 131.

These commentators are correct to think that the B-Deduction plays a significant role in Kant's campaign against Cartesian scepticism (a campaign which culminates in the 'Refutation of Idealism'), but that role is not what they think it is. As I hope my previous discussions in this chapter have made clear, the suggestion that these commentators make – that the B-Deduction is an attempt to prove that we experience 'external things' that are 'distinct from our subjective states' – presupposes the very model of cognition (i.e., the Cartesian model) that Kant is attacking in the B-Deduction. For in the B-Deduction Kant argues that conscious experience, or cognition, does not begin with an immediate apprehension of 'mere subjective states'; it begins with an act of grasping something *in* those subjective states, and thus with an act of judgment. Hence, as I have argued, there is no longer the philosophical motivation to think of inner sense as being epistemically privileged over outer sense – which is precisely the presupposition that makes Cartesian scepticism seem almost inescapable. In this way, then, the B-Deduction can be seen as a crucially important part of Kant's development and transformation of his representationalist heritage.

Bibliography

KANT'S WRITINGS

Briefwechsel, ed. R. Malter, 3rd edn Hamburg: Felix Meiner, 1986.
Kants gesammelte Schriften, ed. Deutschen Akademie der Wissenschaften, 29 vols., Berlin: de Gruyter, 1902–83; 2nd edn for vols. I–IX, 1968.

TRANSLATIONS OF KANT'S WRITINGS

Correspondence, ed. and trans. Arnulf Zweig, Cambridge University Press, 1999.
Critique of Pure Reason, ed. and trans. Paul Guyer and Allen W. Wood, Cambridge University Press, 1998.
Lectures on Logic, ed. and trans. J. Michael Young, Cambridge University Press, 1992.
'On a discovery according to which any new critique of pure reason has been made superfluous by an earlier one', in *The Kant–Eberhard Controversy*, ed. and trans. Henry E. Allison, Baltimore: Johns Hopkins University Press, 1973, 107–60.
Practical Philosophy, ed. and trans. Mary J. Gregor, Cambridge University Press, 1996.
Prolegomena to any future Metaphysics that will be able to come Forward as Science, ed. and trans. Gary Hatfield, Cambridge University Press, 1997.

OTHER WORKS CITED

Adams, R. M., *Leibniz*, Oxford University Press, 1994.
Aldrich, V. C., 'Mirrors, Pictures, Words, Perceptions', in *New Representationalisms*, ed. E. Wright, Aldershot: Avebury, 1993, 117–35.
Allison, H. E., *Idealism and Freedom*, Cambridge University Press, 1996.
    Kant's Transcendental Idealism, New Haven: Yale University Press, 1983.
Ameriks, K., 'Kant's Transcendental Deduction as a Regressive Argument', *Kant Studien*, 69 (1978), 273–87.

Anscombe, G. E. M., 'The Intentionality of Sensation: A Grammatical Feature', in *Metaphysics and the Philosophy of Mind: The Collected Papers of G. E. M. Anscombe*, vol. II, Minneapolis: University of Minnesota Press, 1981, 3–20.

Aquila, R. E., *Matter in Mind*, Bloomington: Indiana University Press, 1989.

Representational Mind, Bloomington: Indiana University Press, 1983.

Ariew, R. and Grene, M., 'Ideas, in and before Descartes', *Journal of the History of Ideas* 56 (1995), 87–106.

Arnauld, A. and Nicole, P., *Logic or the Art of Thinking*, trans. J. V. Buroker, Cambridge University Press, 1996.

Ayers, M., *Locke*, 2 vols., London: Routledge, 1991.

Baker, G. and Morris, K. J., *Descartes' Dualism*, London: Routledge, 1996.

Baum, M., 'The B-Deduction and the Refutation of Idealism', *Southern Journal of Philosophy (Supplement)* 25 (1986), 89–107.

Beck, L. W., *A Commentary on Kant's Critique of Practical Reason*, University of Chicago Press, 1960.

'Did the Sage of Königsberg have no Dreams?', in *Essays on Kant and Hume*, New Haven: Yale University Press, 1978, 38–60.

Bell, D., *Frege's Theory of Judgment*, Oxford University Press, 1979.

Husserl, London: Routledge, 1990.

Bencivenga, E., *Kant's Copernican Revolution*, Oxford University Press, 1987.

'The Metaphysical Structure of Kant's Moral Philosophy', in *My Kantian Ways*, Berkeley: University of California Press, 1995, 33–46.

Bennett, J., *Kant's Analytic*, Cambridge University Press, 1966.

Kant's Dialectic, Cambridge University Press, 1974.

Berkeley, G., *A New Theory of Vision and other Writings*, London: J. M. Dent, 1910.

Boswell, T., 'On the Textual Authenticity of Kant's *Logic*', *History and Philosophy of Logic* 9 (1988), 193–203.

Brook, A., *Kant and the Mind*, Cambridge University Press, 1994.

Burrell, D. B., 'Distinguishing God from the World', in *Language, Meaning and God*, ed. B. Davies, London: Geoffrey Chapman, 1987, 75–91.

Carriero, J. P., 'The First Meditation', in *Descartes's Meditations*, ed. V. Chappell, Lanham, MD: Rowman & Littlefield, 1997, 1–31.

Charlton, W., *Aesthetics*, London: Hutchinson, 1970.

Collins, A. W., *Possible Experience*, Berkeley: University of California Press, 1999.

Cottingham, J., 'Descartes' Treatment of Animals', in *Descartes*, ed. J. Cottingham, Oxford University Press, 1998, 225–33.

Davidson, D., 'Truth and Meaning', in *Inquiries into Truth and Interpretation*, Oxford University Press, 1984, 17–36.

Dennett, D., *Brainstorms*, Brighton: Harvester Press, 1978.

Descartes, R., *The Philosophical Writings of Descartes*, trans. John Cottingham, Robert Stoothoff and Dugald Murdoch, 3 vols., Cambridge University Press, 1985–91.

Diamond, C., *The Realistic Spirit*, Cambridge, MA: MIT Press, 1991.

Dummett, M., 'Frege and Husserl on Reference', in *The Seas of Language*, Oxford University Press, 1993, 224–9.

Engstrom, S., 'The Transcendental Deduction and Skepticism', *Journal of the History of Philosophy* 32 (1994), 359–80.

Falkenstein, L., *Kant's Intuitionism*, University of Toronto Press, 1995.

Frege, G., *The Frege Reader*, ed. and trans. M. Beaney, Oxford: Blackwell, 1997.

Gardner, S., *Kant and the Critique of Pure Reason*, London: Routledge, 1999.

Geach, P. T., 'God's Relation to the World', in *Logic Matters*, Berkeley: University of California Press, 1972, 318–27.

Mental Acts, 2nd edn, Bristol: Thoemmes Press, 1992.

'Saying and Showing in Frege and Wittgenstein', in *Essays on Wittgenstein in Honour of G. H. Von Wright*, ed. J. Hintikka, Amsterdam: North Holland Publishing, 1976, 54–70.

George, R., 'Kant's Sensationism', *Synthese* 47 (1981), 229–55.

Gram, M. S., 'Intellectual Intuition: The Continuity Thesis', *Journal of the History of Ideas* 42 (1981), 287–304.

Grene, M., *Descartes*, 2nd edn, Indianapolis: Hackett, 1998.

Guyer, P., *Kant and the Claims of Knowledge*, Cambridge University Press, 1987.

Haldane, J., 'A Return to Form in the Philosophy of Mind', in *Form and Matter*, ed. D. S. Oderberg, Oxford: Blackwell, 1999, 40–64.

Hatfield, G. C. and Epstein, W., 'The Sensory Core and the Medieval Foundations of Early Modern Perceptual Theory', *Isis* 70 (1979), 363–84.

Henrich, D., 'Identity and Objectivity: An Inquiry into Kant's Transcendental Deduction', in *The Unity of Reason*, ed. R. L. Velkley, trans. J. Edwards, Cambridge, MA: Harvard University Press, 1994, 123–208.

'The Identity of the Subject in the Transcendental Deduction', in *Reading Kant*, ed. E. Schaper and W. Vossenkuhl, Oxford: Blackwell, 1989, 250–80.

'Kant's Notion of a Deduction and the Methodological Background of the First *Critique*', in *Kant's Transcendental Deductions*, ed. E. Förster, Stanford University Press, 1989, 29–46.

'The Proof-Structure of Kant's Transcendental Deduction', *Review of Metaphysics* 22 (1969), 640–59.

Howell, R., *Kant's Transcendental Deduction*, Dordrecht: Kluwer, 1992.

Hume, D., *Enquiries Concerning Human Understanding and Concerning the Principles of Morals*, ed. L. A. Selby-Bigge, 3rd edn, Oxford University Press, 1975.

A Treatise of Human Nature, ed. L. A. Selby-Bigge and P. H. Nidditch, 2nd edn, Oxford University Press, 1978.

Hurley, S. L., 'Kant on Spontaneity and the Myth of the Giving', *Proceedings of the Aristotelian Society* 94 (1994), 137–64.

Hylton, P., 'The Nature of the Proposition and the Revolt against Idealism', in *Philosophy in History*, ed. R. Rorty, J. B. Schneewind and Q. Skinner, Cambridge University Press, 1984, 375–97.

Ishiguro, H., 'Imagination – II', *Aristotelian Society Proceedings (Supplement)* 41 (1967), 37–56.

'On Representations', *European Journal of Philosophy* 2 (1994), 109–24.

'Representation: An Investigation Based on a Passage in the *Tractatus*', in *Forms of Representation*, ed. B. Freed, A. Marras and P. Maynard, Amsterdam: North Holland Publishing, 1975, 189–202.

Jolley, N., *Leibniz and Locke*, Oxford University Press, 1984.

The Light of the Soul, Oxford University Press, 1990.

Locke, Oxford University Press, 1999.

Keller, P., *Kant and the Demands of Self-Consciousness*, Cambridge University Press, 1998.

Kemp Smith, N., *A Commentary to Kant's 'Critique of Pure Reason'*, 2nd edn, New York: Humanities Press, 1962.

Kitcher, P., *Kant's Transcendental Psychology*, Oxford University Press, 1990.

Kulstad, M. A., *Leibniz on Apperception, Consciousness, and Reflection*, Munich: Philosophia, 1991.

Leibniz, G. W. F., *Philosophical Papers and Letters*, ed. and trans. L. E. Loemker, 2nd edn, Dordrecht: D. Reidel, 1969.

New Essays on Human Understanding, trans. Peter Remnant and Jonathan Bennett, Cambridge University Press, 1996.

Linsky, L., 'Terms and Propositions in Russell's *Principles of Mathematics*', *Journal of the History of Philosophy* 26 (1988), 621–42.

'The Unity of the Proposition', *Journal of the History of Philosophy* 30 (1992), 243–73.

Locke, J., *An Essay Concerning Human Understanding*, ed. P. H. Nidditch, Oxford University Press, 1979.

Longuenesse, B., *Kant and the Capacity to Judge*, trans. C. T. Wolfe, Princeton University Press, 1998.

McCann, E., 'Skepticism and Kant's B Deduction', *History of Philosophy Quarterly* 2 (1985), 71–89.

McDowell, J., *Mind and World*, Cambridge, MA: Harvard University Press, 1994.

McRae, R., ' "Idea" as a Philosophical Term in the Seventeenth Century', *Journal of the History of Ideas* 26 (1965), 175–90.

Leibniz, University of Toronto Press, 1976.

Palmer, A., *Concept and Object*, London: Routledge, 1988.

Parsons, C., 'The Transcendental Aesthetic', in *The Cambridge Companion to Kant*, ed. P. Guyer, Cambridge University Press, 1992, 62–100.

Pereboom, D., 'Kant on Intentionality', *Synthese* 77 (1988), 321–52.

'Self-Understanding in Kant's Transcendental Deduction', *Synthese* 103 (1995), 1–42.

Pippin, R. B., 'Kant on the Spontaneity of Mind', *Canadian Journal of Philosophy* 17 (1987), 449–75.

Kant's Theory of Form, New Haven: Yale University Press, 1982.

Pitkänen, R., 'The Resemblance View of Pictorial Representation', *British Journal of Aesthetics* 16 (1976), 313–23.

Prauss, G., *Erscheinung bei Kant*, Berlin: Walter de Gruyter, 1971.

Robinson, H., 'Intuition and Manifold in the Transcendental Deduction', *Southern Journal of Philosophy* 22 (1984), 403–12.

'The Transcendental Deduction from A to B: Combination in the Threefold Synthesis and the Representation of a Whole', *Southern Journal of Philosophy (Supplement)* 25 (1986), 45–61.

'Two Perspectives on Kant's Appearances and Things in Themselves', *Journal of the History of Philosophy* 32, no. 3 (1994), 411–41.

Rorty, R., 'Strawson's Objectivity Argument', *Review of Metaphysics* 24 (1970), 207–44.

Rousseau, J.-J., *The Social Contract and the Discourses*, trans. G. D. H. Cole, London: J. M. Dent, 1993.

Russell, B., *The Principles of Mathematics*, London: Routledge, 1992.

Sellars, W., *Science and Metaphysics*, Atascadero, CA: Ridgeview, 1992.

Sleigh, R. C., *Leibniz and Arnauld*, New Haven: Yale University Press, 1990.

Sluga, H., 'Frege against the Booleans', *Notre Dame Journal of Formal Logic* 28 (1987), 80–98.

Gottlob Frege, London: Routledge, 1980.

Strawson, P. F., *The Bounds of Sense*, London: Routledge, 1966.

Stump, E., 'The Mechanisms of Cognition: Ockham on Mediating Species', in *The Cambridge Companion to Ockham*, ed. P. V. Spade, Cambridge University Press, 1999, 168–203.

Thomas, A., 'Book Review: D. Henrich's *The Unity of Reason*', *Mind* 105 (1996), 706–8.

Vendler, Z., *The Matter of Minds*, Oxford University Press, 1984.

Walker, R. C. S., *Kant*, London: Routledge & Kegan Paul, 1978.

Waxman, W., *Kant's Model of the Mind*, Oxford University Press, 1991.

Weinberg, J. R., *Abstraction, Relation, and Induction*, Madison: University of Wisconsin Press, 1965.

Wilkerson, T. E., *Kant's Critique of Pure Reason*, 2nd edn, Bristol: Thoemmes Press, 1998.

Williams, B., *Descartes*, Harmondsworth, UK: Penguin, 1978.

Wilson, M. D., 'Kant and "the *Dogmatic* Idealism of Berkeley"', in *Ideas and Mechanism*, Princeton University Press, 1999, 276–93.

Winkler, K. P., *Berkeley*, Oxford University Press, 1989.

Wittgenstein, L., *Notebooks 1914–1916*, ed. G. H. von Wright and G. E. M. Anscombe, trans. G. E. M. Anscombe, 2nd edn, University of Chicago Press, 1979.

Philosophical Investigations, ed. and trans. G. E. M. Anscombe, 2nd edn, Oxford: Blackwell, 1958.

Tractatus Logico-Philosophicus, trans. D. F. Pears and B. F. McGuinness, London: Routledge, 1961.

Wolff, R. P., *Kant's Theory of Mental Activity*, Cambridge, MA: Harvard University Press, 1963.

Wood, A. W., *Kant's Rational Theology*, Ithaca, NY: Cornell University Press, 1978.

Index